THE C ES

CW01629385

CONFLICT OF LAWS

Cavendish
Publishing
Limited

TITLES IN THE Q&A SERIES

BUSINESS LAW
CIVIL LIBERTIES
COMMERCIAL LAW
COMPANY LAW
CONFLICT OF LAWS
CONSTITUTIONAL & ADMINISTRATIVE LAW
CONTRACT LAW
CRIMINAL LAW
EMPLOYMENT LAW
ENGLISH LEGAL SYSTEM
EQUITY & TRUSTS
EUROPEAN COMMUNITY LAW
EVIDENCE
INTERNATIONAL TRADE LAW
JURISPRUDENCE
LAND LAW
PUBLIC INTERNATIONAL LAW
REVENUE LAW
SUCCESSION, WILLS & PROBATE
TORTS LAW
'A' LEVEL LAW

THE CAVENDISH Q & A SERIES

CONFLICT OF LAWS

JCT Chuah, LLM (Hons) (Cantab)
LLB (Hons), M IEx (Dist)
Lecturer in Law
University of Luton

Alina Kaczorowska, PhD, DEA, BCL
Barrister at the Paris Bar
Principal Lecturer in Law
Southampton Institute

Cavendish
Publishing
Limited

First published in Great Britain 1996 by Cavendish Publishing Limited,
The Glass House, Wharton Street, London WC1X 9PX.
Telephone: 0171-278 8000 Facsimile: 0171-278 8080

British Library Cataloguing in Publication Data. A catalogue record for this book is available from the British Library.

ISBN 1 85941 142 8

Printed and bound in Great Britain

Preface

This book is designed for use in a course in private international law as taught in many undergraduate law schools. The materials attempt to cover a wide array of 'popular' issues in these courses. The questions are tailored to the syllabi of most undergraduate programmes.

Whilst the book has been arranged into delineated chapters on jurisdiction, choice of law in specific matters, recognition and enforcement of judgments and awards, it should be emphasised that these are but an artificial vehicle to assist the student in his or her revision. It should not be perceived as presenting the substance of private international law as discrete packages. The law is, of course, the result of the combination of those issues together.

We believe that the introductory notes in every chapter help the student identify the relevant issues for examination purposes. These brief notes and the nature of the book make no apology for the use of the materials in preparation for examinations. The book does not seek to replace the textbook but to complement it. Student numbers have grown considerably over the years and where there was the personal tutorial, now there is mass education. Innovative distance learning modes have also necessitated the use of a book of this size and nature. A book like this, if used carefully and as a supplement, should assist the student in studying intelligently and discovering the acceptable approach and structure of a legal essay. Some of the legal skills this book treats as important include: fact analysis; issue identification; statutory interpretation; legal application; clarity of argument and critical legal analysis.

The academic substance of private international law is not however compromised. There are end notes inviting the student to do further reading. There is a comprehensive index and the table of cases should assist the student in locating the primary sources. The questions have been designed to accommodate recent and potential legal problems in private international law and the theories of private international law (see for example Chapter 1). Students are reminded of the theoretical underpinnings of the 'practical' outworking of the law. In the 'answers', students are exhorted to note that there is very often no 'one right answer'. The essential criterion is a well-structured legal analysis.

Alina Kaczorowska has been primarily responsible for the following topics: domicile, jurisdiction, family law and tort; and her introduction and questions and answers have been marked with an asterisk. Jason Chuah is responsible for the residual areas.

We should like to thank Kate, Cathy and Jo at Cavendish for the support and encouragement in seeing this project to completion. Alina wishes to thank Paula Elliott, Southampton Institute. Jason Chuah thanks Mark Herrett and Isabelle Brodie for providing the vital distraction – *dulce est desipire in loco* (Horace, Od, IV.xii.28) or 'it is pleasant to play the fool on occasion'.

We have attempted to state the law as it stood on 20 April 1996.

JCT Chuah
Alina Kaczorowska

Introduction*

Prior to the actual application of the law selected by the choice of law rules an English court has to solve various problems. First, it has to determine the judicial nature of the question raised by a multi-state problem. The identification of the correct legal category into which the factual situation falls is known as the classification of the cause of action. Usually, the process of classification poses no major problems and an English judge automatically and often unconsciously assigns the question to a particular legal category. However, it may happen that a foreign law and the *lex fori* differ as to the classification of the cause of action. For instance, in the *Maltese Marriage Case* (1891) French law classified the factual situation as raising a question of succession while the Maltese law considered it to be a question of matrimonial rights. In order to solve the conflict of classification English private international law adopts a flexible approach. Although the classification of the cause of action is made by reference to the *lex fori*, an English court will not rigidly adhere to the concepts and legal categories of its domestic law.

Furthermore, a second classification relating to a rule of law may also be necessary. Once the applicable law is ascertained on the basis of an appropriate connecting factor which varies according to a particular legal category, the nature of the rule which governs the matter must be determined. In this respect, the choice is limited but still far from being automatic as a rule may relate to procedure (and thus be governed by the *lex fori*) or to substance (in which case the *lex causae* applies). Once again the *lex fori* and the applicable foreign law may have different perceptions as to the nature of the selected rule.

Moreover, even if the applicable law to the main question is ascertained, the incidental question may surface. It is an issue which not only profoundly affects the main question but also requires the determination of the applicable law different from that which governs the main question. Three conditions must be satisfied for the existence of the incidental question: the main question must be governed by a foreign law which has been chosen by English choice of law rules; the subsidiary question must involve some foreign element which has arisen separately and which has its own independent choice of law rules; and finally the solution to the subsidiary question reached under the law selected by English conflict of laws rules must be different from one determined by corresponding rules adopted by the country whose law governs the main question.

On the conceptual level, once the classification is completed the question of *renvoi* may arise. Indeed, if the applicable law is a foreign law, the forum has to decide whether it refers to the foreign law as a whole which includes its private international law or only to its substantive rules. In the first mentioned case the problem of *renvoi* emerges as the foreign private international law may have different choice of law rules regarding the solution of a particular multi-state problem. Consequently, it may refer the question back to the sending forum (which is called the remission) or indicate a law of a third country as the *lex causae* (which is known as the transmission). There are the two forms of *renvoi*: single or partial *renvoi* and double or total *renvoi*. In England the doctrine of total or double *renvoi* is recognised. As a result, when an English court refers the matter to a foreign law it has to decide as a court in a foreign country if it was seised with the matter.

Also the actual application of a foreign law selected by English choice of law rules may be excluded if it is penal or revenue in nature. In addition, an English court will exclude the application of other public laws which are 'enforced as assertations of the authority of central or local government' of a foreign state. The classification of the nature of the foreign law is left to the *lex fori* which is not bound by the classification adopted by the foreign country concerned. As to the foreign expropriatory legislation it will be recognised in England only if the affected property is situated within the jurisdiction of a foreign state at the time of the foreign decree of expropriation even though the property may have subsequently been brought to England before or during the proceedings there. An English court will also refuse the application of a foreign law which is repugnant to its public policy.

Finally, unless a foreign law is pleaded and proved by the party, an English court will determine a multi-state problem as if it were a purely domestic dispute since according to English private international law a foreign law is treated as a question of fact. The only exception relates to Scottish law before the House of Lords. Being the final court of appeal in civil matters for both England and Scotland, their Lordships have judicial knowledge of Scottish law.

Contents

Table of Cases

C

M

N

O

P

Q

R

S

T

U

V

W

X

Z

Table of Statutes

Chapter 1

General Introductory Issues in Private International Law

Private international law or conflict of laws is a body of rules which is designed to determine whether English or foreign law is to be applied when an English court is faced with a claim that contains a foreign element. The peculiarity of private international law is that it has no material content in the sense that it does not provide any immediate solution for a particular dispute but merely indicates the legal system which is competent to provide the rules to be applied. Furthermore, private international law is part of English law and, consequently, it is neither private nor international. Private international law operates indirectly by providing a technique which is used to solve multi-state problems; it is not at all a system of independent substantive rules. As Voltaire said the 'Holy Roman Empire!' was not holy, nor Roman, nor an empire, but we still use the term.

Three successive stages can be distinguished when an English court is faced with a claim that contains a foreign element. First, it must decide whether it has jurisdiction over the parties and the cause of action. At the jurisdictional stage, an English court has to decide whether the trial should take place in England. In this respect, two sets of rules may be invoked: the traditional common law rules with the accompanying *forum non conveniens* discretion and the new conventional rules set out in the 1968 Brussels Convention on Jurisdiction and Enforcement of Foreign Judgments in Civil and Commercial Matters as amended. Once the court decides that England is an appropriate forum for trial, it has to select the choice of law rule which will indicate the law applicable to a multi-state problem. This task is far from easy as different preliminary problems may arise such as the question of classification, the incidental question, the *renvoi* etc. At this stage the connecting factor which changes according to circumstances of the case will be decisive as to the determination of the law that will be applied to a multi-state dispute.

The next stage involves the actual application of the selected law which can be English law or foreign law. Indeed, choice of law rules are bilateral and thus may lead to the application of the *lex fori* or the foreign law and neutral as they indicate the competent law regardless of the content of thereby selected law. If the *lex fori* is selected no major problems arise. However, the application of a particular foreign law poses delicate questions. On the one hand, the foreign law which would otherwise apply according to the ordinary principles of private international law may be excluded in some circumstances. Indeed, an English court will not enforce and often not even recognise penal, revenue or other public laws of a foreign state. In addition, foreign expropriatory legislation and foreign laws repugnant to English public policy will not be given effect in England. On the other hand, under English private international law a foreign law is treated as a question of fact. Thus it must be pleaded and proved by the party which has invoked it. Consequently, the question of the proof of foreign law arises.

Finally, English private international law also deals with the recognition and enforcement of foreign judgments and foreign arbitration awards. At common law English courts have no jurisdiction to directly enforce foreign judgments. Consequently, the plaintiff has to commence proceedings against the defendant in England and Wales on the judgment debts. His situation is alleviated when the 1968 Brussels Convention, the Foreign Judgments (Reciprocal Enforcement) Act 1933, the Administration of Justice Act 1920 or the 1958 New York Convention on the Recognition and Enforcement of Arbitral Award apply. In this area, public policy becomes all important as the defendant may raise in defence that the recognition and enforcement of the judgment or the arbitral award is in breach of English public policy.

Private international law as a branch of English law has been relatively neglected until recently. The new interest is due to many factors: internationalisation of our every day life, the developments of telecommunication, the increasing economic interdependence among states and finally the accession of the United Kingdom to the European Community. Paradoxically, those factors challenge traditional conflict of law rules. Indeed, now more than ever, the traditional recourse to choice of law rules which change from state to state just as the substantive laws vary from forum to forum emphasise the need to harmonise both. As the universal unification of substantive laws which is the only way to eliminate the conflict of law rules is quite impossible to achieve, the need to apply conflict of laws remains, although considerable progress in the unification of substantive and conflict of law rules has been accomplished. Many international, intergovernmental and non-governmental organisations at the universal and regional level have promoted the process of unification. However, the most successful are certainly the developments which have taken place in Europe. The creation of common rules regulating many areas of law in the Member States of the European Union and which are interpreted and enforced by the Court of Justice of the European Community constitutes the best and most effective attempt at the unification of law. Within the subject of this book, it is necessary to mention Article 220 of EC Treaty which constitutes a legal basis for the adoption of two very important conventions: the 1968 Brussels Convention on Recognition and the Enforcement of Judgments in Civil and Commercial Matters and the 1980 Rome Convention on the Law Applicable to Contractual Obligations, both in force in the United Kingdom.

Checklist

- nature and scope of private international law
- proof of foreign law
- exclusion of foreign law
- role of public policy
- sovereign and diplomatic rights
- the distinction between substance and procedure
- *renvoi*
- characterisation
- the incidental question
- the time factor
- theories and methodology applied in private international law
- the progressive unification of the rules of private international law

Question 1

Distinguish the theory of double *renvoi* from the theory of simple or partial *renvoi*. Comment on the total *renvoi* doctrine as applied by English courts.

Answer plan

The question of *renvoi* is a popular examination topic, especially in the context of formal validity of wills. The student must be able to distinguish the difference between double *renvoi* and single *renvoi*. An understanding of the context within which the doctrines have been formulated and applied is particularly useful.

The problem of *renvoi* usually arises when the court has characterised the matter in dispute but the private international law rules of the *lex causae* suggest that the law of the *lex fori* should be used. To alleviate this problem, the courts in different jurisdictions have adopted various solutions; including single *renvoi*, double *renvoi* or simply ignore the issue entirely. It is imperative to set out this context in answering a question of this nature, which seeks to examine the student's understanding of the overall perspective.

Some of the cases that should be alluded to include *Re Annesley* (1926), *Collier v Rivaz* (1841), *Re O'Keefe* (1940) and *R v Brentwood Superintendent Registrar of Marriages* (1968). Bear in mind that a pure recitation of the facts without any commentary is of little merit.

Answer

The term *renvoi* is used to define the practice where the law of more than one country may be applicable in the choice of law question. It is to the effect that if a judge is seised of a case in one country, X whose law requires him to apply the law of another country, Y and the rules of private international law in Y refers to the laws of X, then the judge is to apply the law of country X. The alternative to this is the English doctrine of *renvoi*, also known as the foreign court theory. According to this theory, an English judge who is referred by English law to a foreign legal system must apply whatever law a court in that foreign system would apply. This naturally depends on whether that foreign legal system recognises the doctrine of *renvoi* or not.

In the mid-19th century, the continental doctrine of single or partial *renvoi* was primarily confined to the area of formal validity of wills. The situation was that under the then English rule (1), compliance with one form alone was required of wills. Under continental law on the other hand, compliance with the forms permitted by the testator's personal law or the law of the place where the will was made is deemed sufficient. In view of the stricture expected under English law, the probate court in *Collier v Rivaz* (1841) admitted the doctrine of single *renvoi* to admit codicils in question. The codicils were opposed on the basis that while they conformed with the English forum, they should have been made consistent with the Belgian form since the testator dies domiciled in Belgium and hence only Belgian law should be used to test formal validity. Sir Herbert Jenner admitted the codicils by stating that Belgian law would have referred the validity of the codicils to the law of the testator's original country of nationality. Where the conflict rules of the foreign state identified by the English forum would have referred the matter back to the English forum, acceptance of the *renvoi* constitutes the application of the doctrine of single *renvoi*.

This status of the *renvoi* doctrine remained until 1926 when Russell J in *Re Annesley* (1926) introduced the double *renvoi* doctrine into English law. The doctrine necessitates not only reference to the conflict rules of the chosen system but to that system's *renvoi* rules as well. In *Re Annesley*, according to English law the testator had died domiciled in France but according to French law he was domiciled in England. The distinction was fundamental because under French law the testator could not bequeath more than one third of her property because she had surviving children. This would have been possible under English law. The probate court held that as a French judge hearing the case was bound to turn to English law as the applicable law but subsequently would have to accept the *renvoi* back to French domestic law, French law should apply.

A few points of interest can be raised in this case. First no authority was cited for making such introduction into English law as it stood then. Secondly, the judge presumably took a 'common sense' approach and applied French domestic law as the law of the domicile on the basis that the French court would have arrived at the same result. Third, it is noteworthy that Russell's *dicta* suggest that a more direct reference or route is preferred but His Lordship nevertheless applied the doctrine of double *renvoi* without giving any reason.

A case applying the doctrine but arriving at a different conclusion is *Re Ross* (1930) where the court found that although the testator was domiciled in Italy under English law, it was proved that the Italian court would not have accepted the *renvoi* following its rules of private international law and hence the probate court could apply English law. This evidences the dependency the doctrine of double *renvoi* has on proof of how the foreign court would respond to the *renvoi*.

In *Re Duke of Wellington* (1948) it was remarked that where there exists a difference in opinion and conflicting decisions in the foreign system on the *renvoi*, the application of the doctrine would lack certainty and could lead to injustice. The practice of the foreign court becomes a fact in issue which counsels will attempt to prove the existence of when it is patently clear that there is no consistency of practice within the foreign system. The English court is under a duty to make a finding of fact at the conclusion of arguments, and this could very well be contrary to subsequent practice of the foreign system. This was seen in *Re O'Keefe* (1940). In that case the intestate had lived in Italy for the last 47 years of her life and was clearly domiciled there. Under the *renvoi* doctrine, however, movable property had to be distributed according to the domestic law of the Irish Free State. She was not a citizen of the Irish Free State and had never visited the country except for a short holiday 60 years before her death. Yet according to Crossman J, her nationality is crucial under Italian choice of law and hence the law must refer to the country where her father was domiciled at the time of her birth.

On the issue of nationality, the problem caused by authorities like *Re O'Keefe* in the application of the foreign court theory doctrine is that the law of the nationality is frequently referred to by the foreign choice of law system. As far as the British subject is concerned, this raises the absurdity of having to apply 'British' law which is non-existent. On the other hand there is no such thing as English nationality. The assumption adopted by the courts in *Re O'Keefe* and *Re Johnson* (1903) was that the national law of a British subject meant the law of his domicile of origin, without any evidence of foreign law. On the other hand, in *Re Ross* (1930), expert evidence was adduced to the effect that the foreign court in question would determine the case on the footing that the English law applicable is that part of the law which would be applicable to a British national domiciled in England. From these cases, it may be argued that there are no guidelines as to the application of the doctrine in cases of nationality and domicile of origin. The English court's assessment of how the foreign court would decide is not necessarily the way that the foreign court would respond.

There is yet another difficulty as pointed out by the Private International Law Committee (2). Successful invocation of the doctrine relies on the foreign court rejecting the *renvoi* or adopting only the doctrine of single *renvoi*. Where the foreign court also adopts the doctrine of double *renvoi*, the *renvoi* will move to and from that system leading to no solution at all.

Finally, it is foreseeable that in the application of the doctrine of double *renvoi*, the conflict rules of the *lex causae* (the foreign system in question) may refer the case to a third system of law. *In R v Brentwood Superintendent Registrar of Marriages, ex parte Arias* (1968), the Italian choice of law rules referred to the *lex patriae* of the French national who was domiciled in Italy; the *lex patriae* in this case being French law. In that case, the English court could choose to apply French law and by doing so it would achieve some form of consistency with the Italian court. However, the problem is where does the transmission end? It seems to be the suggestion of jurists that where the foreign court and the English court would both turn to a third system, then for the sake of consistency and practicality that third system should be given effect to. Where there is no consistency however, then the *renvoi* should be rejected and ignored. This position on transmission is still not entirely clear and a reading of *R v Brentwood* does not produce a coherent theme as to the logic of the application.

While the problem is undesirably uncertain and in some cases, severely applied, it is to be noted that the *renvoi* has not been extended beyond the area of succession of property and legitimacy. Further, the area of formal validity of wills is now covered by legislation, the Wills Act 1963 (3). In the area of contract law within the EC, the application of the doctrine is expressly excluded by Article 15 of the Rome Convention. There is opinion to suggest however that questions of formal validity of instruments and other arrangements (non-contractual) may still be subject to the doctrine.

Notes

1 The law as preceded the Wills Acts 1968 and 1861.
2 See 1st Report (1954) Cmd 9068 para 23 for a full account of the proposition.
3 Note in particular ss 2(1)(b) and 6(1).

Question 2

> 'Laws do not remain stagnant. Hence although conflict rules may refer to a particular system of law, the problem still remains that changes may have occurred to the connecting factor or to the *lex causae* itself.'

Comment on how English judges have responded to such an observation.

Answer plan

This is an area of growing importance amongst English lawyers. The time factor is one which private international law rules cannot afford to disregard indefinitely, although in many situations the courts have approached the matter from a piecemeal basis. The student may expect questions in this area to deal with any of the following three situations:

- changes in the forum's private international law rules;
- changes in the connecting factor in a rule of conflict of laws;
- changes in the *lex causae*.

The student should be able to present the difficulties created by these changes (if any) and assess how the courts have responded to them. An understanding of the court's judgment in *Lynch v Provisional Government of Paraguay* (1871) is especially helpful in setting out the common sense approach. Policy considerations should not be omitted, and perhaps equally important is the English court's manner of addressing issues of policy.

Answer

The situations identified, ie changes in the connecting factor and the content of the *lex causae*, form two of the three areas where the time factor may be of particular importance in conflict of laws. The third is where there has been change to the conflict rule of the forum. For the purposes of this essay, that third area shall be excluded from discussion.

With regard to the possibility of changes made to the content of the connecting factor, it is foreseeable that while English conflict rules may refer to a particular connecting factor, the character of the connecting factor may be such that it is time dependent. This is to say that the connecting factor is 'variable' instead of being constant. A good illustration may be found in the legitimation of children. The conflict rule is that the child's legitimation is dependent on the law of his father's domicile. In this connection it is crucial for the law to identify the time when the father's domicile becomes relevant since the father's domicile could change according to his intention and *de facto* residence. Section 3 of the Legitimacy Act 1976 provides that the father's relevant domicile is that when he was married.

On the other hand changes could also occur to the *lex causae*. Problems become exacerbated when these changes purport to have retrospective effect.

How have the English courts taken to these intervening factors when it comes to determination of the choice of law? The first point to note with reference to the first situation is that the courts will always endeavour to proceed on the premise to secure some certainty although this is not always possible. Professor McClean finds that there is in fact no general principle identifiable from judicial authority (1). The reason is simple – the diversity of cases are such that it is impossible to discern how one case in, say, legitimacy may provide any rational guidance for the resolution of a case in property. It is not easy to locate any discernible trend of judicial thought that is general enough to accommodate situations involving a different subject matter.

In any event the starting point with most cases is the determination of whether there is any statutory provision that may offer some kind of direction. Where statutes provide a solution, the matter quite speedily resolves itself.

In more vexing cases however, there is unfortunately no consistency in practice as highlighted earlier. Grodecki suggests that the better approach is to resolve the problem at hand by framing the most convenient and fair conflict rule and not to be swayed by the time factor (2). The lack of a metanarrative is resolving the matter is seen in the tremulous decisions on formal validity of wills. In *Coppin v Coppin* (1752) we are reminded that the old common law which states that a will of immovable property must conform to the formalities set out by the *lex situs*. This old rule is perhaps one that has frequently given cause for concern as regards the time factor. In *In bonis Lacroix* (1877) for example, hardship and inconvenience could result if the testator changed his domicile after executing his will. The court in that case purportedly gave recognition to the time factor by admitting to probate wills which met the formalities required by either the domestic law of the testator's last domicile or the domestic law of any system of law identified by the conflict rules of that law (3).

Still on the matter of wills, a 'worse' scenario is found in the area of construction of wills. The law is that a will of movable property must be construed according to the provisions of the law intended by the testator. Generally as pointed out in *Anstruther v Chalmer* (1826) which was later affirmed in *Re Cunnington* (1924), the court will apply the law of testator's domicile at the time the will was made and contrary to certain views, not at the time of his death. This is however only a presumption, and a rebuttable one at that. What is interesting for our purposes is that any change in the testator's domicile is not relevant according to the Wills Act 1963, s 4. The qualification is that this is only operative once the presumption has been activated. Where it is proved that the testator had intended a different system of law to govern the construction issue then that intention will be given effect to, whether or not the intention was expressed at the time of the making of the will or after.

In this case two matters are pellucid. First, where the time factor is treated as relevant, the position seems to be that which coincides with common sense and convenience. Second, it provides support for Grodecki's argument that the time factor is not a relevant factor at all. All the court has to do is to formulate the conflict issue according the essence of the subject matter. Accordingly in the above cited case, there was a will and its construction is in issue; as with all construction of deeds, the intention of the maker is fundamental and hence the conflict rule should be applied consistent with that intention.

Other areas of dispute have produced similar results in that there is no uniformity of application of the time factor issue and in many situations the time factor has been presumed or ignored in the light of the citation of a wider conflict rule.

With reference to the second situation, it is here where some of the most important problems of the time factor have surfaced, especially when the change necessitates the retrospective effect.

Broadly speaking, the forum should apply the *lex causae* in its entirety and this would naturally include all transitional rules. The qualifier must be that there is a real distinction between constant and variable connecting factors. Where the connecting factor is a constant, the application of the *lex causae* in its entirety would raise few objections. Where the connecting factor is not constant but changes from time to time, the formulation of the applicable conflict rule has to be made more precise.

The main issue for the courts is whether subsequent changes in the *lex causae* should be applied or simply ignored. The problem is aggravated by the fact that policy in this country has always been to treat retrospective laws with some degree of circumspect and apprehension. There is little authority directly on this issue but the vacuum may be treated as with all matters in private international law concerning public policy. As a paradigm the courts are slow to find a public policy cause and will apply severe tests as to whether judicial notice should be taken of the existence of the alleged public policy. Finally the courts will only apply it as an exception to the rule.

On the issue of applying the *lex causae* in its entirety it may be useful to turn to a few cases that have purportedly grappled with the question subject to their approach to using public policy in a legal context. In *Lynch v Provisional Government of Paraguay* (1871) two months after the death of the testator who was domiciled in Paraguay, there was a revolution in the country. The new government passed a law declaring that the testator's property wherever situated shall be the property of the state and the decree will apply as at the time of the testator's death. This affected the beneficiary plaintiff who was entitled to the deceased's property in England. Lord Penzance granted probate to the plaintiff on the basis that English law adopts the law of the domicile as it stands at the time of the testator's death. Any subsequent retrospective change in that law cannot be given effect to.

Two points may be raised here. First, Lord Penzance's formulation of the conflict rule and secondly, the common sense perception of justice and convenience which His Lordship applied. On the first, Professor FA Mann's criticism is that such a formulation does not take into account any transitional rules of the *lex causae* and hence derogates from the practice of applying the *lex causae* in its entirety (4). There is also cause for concern that this judgment does not consider the content of the transitional rule. Professor McClean cites the example where the will had been defective in point of form at the time of death but had subsequently been validated by retrospective legislation in Paraguay: 'it is hard to suppose that Lord Penzance would have thought it "inconvenient and unjust" to give effect to that legislation'.

On the second issue it could be submitted that a better approach to the resolution of that which is perceived to be ostensibly 'inconvenient and unjust' is not simply to rely on the technical formulation of the conflict rule alone but to place the application of that rule in the context of policy considerations of the highest eminence. This contextual approach is probably a suitably effective compromise following the House of Lords' recognition of the Lynch principle as the 'correct principle' in *Adams v National Bank of Greece* (1961). In that case the House of Lords refused to apply a retrospective Greek law which would have otherwise freed a Greek bank from its existing contractual liability. It was held unanimously that the principle in Lynch was correct and while only Lord Tucker relied squarely on that case to refuse the Greek bank's defence, it was quite obvious that in the formulation of the conflict question the House found that the Greek law was not the *lex causae* and hence should have no relevance.

This is not to suggest however that there is complete consistency in the application of the rule in *Lynch*. The House of Lords in *Starkowski v Attorney General* (1954) had to decide whether the law of the place where the marriage was celebrated as it stood at the time of the marriage or as it stood when the problem of validity arose should be applied. The House distinguished Lynch's case on various grounds, *inter alia,* that the case was of an entirely different subject matter. Taking this case and the problems faced by the House of Lords, it is opined that the major difficulty is attempting to find some semblance of congruity in the quagmire policy considerations. There is predictably represented in this legal perplexity the tussle between flexibility and certainty.

Notes

1 McClean, *The Conflict of Laws* (4th edn, 1993) Sweet & Maxwell, (London) p 431.
2 Grodecki (1959) 35 British Yearbook of International Law 58.
3 See too *Collier v Rivaz*.
4 Mann (1954) 31 British Yearbook of International Law 217.
5 McClean (*supra*) at p 433.

Question 3

> '... As has often been said private international law is really a branch of municipal law and obviously there can be no branch of municipal law in which the general policy of such law can be properly ignored' *per* Lord Parker, *Dynamit A G v Rio Tinto Zinc Co* (1918).

Examine the role English courts have placed on public policy in the application of private international law.

Answer plan

The emphasis in this question is the role of public policy in private international law. The starting point as suggested in the quote is the definition of private international law as a branch of municipal law. The chief implication of this proposition is that it is thus subject to the operation of English public policy regardless of the *lex causae*.

Students attempting a question like this must be familiar with the labour exerted into defining and arguing for a set of coherent rules concerning the application of public policy rules. The cases that deal with penal foreign rules, discriminatory measures in status, the importance of natural justice and fraud, to name a few, are useful to reveal the lack of consistency on the one hand but the serious difficulties involved on the other. It is needful for the good student to highlight the general approach taken by the English courts in this connection.

It would also be of value to refer to the importance of policy applied not only in the common law, but also through the Brussels Convention and the Rome Convention.

Answer

As is clear from Lord Parker's observation, private international law unlike public international law is very much a part of the domestic law of this country. Public international law arguably stands on a different footing, rules of public international law as found in custom, state practice and treaties are not usually subject to public policy concerns in the same manner. The application of any rule of conflict of laws must consequently meet the demands of public policy as understood, construed and applied within the domestic system. Scarman J in *In the Estate of Fuld (No 3)* (1968) said in no uncertain terms that an English court will refuse to apply a law which outrages its sense of justice and decency. There is however a qualifier in that before the court refuses to do so on the ground of failure of public policy, the court must consider the relevant foreign law as a whole and determine if proof of that foreign is consistent with the allegation.

In *Fender v St John Mildmay* (1938), this qualification is explained in the following terms. The doctrine should only be called upon in clear cases in which the harm to the public is substantially incontestable and does not depend on the idiosyncratic inferences of a few judicial minds. This is an important demarcation of the boundaries of public policy. It does not seek to define the exact parameters of public policy but it sets out one paradigm, that of certainty. It appears that the premise of this exception to the application of rules of conflict is that public policy having a fundamental role in the municipal system should be clear and unambiguous.

The public policy as applied must be clearly identified and then raised in the context against the foreign law in question. Abstract or purely esoteric reasons will be regarded as insufficient proof of public policy. For example where English public policy would have rejected the giving of effect to any foreign law which is penal, that provision which is contended as being so must be obvious as being penal. A case which has been the subject of criticism on this basis is *Re Selot's Trusts* (1902). In that case a testator domiciled in England gave a legacy to his grandson, a French national who was domiciled in France. The grandson was found under French law to be a prodigal and as a result could not execute a charge over the property without proper consent. He charged the property as security for a loan without the requisite consent. It was held by the English court that the charge was valid and that the French rule on consent was bad for transgression of English public policy. It was decided by Farwell J that the French status rule was penal. 'Penal' however was not defined by the judge and hence the conclusion arrived by the judge in that case is open to criticism on that basis.

There is a distinction between cases which simply requires adjudication and enforcement of English law and those which have a significant factual connection with England although they are governed by a foreign system. Where the factual connection between the case and England as a forum is tenuous, English public policy should only be applied to reject the result of the application of the foreign law where that application flies in the face of fundamental principles of English law or its basic morality. Where there is a substantial connection with England, policy considerations of a lower degree in the hierarchy of norms may be applied to refuse application of the foreign rule.

A model of this first proposition is perhaps best displayed in *Robinson v Bland* (1760). In that case the English court felt bound to refuse recognition of a contract of prostitution (which was otherwise valid under the foreign law) even though the contract was not connected with the *lex fori* because to do so would be to derogate from the basic morality of English law. It would have constituted a fundamental departure from the morality of this country. Lower order policy considerations may include, as in *Grell v Levy* (1864) the rule under English law against the acceptance of contingency fees to maintain litigation. Although it was not a fundamental policy or a rule of basic morality, the court declined in that case to enforce the arrangement because the maintenance of the action was to take place in England, hence providing that substantial connection.

Besides these common law considerations, statutory provisions on enforcement and recognition of foreign law and judgments also make exception of matters contrary to public policy. Under the Administration of Justice Act 1920 for example, the defences to the recognition and enforcement of foreign judgments at common law such as fraud, denial of natural justice and other grounds of public policy are directly relevant. Under the Brussels Convention as ratified and put into force by the Civil Jurisdiction and Judgments

Act 1982, Article 27 provides that a judgment given by a contracting state will not be recognised if such an action would be contrary to public policy of the recognising state. The precise scope of application is however unclear in the light of Article 28(3) which rules out expressly any public policy objections to the original court's jurisdiction. Further Article 29 states that under no circumstance may a foreign judgment be reviewed as to its substance. The Jarrad Report takes the view that public policy objections vitiate the act of recognition of the judgment and not the judgment itself. This seems to suggest that while the nature and substance of the judgment cannot be challenged, the recognition and subsequent enforcement could be subject to the test of the recognising state's public policy under Article 27.

Under the Contracts (Applicable Law) Act 1990 and consequently the Rome Convention 1980, it is clear from Article 16 that the application of a rule of law otherwise applicable by virtue of the Convention may be refused if its application is manifestly incompatible with the *ordre public* of the forum. It is somewhat translucent how the *ordre public* will be construed by the English courts and whether its interpretation will depend on the common law distinction made between cases having a substantial connection with England and those that do not.

Another area where the exclusion of foreign law on the grounds of public policy is relatively rare is that which involves the question of status. In general, according to *Re Metcalfe Trusts* (1864), the rule is that English courts will not give effect to the implications of any status existing under a foreign law which is penal or discriminatory. The status or incapacity imposed on certain individuals will not be given effect to where to do so would be to act as the foreign state's agent in executing an order contrary to the morality of English law. A distinction was made in *Re Selot's Trusts* (1902) between status which is penal and that which is merely protective or discriminatory. The extent this distinction will sway a case either way is not exactly clear from *Re Selot's Trusts*. Further the issue may be better resolved by considering the *lex causae* or the connection between the facts of the case and the forum. In *Re Selot's Trusts*, the question was whether the legatee petitioner could take under the will of a testator domiciled in England. English law appears to be the *lex causae*, hence the foreign rule on incapacity to claim was not applied. Where the foreign law had been the *lex causae*, the result would probably have been quite different.

In the area of matrimonial relations, English public policy has occasionally dictated that a status under foreign law should be disregarded. For example, English courts for some purposes (1) have given recognition to polygamous marriages and other 'unlawful' marriages (2).

The courts have also been known to hold that they possess a 'residual discretion' to refuse recognition of foreign status (*Re Langley's Settlement* (1962)) if the recognition would be improper or unjust in the circumstances of the case. It must be submitted that such a position will cause even more uncertainty to the already watery perimeter of what public policy is (3). The exercise of such discretion is clearly not relevant where the recognition of the status has the effect of contravening public policy under the circumstances of the case.

Public policy may also operate where the litigants raise provisions of foreign public law in the proceedings before the English court. According to *Regazzoni v KC Sethia (1944) Ltd* (1956), the English courts do not act as the executive agents for any foreign sovereign. The court's traditional position as per foreign revenue laws, for example, is that they will not act as the foreign state's tax collectors. Also as was the case in *Rossano v Manufacturers' Life Insurance Co Ltd* (1963), direct or indirect attempts by any party to enforce foreign revenue laws will not be entertained. This is however not to say that these laws will never be recognised in every circumstance. In *Re Emery's Investment Trusts* (1959), the English court refused to abet any scheme to evade the operation of foreign revenue law. The clearest observation that may be made, as matters stand currently, is that English courts choose actively to remain neutral, neither enforcing nor ignoring the public laws of a foreign state.

A stronger prohibition under public policy is the refusal to permit the recovery of a penalty imposed by a foreign tribunal, *a fortiori* a criminal court of the foreign state. This must be confined to actions at the suit of a foreign state, not individuals who stand to benefit from such penal provisions (*Huntingdon v Attrill* (1893)). Hence, in *SA Consortium General Textiles v Sun and Sand Agencies Ltd* (1978), a foreign award of exemplary damages was enforced even though such awards are deemed to be punitive at English law. Here the position of public policy is clearer in that while the English court will actively remove itself from being perceived as the police agency of the foreign state, the matter is entirely different where rights of individuals are concerned. In the latter situation, regardless of nationality or domicile, any litigant who appears before the English court is subject to both the governance and protection of the court.

In conclusion, it may be said that while the role of public policy in conflict of laws has always been treated by the courts as a necessity, its application and definition have eluded the best of judicial endeavours. In the 1960s and 1970s, the view of writers was that more precise delineation of the role and operation of public policy was needed. The position has somewhat shifted since; the emphasis being placed on proving connection between the case in question and the forum. Instead of applying a blanket defence of public policy, the shift healthily suggests a more objective placing of the conflict rule.

Notes

1 See *Shahnaz v Rizwan* (1965); *Mohamed v Knott* (1969). Purposes include legitimacy of children, succession and some social security cases.

2 Some cases of interest in this area include *Re Bozzelli's Settlement* (1902); *Re Pozot's Settlement* (1952) and *Cheni v Cheni* (1965).

3 See for instance Nygh (1964) 13 International and Comparative Law Quarterly 39.

Question 4

'Characterisation of issues in conflict of laws are usually resolved in a practical and rather common sense manner.'

Discuss the above statement and demonstrate the relevance of characterisation in the light of the Contracts (Applicable Law) Act 1990.

Answer plan

This is not an easy question to attempt. The student will need to analyse how characterisation remains important even after the passage of the Contract (Applicable Law) Act 1990. Little has been written on it and the student will have to draw on his understanding of the Act and of how characterisation works to deal with this question adequately.

He will need to define characterisation and demonstrate how it was relevant under the common law regime on conflict of laws. An outline of the Contracts (Applicable Law) Act 1990 is useful to show how much the law has changed, and subsequently how the new law may be affected by characterisation.

Pay close attention to the *lex fori* approach as against what some jurists label the *lex causae* perspective. Examine the distinction in the light of case law. This examination should enable the student to comment on the trend of legal development in this segment of conflicts.

Answer

Under the common law before the passage of the Contracts (Applicable Law) Act 1990 the position was that where the parties' intention could not be ascertained as to the applicable law for the contract, the courts would have to locate the connecting factor between the foreign law that is pleaded and the contract in question. The choice of the connecting factor is dependent on the nature of the issue before the court; whether the issue is one of tort, contract, real property, family etc. The question of classification is known as characterisation of issues.

The question that begs resolution is whether the practice of characterisation of issues has changed following the enactment of the Contracts (Applicable Law) Act 1990. Under the Act the position has not changed too much. It starts with the same premise; that the intention of the parties be given eminence. Therefore if the parties decide to insert a choice of law clause in the contract, that choice will govern the contract (Article 3, Rome Convention). In the absence of a choice of law agreement, unlike the position before the Act there are now a few presumptions to determine the connecting factor. Article 4 reiterates the old position by requiring the courts to identify the law of the country that has the closest connection with the contract, however it does not stop there. Article 4(2) provides that the presumption is that the law of the party who has to effect the performance which is characteristic of the contract will apply. This is usually the law of the country where that party has his place of residence or business. Article 4(4) however comes in by providing that the presumptions will not apply if it appears on the whole from the circumstances that the contract is more closely connected with another country.

Characterisation arises in at least two situations under the new regime:

- characterisation of whether a dispute is contractual or not is fundamental. For example in a matter of obligation which may be both tortious and contractual, the Act will only apply to the latter;
- characterisation of the performance in question is equally important as it predicates the application of the presumptions.

Additionally characterisation is also involved where a matter has to be properly distinguished as being procedural or substantive.

The characterisation approach is often assumed to be governed by the *lex fori* as was held in *De Nicols v Curlier* (1900). What this means is that the courts will apply their own law to determine the nature of the issue in question. In *Ogden v Ogden* (1908) the probate court classified the issues based on English, the *lex fori* on the implied basis that English law is the best known law to the court and this makes the determination or characterisation process straightforward. Issues of foreign law or of the subject matter as it involves foreign law need not be delved into. All that needs to be done is the pigeonholing of that dispute into the already known causes of action at English law. In that case this pigeonholing exercise was done almost unconsciously. This form of characterisation that uses the *lex fori* reduces or modifies the subject matter into a so-called acceptable recognised pigeonhole in English law. In *G & H Montage v Irvani* (1990) an aval had to be characterised to determine the nature of the subject matter. The aval as it is properly known and practised in the continent does not exist in English law. What was alleged by writers about this case was that the court performed a superficial task of surgery by cutting down in size, shape and substance the issue at hand because it was a matter alien in the eyes of the common law.

An alternative or rather complementary approach should be adopted, in that while the *lex fori* approach has some merits, the process of characterisation should also take into account the *lex causae* of the subject matter. In *Re Maldonado* (1954) the Court of Appeal turned to Spanish law to decide if the claim of the Spanish government to the moveable property of a Spanish domiciliary who died intestate was a matter of succession or a *jus regale*. If it was the former then the dispute must be governed by Spanish law but were it was the latter, English law will preside. There was, however, no express reference to why the *lex causae* was used. In fact what could be deduced from the case is that the court was using the *lex fori* in a way that enabled it to take into account elements of Spanish law.

There is a further problem of using the *lex causae* in that when the court is uncertain as to what the *lex causae* is, it has to set out to determine what it is. To determine what it is, the court will have to consider the nature of the subject matter. This is not possible without the *lex causae*. Hence the entire process meanders in a circular motion. Further cumulation will result in the court having to contend with more than one *lex causae*. This happened when the court tried to solve the chicken and egg situation by resorting to classifying all the possible relevant *lex causae* and then reducing the cumulation by removing the less probable links. This form of solution could lead to the outrageous conclusion that there is a gap in the dispute, ie no law applies at all.

The English courts have tended to characterise simply by impulse and common logic (common logic appurtenant to English law, that is) as in *Huber v Stenier* (1835). The clear demarcation between *lex fori* and *lex causae* does not appear to stand in the way of the approach adopted by the judges. In *G & H Montage v Irvani* for example the court construed the concept of 'indorsement' so widely that it could support the instrument of an aval. The tenor of this case indicates that while the courts would prefer to use the *lex fori* approach they have no qualms in resorting to foreign law, usually the *lex causae* without making an opera about it. This has however been criticised as not providing a coherent and clear theoretical basis for the practice. Kahn-Freund argues, for example, that the courts of the *lex fori* should adopt what is known as the 'enlightened *lex fori*' approach to solve the conundrum. The courts should devise a system within the common law (ie the *lex fori* itself) which could accommodate the characterisation issue, by so doing the court itself could not be indicted for turning to the foreign element for assistance. The *G & H Montage v Irvani* situation where the court used rules of construction in the widest possible way to deal with the alien instrument displays the unconscious development of practice, and unless this haphazard practice is properly justified by legal principles the practice becomes difficult to defend for lack of a theoretical foundation.

Another method used by the courts is *petitio principii*. This is where the court pre-supposes that which is in issue. To borrow an illustration from Professor Goode (1) whether a contract has come into existence through offer and acceptance and *consensus ad idem* is generally considered a matter for the putative proper law of the contract ie the contract is assumed to be valid for the exercise of considering by what law its validity is to be determined. While it may be hard to see the logic in such a presupposition, it is justifiable in that whether there is a valid contract or not, the putative proper law of the contract has the closest connection with the contractual events contemplated by the parties. What is apparent in this device is the use of common sense.

In conclusion while it is safe to say that common sense in the matter of characterisation appears to have led to some semblance of a framework, this is not entirely a satisfactory state of affairs. In many respects it is not coherent and provides no solution to the lawyer faced with problems of conflicting characters of the dispute as a result of the foreign element.

Notes

1 Goode, *Commercial Law* (1983) (1986 Reprint), Penguin, p 924.

Question 5 *

Judge Peirson Hall in *Re Paris Crash* (1974), described the American revolution in conflict of laws as follows:

> 'The law on "choice of law" in the various states and in the federal courts is a veritable jungle, which, if the law can be found, leads not to a "rule of action" but a reign of chaos.'
>
> Comment.

Answer plan

In order to answer the question, each important theory should be examined. First, it will be necessary to discuss the points common to all theories such as the 'rule-selection' approach and the determination of the 'true' and 'false' conflict. Once a particular theory is presented it should be critically assessed. The main theories to be examined are:

- the Restatement (Second) of the conflict of laws elaborated by Professor Reeds which contains his theory of the most significant relationship
- the choice-influencing considerations theory of Leflar
- the governmental interest analysis theory of Currie
- the comparative impairment theory of Baxter
- the principles of preference theory of Cavers
- the interpretation of forum policy theory of Ehrenzweig

Answer

The American revolution in conflict of law has its source in the dissatisfaction with traditional choice of law rules which were criticised for their excessive rigidity. They were also considered as being too general and an obstacle to the unification of private international law. Indeed, the traditional conflict of law rules, in the terminology of the recent American scholars, are based on the 'jurisdiction-selection' approach which requires that once the conditions for their application are satisfied, the court has to apply them irrespective of the content of the substantive rules selected by the choice of law as competent to solve the multi-state problem. As a result, the traditional conflict of law rules may produce unjust and unfair solutions since the substantive rules of the selected law are applied without taking into account the circumstances of a particular case. The objective of traditional conflict of law rules is not to find the best solution in each individual case but to provide a mechanism for solving multi-state problems. The essence of the theories espoused in the USA is that in the search for the best solution to multi-state problems each case has to be examined individually.

American scholars were hostile to generalisation. However, the concept of the best solution is perhaps as elusive as the concept of happiness. Thus, the American authors provided some guidelines to judges as to how to proceed to find the best solution to each case. This approach is based on the 'rule-selection' techniques which require the court to compare substantive rules of law of two or more apparently involved legal systems and to select the one which would produce the best result in a particular case. In this respect, the American theories can be divided into two categories: the first provides a technique which judges should use in order to select the appropriate law and the best example of it is the proper law approach. The second requires that some objectives must be achieved by the court such as the application of the substantive law which has the prevailing legitimate interests in a case according to Brainerd Currie or to do justice between the parties on the basis of the 'principles of preference' advocated by David Cavers.

The second feature common to new theories is the distinction between 'true' and 'false' conflicts. A basic assumption of the traditional conflict of law rules is that the substantive laws involved in the dispute always claim their application irrespective of the circumstances of the dispute. The 'rule-selection' approach makes a distinction between 'false conflict' in which the analysis of the substantive laws indicate that only one law has a legitimate claim to application and thus there is no choice to be made and 'true conflict' when two or more substantive laws have legitimate interests to be applied. However, it may happen that neither law has a legitimate claim to be applied and thus the third possibility called a 'no-interest case' emerges. The classic 'no interest' case arises when the substantive law of the plaintiff's state in favourable to the defendant and the defendant's state has the substantive law favourable to the plaintiff. Thus the plaintiff's state has no interest in protecting the defendant from another state and the defendant's state is not interested in affording a more favourable treatment to the plaintiff than he would get under the law of his own state.

Most significant relationship

Amongst the various approaches, the theory of the most significant relationship provides a technique under which the applicable law is selected by reference to a variety of choice of law factors. This theory is favoured by the moderate fraction of the American scholars and based on the English 'proper law' approach which has been elaborated by Dr Morris. According to him, in multi-state torts, the applicable law should be selected on the grounds of 'the most significant connection' with the particular case and the specific issue posed. Instead of applying automatically the *lex loci delicti*, the law of the place of injury to all torts, the court should be more flexible and take into account other factors such as the residence of the parties, the relationship between them, etc, in order to determine the law which has the most significant significant connection and which would be the most appropriate to solve a multi-state tort. Furthermore, he advocated that different laws might be applied to different issues.

His theory promotes a more flexible, and according to him, rational approach to choice of law problems in multi-state torts. The proper law idea served as a foundation for Professor Reeds theory of 'the most significant relationship' which is explained in the Restatement (Second) of the conflict of laws. He considered that courts should follow the directive of its own state on choice of law but in the absence of such directive they should apply the law which has the most significant relationship to the particular issue. In order to ascertain that law he provided a list of factors which should be taken into consideration in para 6 of the Restatement. Those factors are: (a) the needs of interstate and international system; (b) the policies underlying substantive laws of the forum; (c) the interest and policies of other states apparently involved in the dispute; (d) the protection of justified expectations of the parties; (e) certainty, predictability and uniformity of result; (f) difficulty in application of the selected law.

Thus Reeds blended the proper law theory with the governmental interest analysis and the principles of preference.

However, he did not advocate the abolition of traditional choice of law rules but a technique in determination of the most appropriate law to a multi-state problem. The Restatement Second enjoys considerable support of scholars and courts in the USA (*Babcock v Jackson* (1963)). The main drawback of his theory is as Cavers remarked, that 'the factors often point in different directions and carry in themselves no measure of their significance'.

The choice-influencing consideration

A variation of Reeds' theory is the 'choice-influencing consideration' approach advocated by Leflar. He elaborated his own list of factors which should guide the courts in determining the applicable law and added a factor absent in the Restatement Second: the application of the better rule of law. This new ingredient is quite dangerous as it may encourage the court to apply the *lex fori* as a better law.

Governmental interest analysis

With reference to the second category, the most important doctrine is the governmental interest analysis elaborated by Currie. Brainerd Currie advocated the abolition of the traditional conflict of laws rules. He was also against multi-lateralism. He argued that states have interests in promoting their policies. The role of the judge is to identify and assess the policies and interest of substantive rules apparently involved in a dispute. Currie like Wachter considered that courts have a duty to promote forum interest. As a result, the *lex fori* should be applied as a matter of principle and foreign law should displace local rules only if the forum has no legitimate interest in the case. The distinction between 'true' and 'false' conflict is vital to his theory as it applies only in the first mentioned case. In a 'no-interest' situation he suggested the application of the *lex fori*.

In order to discover the policies underlying the substantive laws Currie suggested that courts should use the ordinary process of construction and interpretation. He examined real and hypothetical cases and almost always deduced the legitimacy of asserting a governmental interest from the fact that one of the party was domiciled in that state. The main characteristics of his theory is that a separate analysis is necessary for each issue raised by a multi-state dispute in order to assess which substantive law claims its application. The personal connection of a party with a state constitutes a base for assuming the interest of the local law and the territorial contact is less important. In case of 'no-interest' the *lex fori* should be applied. Similarly all doubts should be resolved in favour of the forum.

The theory of Currie unfortunately introduces uncertainty and unpredictability of results. Also for judges to assess the policies and interest of the substantive laws, if they are able to do so taking into account that even Curries had difficulty in doing so, it is only relevant as to the determination of the 'false' and 'true' conflict but useless as to the solution of the particular case. Indeed, the theory of governmental interest analysis provides little guidance as to how the interests should be weighted and which should prevail. This is particularly obvious in cases where the forum has no legitimate interest in application of its substantive law but substantive laws of two or more other states claim such interest. It is submitted that the theory provides a complicated system to justify the exclusive application of the *lex fori*.

Comparative impairment

The theory of comparative impairment has been introduced by Baxter and applied by the Supreme Court of California. It diverges from the governmental interest analysis in one respect. In case of a 'true' conflict the court should not automatically apply the *lex fori* which is the practical result of Currie's theory but should assess the conflicting interest on the basis of 'comparative impairment', that is, they have to determine which of the conflicting states' interest would be more impaired if its interests were substantially subordinated to the interest of the other state. The theory of comparative impairment suffers the same drawbacks as the theory of governmental interest analysis.

Principle of preference

David Cavers like Aldricus considered that the substantive law which is 'better' in the individual case should be applied. In order to determine the 'best law' he has elaborated seven principles of preference to help the court to determine the applicable law where there is a 'true' conflict. Five of those principles deal with tort and two with contracts and conveyances. The objective of his system, which he himself admitted was incomplete, is to do justice between the parties in each case. His theory is confined to tort and contract and as he himself admitted it would be more appropriately applied in the context of federal state when it is necessary to resolve inter-state rather than international conflict. The main criticism is that as any 'rule-selection' approach it introduces uncertainty and unpredictability.

Interpretation of forum policy

Finally the theory presented by Ehrenzwieg which criticises the traditional conflict of law operation and the government interest analysis approach without introducing any substantive innovation in the latter. He considered that the court should give preference to the *lex fori*. The 'interpretation of forum policy' amounted to the systematic application of the *lex fori* which according to him should be a rule. A foreign law should be applied in exceptional circumstances where the application of the *lex fori* would be unfair to the parties. His theory, if applied, would result in the demise of private international law and further, the unbridled rise of the forum shopping.

It is submitted that the different American theories instead of introducing certainty, predictability and uniformity of solution, sacrifice them. In most cases they justify the systematic application of the law of the forum and thus virtually eliminate the application of a foreign law. This approach not only promotes the forum shopping but is fundamentally contrary to the objectives of private international law. In practice the American revolution in conflict of law produces, as Judge Peirson Hall stated, chaos and confusion. Indeed, the American courts apply whichever theory, alone or in combination with another, suit them best in any one case.

* by Alina Kaczorowska

Question 6

Critically examine the common law rules on proof of foreign law.

Answer plan

This question looks at the general question of proof of foreign law. Students should be able to state the general principle that foreign law has to be proved as a matter of fact. There should also be an account of the statutory exceptions to the general rule.

It would be useful to comment on the attitude of the common law in determining who an expert witness on foreign law is.

Answer

The starting point is that foreign law, as adduced and pleaded at the common law courts, is asserted as a matter of fact. The burden of proving the fact of the foreign law is with the party who relies his claim or defence (as the case may be) on it (*Dynamit AG v Rio Tinto Zinc Co* (1918)). This issue of proof is mandatory in the light of the rule in *Lloyd v Guilbert* (1865) which states that if the party provides no evidence or insufficient evidence of foreign law, the court will disregard the plea and only apply English law. This rule is reflective of the oft-cited presumption that foreign law is the same as English law until the contrary is proved.

The general rule is that if a party wishes to rely on a principle of foreign law as applicable to the cause in action or the defence, he must adduce evidence to prove as with all questions of fact. The one exception where judicial notice may be applied is found in the British Law Ascertainment Act 1859 which provides that where the case is governed by the law of certain British territory, the court may take cognisance of the foreign law even though the party has not provided evidence in support (see below).

Other attempts to raise foreign law by relying on the doctrine of judicial notice have been unequivocally rejected by the courts. Although in *Saxby v Fulton* (1909), judicial notice was taken with reference to the 'notorious' fact that roulette was lawful in Monte Carlo, this is not indicative of the general approach. The general approach is that foreign law is a matter of fact but does not possess the element of notoriety required for the application of the doctrine of judicial notice. The roulette case may be explained on the basis that the foreign law in question was a notorious fact.

Proof of foreign law being a matter of evidence means that the party adducing it as evidence must rely on 'fresh' evidence in every case. He may not plead that as the foreign law has been applied in another English case, that foreign law stands as it did then (*Lazard Brothers v Midland Bank* (1933)). While in the past the jury needed to be convinced of the principle of foreign law as a matter of fact, the Supreme Court Act 1981 (s 69(5)) makes it the duty of the judge alone.

There is one exception to this general approach though. The House of Lords (or its alter ego, the Judicial Committee of the Privy Council) which has the power to hear appeals from different countries may rely on its previous decisions to take judicial notice of the laws of any of the countries when it hears an appeal from them. In these cases, the position is that proof of foreign law becomes a matter of law rather than of fact.

The question of foreign law is, however, a question of fact *sui generis*. It is peculiar in that it must be proved by expert evidence. The adduction of legal literature, whether official or unofficial, before the court is not considered sufficient without the assistance of an expert witness. The justification of this approach to the adduction of evidence is perhaps the fact that legal materials alone may be subject to different interpretative canons and unique rules of construction. It would not be proper for the English lawyers and judges to apply English rules of construction on foreign legal materials. When the legal expert refers to legal materials, the English court may then look at the materials and draw some of its own conclusions from both the texts and the expert evidence.

This begs the question of who is an expert in the foreign law concerned. Under s 4(1) of the Civil Evidence Act 1972, it is declared that in civil proceedings, a person who is suitably qualified to do so on account of his knowledge or experience is competent to give expert evidence as to foreign law, irrespective of whether he has acted, or is entitled to act, as a legal practitioner in the foreign country. The old rule in *Bristow v Sequeville* (1850), where the person called to testify on foreign law must be a person qualified to act as a legal practitioner in the foreign country, has been abolished by the Act. It should be borne in mind at this juncture that any legally competent witness need not necessarily be the most suitable. While a person may be suitably qualified, the higher his standing in the legal profession of the foreign country concerned the more weight his evidence carries.

As regards non-lawyers, the law allows various professionals or persons who by virtue of their status and office are in the position to testify on a fact of foreign law. In *Lacon v Higgins* (1822), a vice consul was held to be suitably qualified to act as an expert witness. Other 19th century cases have permitted ambassadors, notary publics, bishops, merchants and other professionals to act as expert witnesses. It should perhaps be pointed out that in the light of technological advances and the mobility of legal professionals, whilst the rules should not be made more restrictive, greater weight should be given to testimonies of legal practitioners or academics.

The court will usually accept the evidence of an expert where he is not contradicted as was the case in *Buerger v New York Life Assurance Co* (1927). The court may, however, reject his evidence where to do so is to provide an absurd result. Further the court held in *Tallina Laevauhisus A/S v Estonian State SS Line* (1947), where his evidence is inconsistent overall, then it should be rejected on the grounds of lack of credibility.

Where the evidence is challenged, the court may look at the legal texts or sources to confirm and assess the consistency of the testimonies. In this regard the court will also take into account judgments given by the foreign courts in question and some considerable importance is usually attached to these judgments provided that they are clear and unambiguous (*Beatty v Beatty* (1924)).

There are a few situations where the proof of foreign law may be unnecessary. Under the Civil Evidence Act 1972 for example, s 4(2)–(5) provides that where any question of foreign law has been determined in civil or criminal proceedings at first instance in the High Court, the Crown Court, or in any appeal therefrom, or in the Privy Council on an appeal from any court outside the United Kingdom, then any finding of that question may be admissible in evidence in any civil proceedings. Subsequent foreign law issues shall be taken as in accordance with that finding or decision unless the contrary is proved. The finding or decision as to foreign law must be recorded in writing in a document which could be cited as an authority in legal proceedings in England if the question had been one of English law.

The second exception comes in s 1(3) of the Evidence (Colonial Statutes) Act 1907. This provision states that copies of laws made by the legislature of any British possession, if purporting to be printed by the government printer of the British possession, can be received in evidence in the United Kingdom without proof that the copies were so printed. Whilst under the law the substance of these laws may be admitted without the need of expert evidence, the court may require evidence to the effect that these laws are still in force and have not been repealed.

Finally, under the British Law Ascertainment Act 1859, a court may state a case for the opinion of a court in any other part of Her Majesty's dominions in order to ascertain the view of that court as to the applicable law of the case in question. This is subject to the condition that the applicable law is vital to the disposal of the case in question. This is a matter left purely to the discretion of the court. The court may or may not state a case depending on the seriousness of the issue involved as was held in *Lord v Colvin* (1859). The opinion of the foreign court is binding on the English judge with the general exception of the House of Lords or the Privy Council where the foreign court is binding on the English judge with the general exception of the House of Lords or the Privy Council where the foreign jurisdiction relies on either of the two judicial bodies for appeals.

It should be noted that the latter two statutes will still apply to commonwealth countries which are no longer British dominions or possessions.

Chapter 2

Domicile

Introduction

No person natural or legal may be without a domicile at English law. The concept of domicile determines that person's personal law and refers to the person's civil status. Students should note the distinction between the various types of domicile:

- domicile of origin
- domicile of dependency
- domicile of choice

Domicile of origin is the domicile the person acquires at birth. As a rule, a legitimate child will acquire the domicile of his father at birth whilst an illegitimate child will acquire the domicile of his mother. The importance of the domicile of origin is seen in *Winans v Attorney General* (1904) where it was held that the character of the domicile of origin is more enduring than other types of domicile and is less easily shaken off. Further, where the domicile of choice is lost by the person, his domicile of origin will be operative in lieu until he has acquired another domicile of choice.

The fact that the child's domicile follows that of his father or mother depending on his legitimacy is a manifestation of the common law rules on domicile of dependency. Besides children, wives at common law should acquire the domicile of their husbands. These rules have been modified in the Domicile and Matrimonial Proceedings Act 1973.

As far as children are concerned, s 4 of the Act provides that 'a child whose parents are living apart has the same domicile as its mother if he then has a home with her and has no home with his father'. As for married women they are now entitled to have their own domicile as distinct from their husbands', to be determined 'by reference to the same factors as in the case of any individual capable of having an independent domicile' (s 1(1)).

A domicile of choice is determined by the proof of the person's intention to remain in the place of their residence indefinitely and the fact of their residence there. These are elements of fact rather than of law. Residence need not be of a very long time as long as it can be proved that the person has the intention of remaining there permanently. In *Puttick v Attorney General* (1980), however, the law is that the residence must be lawful residence and settlement in a country by an illegal immigrant will not suffice. Where proof of intention goes, the law will take into account almost any act or circumstance, however trivial.

Checklist

It is essential to be familiar with the following areas:

- importance of the concept of domicile
- domicile of origin
- domicile of dependency and the Domicile and Matrimonial Proceedings Act 1973
- domicile of choice – proof of residence and intention
- loss of domicile
- reform in the area of domicile – Law Commission Working Paper No 88

Question 7

In 1973 when Lee and Mary were visiting Aaland, their son, Keith was born. Lee who was then domiciled in Aaland had met Mary three years ago in Beland. They were married in Beland and had set up home there.

In 1980 Lee and Mary decided to separate but because of family pressure, ruled out a formal divorce. A year later Lee killed himself by slashing his wrist because his application to join the Beland civil service was rejected on the basis that he was not a Beland national.

Mary then left Beland to start a new life in Celand with Keith. Unfortunately, finding it impossible to secure suitable employment, Mary fell into severe depression. She began neglecting Keith and as a result Keith was subsequently taken into care by Celand social services.

In 1984 Mary returned to Beland but left a note for Keith telling him how much she loved him and promising to return to Celand someday to be with him.

In 1987 Keith was returned to Mary but Mary had then moved in with her boyfriend. The mother-son relationship had then become quite strained. Keith then decided to go backpacking and see the world.

Trace the domiciles of Mary and Keith under English law.

Answer plan

It would be preferable to deal first with Mary's domicile since Keith as her son would normally take his domicile of dependency after hers following the death of his father. On Mary's domicile, the student must be able to explain the situation before the Domicile and Matrimonial Proceedings Act 1973 because the marriage was contracted before the passage of the legislation. However the effect of the Act in relation to subsequent events cannot be ignored.

On the issue of domicile of choice and the acquisition or loss of domicile, the student should highlight the proof of not only de facto residence but the *animus residendi*. The presumption of continuance of the domicile of origin deserves mention as well.

As regards Keith's domicile, the distinction between the old common law prescription and the 1973 Act should be examined. In addition, it is imperative to apply the law to facts. Never deal with the law in isolation of the facts. Trace Keith's domicile by reference to the rule in *Re Beaumont* (1893) and s 4 of the Act.

Answer

The notion of domicile according to Lord Westbury in *Bell v Kennedy* (1868) is an idea of law and as a legal concept, the distinction between an independent person and a dependent is quite crucial. The tracing of a dependant's domicile will very much be dictated by the acquisition and loss of domicile of the person on whom he is dependent. This being the case, it is appropriate to trace Mary's domicile first.

Since Mary married Lee in 1970, which is before the Domicile and Matrimonial Proceedings Act 1973 had come into operation, her domicile will be determined according to the rules of common law. The Act has no retrospective effect and so although the case becomes a matter of dispute after the passage of the Act, we must still refer to the common law rules. The general rule is that a married woman's domicile will follow that of her husband, because the law views her as being dependent on the husband. In *Lord Advocate v Jaffrey* (1921) it was unequivocally held that the wife's domicile will follow that of her husband and will change as and when his changes.

At this juncture, therefore, even though Lee is deceased, it becomes imperative that his chain of domicile is to be considered. It may be assumed that Lee's domicile of origin is that of Aaland, of which he was a national. When he married Mary and moved, his domicile may be said to have changed if there is evidence that he had set up his principal residence there. The occasional visits to Aaland should not detract from this finding. The length of residence is not particularly relevant in proving physical residence. It only goes to show the intention of the party in treating that country in question as his place of domicile. From the facts we may be permitted to assume that as he was keen to join Beland's civil service, this is good indication that his intention was to remain there and to treat it as his home. Once the animus and fact of residence are met, domicile is usually proved.

Following the coming into effect of the Act, Mary becomes possessed of the capacity to obtain a different domicile to her husband's under s 1(1). As far as s 1(1) is concerned, even though Mary's marriage to Lee was contracted before the Act, the right to acquire a different domicile is available to her regardless of whether she remained married to Lee or not. Under the section the domicile of a married woman like Mary will be ascertained by reference to the same factors as in the case of any other person capable of having an independent domicile. The factors like residence and intention must be proved to coexist before the law finds an acquisition of domicile. Hence, without evidence to the contrary, until the separation from Lee, Mary appeared to have intended to remain in Beland. This intention coupled with her actual residence in the country means that she has been domiciled there.

It should perhaps be pointed out that this may be all superfluous because she might have been born to parents with Beland's domicile and hence, had never lost her domicile of origin there; and her domicile of dependence (under the old law) is also that of Beland.

Be that as it may, there is also the added provision in s 1(2) which states that a married woman was to be treated as retaining her husband's domicile until and unless it is changed by an acquisition or revival of another domicile. This means that she will remain domiciled in Beland until she acquires a new domicile by conduct.

The issue coagulates when she moved to Celand upon Lee's death. Whether this has the effect of her acquiring a new domicile depends on proof of whether she has relinquished her former domicile. As was held in *Bell v Kennedy* (1868) a new domicile is not acquired until there is not only a fixed intention of establishing a permanent residence in some other country but when this intention is solidified by actually taking up residence there. It would appear that when Mary moved to Celand she did so to secure a better livelihood. The duration of her stay there is normally indicative of her intention although not to be attributed conclusiveness. She lived in Celand presumably between 1981 and 1984. This length of time is a relevant fact although other factors like whether she lived there without moving elsewhere, whether she owned the property she was living in, whether she simply lived in lodgings or hotels, whether she made any plans to be naturalised and other personal factors. The court held in *Drevon v Drevon* (1864) that there is 'no act, no circumstance in a man's life, however trivial it may be in itself, which ought to be left out of consideration in trying the question whether there was an intention to change the domicile'. A trivial act might possibly be of more weight than an act which was of more importance to a man in his lifetime.

The burden of proof however is no mean matter; if the House of Lord's pronouncement in *Winans v Attorney General* is anything to go by, there appears to be an almost irrebuttable presumption against the change of domicile. In that case the House of Lords found that although Winans had lived the last 37 years of his life in England he was still not domiciled in this country because he had always harboured loyalty to America and his hatred for England is notorious. It was his poor state of health that had kept him in England over the latter days of his life. This fact was taken by the Lords as indicating his lack of intention to adopt a new domicile, his *animus non revertendi* is pellucid. Whatever the criticisms that may be lodged against the emphasis on Winan's neurosis, the presumption of continuance of domicile remains doggedly a very strong presumption.

In *IRC v Bullock* (1976) the Canadian had lived in England for more than 40 years was held not to have acquired an English domicile of choice because he had intended to return to Canada after the death of his English wife. These cases reflect the reluctance of the courts to dismiss the domicile of origin lightly. In Mary's case if the presumption of *animus non revertendi* is to apply, her domicile (both of dependency and origin) at will be hard to displace.

Assuming that she has successfully acquired a new domicile of choice in Celand, the question is whether she lost it when she returned to Beland. According to Lord Buckmaster in *Ross v Ross* (1930) declarations as to intention are rightly regarded in determining the question of a change of domicile but they must be examined by considering the persons to whom, the purposes for what and the circumstances in which they are made and they must further be fortified and carried into effect by conduct and action consistent with the declared expression. Conduct consistent with the declared intention goes that extra furlong at supporting or rebutting the alleged *animus residendi*. This is directly relevant when Mary expressed in her note that she intended to return to Celand 'to be with' Keith. In this connection the frame of mind that Mary was in when she was in Celand would be a relevant factor. While it may be argued that she had not acted to disprove the intentions in her note, moving in with her boyfriend suggests that her intentions were probably to remain with him. Further, the intention to return was dependent on the eventuality of being with Keith; it was a conditional declaration.

On whether she had lost her domicile simply by not returning to Celand, authorities indicate that a domicile of choice is not lost merely by giving up residence (*Bradford v Young* (1885); *Re Lloyd Evans* (1947)). On the other hand, there appears to be a tacit giving up of the intention as well since she has settled back into 'normality' in. Subject to further evidence, it is contended that if she had acquired Celand domicile in the first place, she must have intended to relinquish it when she settled down in Beland.

Keith's domicile

Under the common law on domicile of dependency, the child has his domicile of origin, the domicile of his father at the time of his birth (*Henderson v Henderson* (1967)). Where the child is illegitimate, he takes on the domicile of his mother at the time of his birth. In Keith's case since he is the legitimate child of Mary and Lee, his domicile of dependency will be that of Lee at the time when he was born. While it may be that the court will find Lee to have chosen Beland as his place of domicile, it should be highlighted that when Keith was born the intention of Lee to relinquish his domicile is not entirely clear. This is the position at common law.

Following the passage of the Act of 1973, the rule as regards Keith has changed somewhat. According to s 4 the child shall take the domicile of the mother if he then has his home with her and has no home with his father or where he has had his mother's domicile by virtue of having his home with her and not his father and he has not since had a home with his father. The domicile of a child is subject to change according to who he lives with (1). It may be the case that until Lee's death Keith was living with both his father and mother, implying that the child's domicile during that time is that of his father's.

After his father's death, when living with his mother, his domicile would follow hers. The problem is exacerbated when he was subsequently taken into care. The position is best studied based on the rule in *Re Beaumont* (1893) which states that at common law the mother can exercise a power to change the domicile of a child who is dependent on her for its domicile. In that case, the widow then domiciled in Scotland subsequently remarried and moved to England taking all but one of her children with her. The court held that this was indicative of her intention to retain the child's Scottish domicile. Although an analogy may be drawn, this case should be distinguished from the present situation on the ground that Mary did not leave Keith in Celand voluntarily but the child had in fact been forcibly removed from her control. Further the rule should be confined to the case of the mother who changed her domicile but left the child in the care of a relative in its domicile of origin.

It would appear to be the case that a mother who is bereft of the care and custody of the child is incapable of changing the domicile of her child. The end result would be that since Keith was no longer subject to Mary's care and custody (if that is the effect of the Celandic law following the taking of Keith into care), when Mary changed her domicile she could dictate his. However while Keith was still a minor, he could not change his domicile by his own accord. Where the issue is indeterminate, the prescription in *Udny v Udny* (1869) is that the person's domicile of origin shall prevail.

When Keith reached the age of 14 in 1987 he was returned to his mother, under s 4 of the Act his domicile will take on that of his mother who at this time was probably domiciled in Beland. The fact that he was going to go travelling and will not take up residence with his mother does not affect his domicile of dependency under s 4 because the latter limb of s 4 applies. That latter limb provides that where the child has at any time had his mother's domicile by virtue of having his home with her, and has not since had a home with his father, his domicile shall take that of his mother. That domicile in the present case is presumably that of Beland.

Notes

1 It should be noted that living apart does not necessarily imply a breakdown in the relationship between the parents, legal or factual.

Question 8

Mister and Missus were domiciled in Utopia where divorce is illegal. They then decided to move to Thailand and were subsequently legally separated under Thai law. This separation is not recognised in Utopia.

Two years after the separation Mister and Missus moved back to Utopia. Last month when Missus was on holiday in Colonia, she met Man and decided to marry him.

Utopian law states that the validity of matrimonial relations and separations is to be determined by the law of the domicile of the husband when the marriage was contracted.

Colonia is a newly independent country that applies English common law as it stood in 1970. Colonian law recognises the separation made under Thai law. Under Colonian law, bigamy is an offence.

Discuss whether Missus can remarry legally in Colonia, paying specific attention to the issue of the incidental question.

Answer plan

This question is primarily about the incidental question in the area of recognition of divorces and separations obtained abroad before the passage of the Family Law Act 1986 and the Recognition of Divorces and Legal Separations Act 1971. It should be borne in mind that Colonia is a country that applies the common law before the enactment of these two Acts.

It is crucial to define what the incidental question is. This should then be followed up with a discussion of the approaches suggested by writers. The application of the rule in *R v Brentwood Registrar of Marriages* (1968) must not only be cited but analysed. Examine how the court approached the matter and discuss whether this is justified. It would also be useful to refer to *Lawrence v Lawrence* (1985) where the court did not make a distinction between the main and incidental questions.

Answer

Since Colonia applies the common law as it stood in 1970, in order to advise Missus it would be useful to refer to rules of the common law in dealing with the incidental question which this case reveals. At common law, the incidental question is one that arises in the course of considering the question in issue but because it carries foreign elements, the problem is whether it should be resolved by referring to the forum's conflict rules or whether the court should use the appropriate conflict rules of the foreign system. According to Professor McClean three conditions must be fulfilled before a true incidental question may be said to be in existence. First the main question must by the application of the English (or in this case, Colonian) conflict rules be governed by the law of a foreign system. Secondly, a subsidiary question involving foreign elements must be found which is capable of arising in its own right or in other contexts, and for which there is a separate conflict rule. Thirdly, the English (or Colonian) conflict rule for the determination of the subsidiary question must lead to a different result from the corresponding conflict rule of the country whose law governs the main question.

Referring to the problem at hand, the main issue for the Colonian court is whether Missus has the capacity to remarry under the common law as it stood in 1970 (in this regard, the application of the two English relevant statutes – Family Law Act 1986 and Recognition of Divorces and Legal Separations Act 1971 – must be excluded). The main question would be referred by the common law (Colonian law) to the law of her domicile. This would presumably be the laws of Utopia where she is probably domiciled. The incidental question is the validity of the separation obtained in Thailand.

The Colonian court is faced with two options, the first is that the incidental question should be resolved using Colonian conflict rules whilst the second is to turn to the conflict rules of Missus's domicile, Utopian law. Writers are divided on which option to take.

On the first option, by applying Colonian conflict rules, the court may be compelled to give a decision which is contrary to its notions of public policy. Conversely by applying the conflict rules of the foreign system or by referring to the *lex causae*, Gotlieb (1) argues that uniformity of decisions can be ensured. Whether the case is tried and heard in Colonia or Utopia the result will be the same. The main problem with this approach is that sorting the incidental question from the main question is not always as a straightforward process. There is no fixed method in identifying the incidental question from the main question. It is not unforeseeable that in some cases the incidental question and the main question are inextricably linked (2). In such a situation determining what the *lex causae* is not free from difficulty. This makes the whole practice of looking to the *lex causae* for assistance highly unreliable. Hence instead of promoting consistency and international judicial harmony, it can lead to the opposite.

Under the common law before the passage of the 1971 and 1986 Acts as enunciated in *R v Brentwood Marriage Registrar* (1968), the respondent whose law of domicile refuses to recognise his or her legal separation or divorce may not remarry in England even though that divorce or separation is recognised in England. The choice of law rules as to capacity to marry prevailed over the rules on the recognition of foreign divorces and legal separations. In that case the Italian respondent had married a Swiss woman and had later obtained a divorce from her in Switzerland where they were both domiciled. Under Swiss law capacity to marry is governed by the law of the nationality of the party concerned, and since Italian law did not recognise divorces of Italian nationals, Swiss law could not give recognition to that divorce even though it was obtained in Switzerland. The English court's problem was deciding whether that divorce should be dealt with by the English conflict rule (which would have recognised the divorce) or by Swiss conflict rule (which would have pointed to Italian law). The Divisional Court applied the conflict rule of Swiss law (3). It must however be said that it was not clear how much attention the court actually gave the incidental question. It appears that the court only applied what seemed to achieve the best harmonisation of decisions between the fora concerned.

In *Lawrence v Lawrence* (1985), Lawrence married a Brazilian national who had obtained her divorce from her former husband in Las Vegas the day before the marriage to Lawrence. Lawrence was domiciled in England at that time. The question was whether the parties had capacity to marry. The incidental question is whether the domicile is valid according to the relevant choice of law rules. Under Brazilian law the divorce would have no effect. The Court of Appeal held that as the divorce was entitled to recognition in England, 'the plain man's view' that the parties to the divorce were free to remarry was to be applied (4). This is not the application of the conflict rules of the forum to the incidental question. As a matter of fact, the Court of Appeal in the case did not even make a distinction between the main question and the incidental question. It may be observed that there is no strict principled way to resolve the issue; the imperative seems to predicate on the need to achieve uniformity (5).

If the approach in *R v Brentwood* is correct, the incidental question in Missus' case would be dealt with by the conflict rule of the law of her domicile. Utopian law as the *lex causae* to the incidental question does not recognise the divorce. Thus, if the incidental question is to be separated from the main question, the result at Colonian law would be that Missus is not free to remarry. However as highlighted in *Lawrence*, the court may perhaps not make a distinction between the incidental question and the main question. Where the court takes the 'plain man's view' approach, the result may be quite different.

There are no guidelines as to when the incidental question should be distinguished from the main issue. In general though, it may be safe to suggest that where the courts agree to the distinguishing of the incidental question from the main question, then the *lex causae* should normally apply in order to achieve some degree of uniformity. The problem is not simply a choice between applying the *lex causae* or the law of the forum but perhaps the frequently overlooked issue of whether the incidental question can and does exist in its own right (5).

Notes

1 (1977) 26 International and Comparative Law Quarterly 734.
2 See *Lawrence v Lawrence* (1985) below.
3 In England the judgment should be read in conjunction with s 50 Family Law Act 1986 which provides that where a foreign divorce or nullity decree is recognised in the United Kingdom, the fact that the divorce is not recognised elsewhere shall not preclude either party from remarrying in the United Kingdom or cause the remarriage of either party to be regarded as invalid in the United Kingdom.
4 The 1971 Act had no application because the remarriage was entered into outside the United Kingdom.
5 Another interesting case is *Perrini v Perrini* (1979) where the remarriage contracted by the Italian domiciled man with an English woman was valid even though the decree of nullity obtained against him by his former wife is not recognised in Italy.
6 See for example, Woolf, *Private International Law* (2nd edn, 1950) ss 196-200; Gotlieb (1955) 33 Canadian Bar Review 523; Hartley (1967) 16 International and Comparative Law Quarterly 680.

Question 9 *

Compare and contrast the domicile of origin with the domicile of choice.

Answer plan

The importance of a domicile as a connecting factor in determining the personal status should be emphasised. The fundamental differences between the domicile of origin and the domicile of choice should be examined as well as the capacity of the domicile of origin to revive. Finally, the Law Commission reforms in this area should be discussed.

Answer

English private international law refers to the domicile in matters relating to personal status. Thus the domicile constitutes the most important connecting factor and as such is relevant to determine diverse issues, *inter alia*, the essential validity of a marriage, legitimacy, legitimisation, adoption, tax liability, succession, jurisdiction in matrimonial causes etc. Lord Westbury said in *Bell v Kennedy* (1868) that: 'Domicile ... is an idea of law. It is the relation which the law creates between an individual and a particular locality or country' (at 312). No person can be without a domicile and a person can have only one domicile at a time (*IRC v Bullock* (1976)). However, in order to acquire a domicile of choice a person of full capacity must first cast off the domicile of origin which the law ascribes to every person at birth. A legitimate child born during his father's lifetime receives the domicile of his father, an illegitimate child or a child born after his father's death has his domicile of origin in the country where his mother is domiciled at the time of birth (*Udny v Udny* (1869)). A foundling is considered to have a domicile of origin in the country where he is found. The domicile of origin is fixed for all times and cannot be changed. Since no one can make the first choice, a person can only shed the domicile of origin when a domicile of choice is acquired. The burden of proof is on the person who asserts it and it is an especially heavy burden when a person changes from a domicile of origin to a domicile of choice (*Cramer v Cramer* (1987)). Thus if one fails to satisfy the requirements necessary to establish a domicile of choice, the domicile of origin revives.

The persistence and tenacity of the domicile of origin implies that it returns as a boomerang during one's lifetime and even after one's death, for example in succession matters. One of the most spectacular cases in this area is *O'Keefe (Deceased), Re Poingdestre v Sherman* (1940) where it was held that Mary Alice O'Keefe who during her life (77 years) spent only three weeks in Ireland had Irish domicile at the time of her death. She was born in India, kept

British citizenship all her life, spent 47 years in Italy where she died. The only connection she had with Ireland was her three-week visit to Ireland and the fact that her father was born in Ennis, Co Clare. Regardless of the fact that her father had acquired a new domicile, through her failure to acquire a new domicile, she was deemed to be a domiciliary of the place where her father was domiciled when she was born. As a result, sometimes there is no connection whatsoever between a person and the country of his domicile at birth, yet he or she still keeps it.

The tenacity of the domicile of origin can only be understood in the light of the complexity relating to the acquisition of a domicile of choice. In order to acquire a domicile of choice, not only a mere physical presence is necessary but, more importantly, the intention to remain indefinitely in that country. The requirement of residence which is also called the factum is easily established. As Lord Chelmsford said in *Bell v Kennedy*: 'if the intention of permanently residing in a place exists, then the residence in pursuance of the actual presence in a new country is of no importance.' Thus the duration of the actual presence is not decisive. In the American case of *White v Tennant* (1888) one afternoon's presence within the jurisdiction was sufficient to acquire a domicile of choice. The residence as the factual requisite of domicile is easy to establish and the only problem which may arise in this context concerns the illegality of the residence. However, the second factor, the intention, poses more difficulty. There are a few reasons why the determination of the intention to reside permanently in a new country is fundamental. One explanation is that the priority given to intention over residency is based on the unhappy influence on the concept of domicile from the law of contract. However, it seems more convincing that there may have been a sense that someone's Englishness should not be sacrificed lightly and, consequently, the mere fact that someone is living abroad should not amount to acquisition of a domicile abroad. Indeed, in order to ascertain the intention to reside indefinitely it is necessary to prove one's state of mind which is extremely difficult since, as Brian J said in the 15th century: 'minds or will are not in themselves existing things that we can look at and recognise. We are restricted in our earthly experience to the observation' (Bryan, CJ in YB 17 Edw IV (1478)). Thus, all circumstances, however trivial, must be taken into consideration. As a result, the decision in each case depends upon the weight the judge attached to the various factors and future contingencies operating on the *propositus*.

The inquiry into the person's state of mind (in succession matters the person is dead) leads to uncertainty and unpredictability of results and the revival of the domicile of origin in many cases. There is no guidance, there is no objective test which would indicate whether the *propositus* intention is sufficient for the acquisition of a domicile of choice. In *Ramsey v Liverpool Royal Infirmary* (1930), a Scot, George Bowie, who spent 37 years of his life in England and did not return to Scotland even for the funeral of his mother was held to retain his domicile in Scotland. In *Re Joyce, Corbet v Fagan* (1946), George Joyce who was born in Galway, twice in his life confined to mental institutions, spent four years in Canada and 37 years of his life in England, was held to acquire English domicile. This case clearly shows that Joyce intended nothing at all as to his domicile. In *Winans v Attorney General* (1904), Winans hatred of England prevented him from acquiring a domicile of choice in England although he lived in the country most of his last 37 years. In *IRC v Bullock* it was held that Captain Bullock had not acquired a domicile of choice in England notwithstanding his long residency in this country (over 40 years) since he intended to return to his native country on the death of his English wife. However, in *Re Furse* (1980), an American who lived in England for 39 years but intended to return to America if his health would have prevented him from working on the farm in England was held to acquire a domicile of choice in England.

Upon the examination of case law in this area it appears that often more weight is given to a trivial act than one which was of considerable importance to the *propositus* as far as the determination of the intention is concerned. Indeed, the standards are so vague that it cannot be predicted which factor on the balance of probabilities will be sufficient to decide that the *propositus* has acquired a domicile of choice in any particular court proceedings. Consequently, very often the domicile of origin revives.

It is submitted that residence should be considered as the main factor in ascertaining whether a person has acquired a domicile of choice. Thus it should constitute a rebuttable presumption. Also the fact that the *propositus* has obtained a foreign citizenship, found a family abroad, established a business abroad, etc, should be held as relevant. These facts are perhaps more convincing in determining the acquisition of a domicile of choice than the dreams or desires to return to a native country on the death of a spouse or a mistress who may survive the *propositus*. Furthermore, often, the *propositus* intends nothing at all. It is not for the judge to make psychological speculations in order to determine whether a person shows the necessary degree of intention to constitute a requisite intention for the acquisition of a domicile of choice, the judge should only confirm the facts. In this respect the emphasis should be put on the residency requirement. Also, the substantial and real connections with a particular place are the best indications of the *propositus* intention. This approach has been applied by the English courts in a few decisions.

Finally, as the acquisition of the domicile of choice is difficult to ascertain, the revival of the domicile of origin which remains in the background ever ready to come back, is likely to happen in many cases. The doctrine of revival has been rejected in the USA, New Zealand and Australia. The Law Commission has taken the view that domicile of origin should be abolished. The domicile of children at the time of the birth and during their childhood would be ascertained but no special tenacity would be given to the domicile of origin and the doctrine of revival would be replaced by the rule that the domicile of choice would continue until an adult acquires another domicile of choice. It will ensure that the domicile of a person is determined in conformity with the law of the place with which the *propositus* has or has had some real connection and also that the ascertainment of the domicile is simplified.

* by Alina Kaczorowska

Question 10 *

Anna was born in Germany in 1909 to German parents. In 1929 she married Jose, whose domicile of origin was Spain. They decided to set up a family home in Italy immediately after their wedding. Their son Marchello was born in 1933 in Rome. In 1937 Anna and Jose decided to settle down permanently in Canada. They submitted an application for a permanent visa at the Canadian consulate in Rome.

In January 1938 their visa had still not been granted. Jose, 'fed up' with waiting, informed the Canadian authorities that he and his family would stay in England until all formalities regarding emigration to Canada were completed.

Two weeks after their arrival to England Jose died. During that time Anna received her Canadian emigration visa. She asked her friend Paula to take care of Marchello intending to return for him once she had set up home in Canada. She boarded a ship at Southampton and arrived at Halifax – there she decided to stay in a hotel whilst she made up her mind whether to go to Quebec or Manitoba. She died a week later in Halifax.

Trace the domicile of each of the persons mentioned above at English law.

Answer plan

Each person should be examined separately. Events which affect the domicile of one member of the family are not necessarily important in relation to the domicile of others. For that reason the following points should be discussed.

Anna

Her marriage to Jose, the death of her husband, her emigration to Canada

Jose

His move to Italy in order to set up a family home, his arrival in England, his death in England

Marchello

His birth, the change of residence of his parents, the death of his father, the death of his mother

Answer

Anna had her domicile of origin in Germany. In 1929 she married Jose, domiciled in Spain. They set up a family home in Italy. According to the old rule upon marriage women acquire the domicile of dependency of the husband and retain it for the duration of the marriage. Anna's domicile changes with the change of domicile of her husband, the person on whom she is dependent. The Domicile and Matrimonial Proceedings Act 1973 abolishes the domicile of dependency of a married woman. Her domicile is ascertained in the same manner as a domicile of any individual who can acquire an independent domicile. However, under s 1(2) of the Domicile and Matrimonial Proceedings Act 1973 which contains the transitional provision regarding women married before 1974, the domicile acquired upon marriage by a woman is considered as her domicile of choice provided it was not a domicile of origin until it changes by the acquisition of a domicile of choice or the revival of the domicile of origin on or after 1 January 1974. As a result, under the 1973 Act the domicile of dependency is re-imposed on a women married before 1974 as a domicile of choice. Therefore, in 1929 Anna acquired the domicile of her husband as a domicile of choice and her domicile followed changes in the domicile of her husband's domicile until his death (*IRC v Duchess of Portland* (1982)). In 1929 Jose was domiciled in Italy. Thus Anna was also domiciled in Italy.

In 1938 Jose abandoned his domicile of choice in Italy and moved to England. His Italian domicile ceased and his domicile of origin was revived and remained attached to him until he acquired a new domicile of choice. He had no intention of setting up a home in England as he was waiting for his Canadian visa. During this period he died. Thus he had his domicile of origin at the time of death. As for Anna, she would have the same domicile as her husband during the duration of their marriage. Even under the old common law rule, a married woman could acquire a domicile of choice if the dependency ended, for example on the death of the husband (*Re Cooke's Trust* (1887); *Re Scullard, Smith v Brock* (1957)). The application of s 1(2) of the Domicile and Matrimonial Proceedings Act 1973 would lead to the same result. After the death of Jose, Anna could acquire a domicile of choice. However she was still waiting for a Canadian visa and had no intention to remain permanently in England. As a result, her domicile of origin is revived. At that time she was domiciled in Germany.

Upon her arrival to Canada she kept her domicile of origin. Although she intended to live permanently in Canada, she could not decide where to go. In order to acquire a domicile of choice two elements must concur: the residence in the country and the intention to stay there permanently and indefinitely. The residence is a physical presence in the country. As to the requirement of residence (*factum*) it is less important from the point of view of the acquisition of a domicile of choice since as Lord Chelmsford said in *Bell v Kennedy* (1868): 'if the intention of permanently residing in a place exists, then residence in pursuance of that intention, however short, will establish a domicile.' The duration of the actual presence in a new country is of no importance (*White v Tennant* (1888)), and an immigrant can acquire a domicile immediately upon his arrival in the country in which he intends to settle permanently (*Bell v Kennedy*), even if he lives in hotels (*Levene v IRC* (1928); *Matalon v Matalon* (1952)). While it may be argued that Anna was physically 'resident' in Halifax, her intention was not to remain there. In the case of a Federal State such as Canada or the USA, the *propositus* has to establish his home in a particular state of the Federation. A person cannot be domiciled in the USA or Canada – only in one of its states or provinces. Consequently, Anna's intention to remain in Canada and her presence there are not sufficient, as she did not decide where to go. Thus the element of residency in a particular province of Canada is missing. During the period of indecision Anna must be deemed to have retained her domicile of origin and consequently she died domiciled in Germany.

Jose had his domicile of origin in Spain. He acquired a domicile of choice when he set up a family home in Italy. At that time both requirements necessary to acquire a domicile of choice were satisfied. He was physically present in Italy and he had an intention to remain there permanently and for an indefinite period. Once he decided to emigrate his intention ceased but not his domicile. A person abandons a domicile of choice by both ceasing to reside in a country and giving up the intention to reside there permanently. If only one requirement is satisfied the old domicile of choice remains. By giving up his intention of residing a person does not abandon his domicile of choice (*The Goods of Raffenel* (1863); *Zanelli v Zanelli* (1948); *IRC v Duchess of Portland* (1982)). As a result his domicile of origin had replaced his Italian domicile upon his arrival to England and remained attached to him until his death.

As to Marchello he is a legitimate child born during the lifetime of his father. Thus he has the domicile of origin in Italy, the country in which his father was domiciled at the time of his birth. Marchello's domicile of dependency would change according to the changes of his father's domicile since he was legally dependent on him. On the death of Jose, Marchello's domicile of dependency changed to that of his mother. He was dependent legally on his mother until her death and any change in her domicile would affect his domicile. His domicile of dependency would follow the changes in the domicile of his mother. At the time of her death Marchello was not *sui juris*. He was only five years old and could not acquire a domicile of choice. If there is no person on whom he may depend, his domicile of dependency cannot be changed at all. If Paula is a legal guardian of Marchello the situation is uncertain. There is no authority on this point but it seems that the domicile of Marchello cannot be changed by his guardian (in *Potinger v Wightman* (1817) the guardian was the child's mother). In any event, the principle is that the domicile of a child without living parents cannot be changed.

It is submitted that Anna had her domicile of origin in Germany. She acquired a domicile of choice in Italy when she married Jose. The transitional provision of s 1(2) of the Domicile and Matrimonial Proceedings Act 1973 applies. Thus Anna changed her domicile with the domicile of her husband. In 1937 when they decided to emigrate to Canada they both abandoned their domicile of choice and the domicile of origin revives. However, under the 1973 Act the domicile of dependency is re-imposed as a domicile of choice on women married before 1 January 1973. As a result Anna acquired the domicile of her husband as a domicile of choice namely that of Spain. On the death of Jose, Anna acquired a domicile of choice. However, she had no intention to settle down in England permanently and for an indefinite period of time. Since no person can be without a domicile her domicile of origin would revive and remain until her death. Indeed on her arrival in Canada she cannot decide where to go and as she dies undecided her domicile of origin subsists.

Jose's domicile of origin was Spain. He acquired a domicile of choice in Italy where he set up his family home. His domicile of choice ceased when he arrived in England. From that time his domicile reverted to his domicile of origin. He consequently died domiciled in Spain.

Marchello's domicile of origin is in Italy. His domicile of dependency would change with the domicile of the person on whom he is legally dependent. After the death of his father his domicile of dependency was in Germany since he was legally dependent on his mother. After her death he should continue to have his domicile of dependency in Germany since the domicile of dependency of a child without living parents cannot be changed at all (1).

Notes

1 However, in Australia, the Family Law Act 1975 provides that for certain proceedings a person is considered to be domiciled in Australia.

* by Alina Kaczorowska

Question 11 *

Paul was born in London in 1990. At the time of his birth, his mother Maria's domicile of origin was German and his father Hank's domicile of origin was French. They lived together but were not married. Hank registered Paul as his son at the French consulate in London.

In 1991 Maria and Hank decided to get married and set up a family home in Belgium. The ceremony of marriage was performed in Hamburg. After their honeymoon in Sicily, Hank took all their family belongings and went to Brussels in order to find a flat for his family. Both Maria and Hank decided that Maria and Paul would join him later.

In the meantime, Maria found a temporary job in London. She could not work and take care of Paul at the same time. Thus she sent Paul to her parent's home in Germany.

After her contract of employment had expired, she took a plane to Brussels. Unfortunately, the plane in which Maria was travelling crashed and she was killed. After her funeral, Maria's mother informed Hank that Maria had an affair with John whilst she was in London and that John, an English domiciliary, was Paul's real father. Furthermore, she intends to keep Paul with her.

Describe the various domiciles of Paul from his birth until now making sure you justify each change of domicile.

Answer plan

The following points should be examined:

- the domicile of origin of Paul. The fact that his parents were not married at the time of his birth will be decisive in this respect
- his domicile of dependency
- the subsequent marriage of his parents and its impact on Paul's domicile of origin and domicile of dependency
- the effect of the alleged paternity of John on Paul's domicile
- the domicile of Paul if Hank abandons him

Answer

The general rule is that no person can be without domicile (*Bell v Kennedy* (1868)). In this connection, it is necessary to determine the domicile of Paul since his birth till now. It was held in *Udny v Udny* that the domicile of origin is attributed to every person at birth by operation of law. The actual place of birth or the place of residence of the parents at the time of birth are irrelevant for the purpose of ascertaining the domicile of origin. The principle is that a legitimate child which is born during the lifetime of his father has his domicile of origin in the country in which his father was domiciled at the time of the child's birth. Consequently, it may happen that neither the father nor his child has ever lived or even resided in a country of their domicile (*Re Kennedy*).

The concept of the domicile of origin has a certain historical justification. In the days of the British Empire, the British moved to faraway countries in the service of the Crown or they settled overseas for various reasons. It is not unforeseeable that some later decided to settle abroad. They often spent their lives abroad, married and had children there. However, they considered themselves to be British and wanted their children to be British. The concept of the domicile of origin allows the transmission of the quality of Britishness through generations since the actual residence or presence in England is not required. Nowadays, the concept of a domicile of origin is highly criticised as artificial and inappropriate to modern life. The English and Scottish Law Commission consider that the concept has 'outlived its usefulness' and should be abolished.

However, at present the old rules apply and thus the domicile of origin of Paul depends upon the domicile of his father if he is a legitimate child or his mother if his is illegitimate. In our case, at the operative time, Maria and Hank were not married. Thus it would seem that Paul has domicile of origin in Germany as his mother was domiciled in Germany at the time of his birth. However, his father Hank has registered Paul as his son at the French Embassy in London. The domicile of illegitimate children is discussed in Question 48. Professor North considers that the personal status of a child should be determined according to the law of his domicile. In order to ascertain that law, reference should be made to the domicile of his natural father. At the time of Paul's birth Hank was considered to be his father since he had registered Paul as his son. Therefore, French law should decide whether Paul is a legitimate or illegitimate child. If under French law the distinction between legitimate and illegitimate children is abolished and all children are regarded as legitimate, Paul would be a legitimate child and would have French domicile of origin. Unfortunately, French law still recognises the distinction. The statute of 3 January 1972 which concerns children and which is incorporated in Articles 311–414 of the French Civil Code provides that the mother's *lex patriae* (nationality) at the time of birth or the child's *lex patriae* whichever is more favourable to the child determines whether a child is legitimate or illegitimate. It seems that German law will determine the question of his legitimacy and unfortunately for Paul under German law he is still an illegitimate child. As a result, he will have the domicile of origin in Germany as his mother was domiciled in Germany at his birth.

Paul also has the domicile of dependency. Under the Domicile and Matrimonial Proceedings Act 1973 until a child is 16, unless he or she is married before reaching the age of 16, the child is incapable of acquiring a domicile of choice and has a domicile of dependency. The dependant person has the same domicile as a person on whom he is legally dependent. Paul has the domicile of dependency in Germany, because he legally depends on his mother. The domicile of dependency contrary to the domicile of origin can change. If Maria changes her domicile, the domicile of dependency of Paul will change as well and will follow that of his mother.

In 1991 Maria and Hank got married. This event has an important impact on the legal situation of Paul. As a principle, the subsequent marriage of the parents of an illegitimate child renders the child legitimate. Under s 3 of the Legitimacy Act 1976 when the parents of an illegitimate child marry one another, and the father is not at the time of marriage domiciled in England but domiciled in a country by the law of which the illegitimate person became legitimate as a result of such subsequent marriage, the child will be recognised as legitimate from the date of the marriage. Section 3 changes the old common law rule which regards a child as legitimate only if the law of his father's domicile, at the time of the child birth and at the time of the subsequent marriage, recognises legitimation by subsequent marriage (*Re Goodman's Trust* (1881); *Re Grove* (1887)). Now, only the law of the father's domicile at the time of marriage determines whether subsequent marriage renders a child legitimate (*Heron v National Trustees Executors and Agency Co of Australasia* (1976)). In our case even the application of the old rule will legitimate Paul as Hank has the same French domicile at the time of Paul's birth and at the time of the marriage. The marriage of Maria and Hank will change Paul's domicile of origin as well as his domicile of dependency. There is no authority on this point but it seems well established that the domicile of an illegitimate child changes as a result of the subsequent marriage of his parents. However, legitimation is not retrospective but prospective. It means that a child acquires a new domicile of origin at the time of his parents' marriage. Until that time his domicile of origin is still with his mother. The marriage of Maria and Hank also changes the domicile of dependency of Paul. Since he is legally dependent on his father his domicile of dependency is French. As a result, from the marriage of his parents until Hank's departure to Belgium, Paul has his domicile of dependency in France. Once Hank settles down in Belgium Paul acquires a domicile of dependency in Belgium. The fact that Paul is sent to Germany has no effect on his domicile of dependency.

After the funeral of Maria, her mother tells Hank that Paul's real father is John, who is domiciled in England. This revelation neither effects Paul's domicile of origin as he is the legitimate son of Hank, nor his domicile of dependency. There is no authority on this point but it is submitted that since Hank has registered Paul as his son at the French Embassy, legally Paul is Hank's son although Paul has his domicile of origin from his birth until the marriage of his parents in Germany (which is the country in which his mother was domiciled at the time of his birth). The fact that the father and his son live in different countries has no effect on the domicile of dependency. The unity of domicile between a father and his legitimate son requires that the domicile of dependency of Paul changes automatically with any change that occurs in the domicile of the father (*D'Etchegoyen v D'Etchegoyen* (1888)). Furthermore, the new rules provided by the Domicile and Matrimonial Proceedings Act 1973 which allow changes in the domicile of dependency apply only if both parents are alive but are living apart and the child is legitimate or adopted. However, the Act will not apply since Maria is dead.

A different question may arise if Hank abandons Paul leaving him with Maria's mother for good. It is not certain whether Paul's domicile will follow his father's domicile as a domicile of dependency. In *Hope v Hope* (1968), a Northern Ireland case, Lord MacDermott LCJ questioned this rule and said: 'Why should it (the rule) apply to the domicile of the child to the will of a father who has abjured his responsibility by walking out of his child's life'.

It is submitted that Paul's his domicile of origin is in Germany which he keeps until the marriage of his parents according to the rule that an illegitimate child has his domicile of origin in the country in which his mother was domiciled at the time of his birth. He is considered illegitimate by English law and his personal law whether German or French. His domicile of origin changes as a result of the subsequent marriage of his parents, however, legitimisation has no retrospective effect.

As for his domicile of dependency, from his birth until the marriage of his parents he is dependent on his mother. Therefore, his domicile of dependency is in Germany. The marriage of his parents changes Paul's domicile of dependency and thus from the marriage of his parents until the arrival of his father to Belgium, Paul's domicile of dependency is France. When Paul settles in Belgium, Paul's domicile of dependency changes as well and follows his father's domicile. From that time until the present Paul's domicile of dependency is in Belgium. However, if he is abandoned by his father and lives with his grandmother he may acquire the domicile of dependency in Germany but his domicile of origin will still be in France.

* by Alina Kaczorowska

Chapter 3

Jurisdiction

Introduction *

When an English court is seised with a dispute containing a foreign element, it must first determine whether it has jurisdiction over the cause of action and the parties involved. This is a preliminary question to conflict of laws. The decision of where to sue has important consequences for the parties: once the court decides to exercise jurisdiction, rules of English private international law will be applied to the dispute even though the parties may seek to enforce the judgment elsewhere. Furthermore, the assumption of jurisdiction by an English court will result in the application of the *lex fori* to the majority of disputes since a foreign law is considered as a question of fact and consequently, the parties will have to plead and prove its content.

In England there are two different schemes for jurisdiction: traditional common law rules on jurisdiction and the rules created by the 1968 Brussels Convention on Jurisdiction and the Enforcement of Judgments in Civil and Commercial Matters as amended many times in recent years.

The traditional common law rules on jurisdiction are simple and liberal. An English court has jurisdiction if the defendant is present within the jurisdiction at the time of service of the writ however short his visit to England may be. The commencement of proceedings in England differs according to the legal status of the defendant as the defendant may be an individual, a partnership firm or a corporation. The service of the writ when the defendant is present within the jurisdiction must be regular, that is, effected in conformity with the Supreme Court Practice current rules in this area. If the defendant is present within the jurisdiction but cannot be served personally the plaintiff may submit an application to the High Court for an order for substituted service and the court can order service of the writ in any way it considers appropriate. Secondly, an English court has jurisdiction if the defendant voluntarily submits to the jurisdiction of that court. Finally, if the defendant is outside the jurisdiction the leave of the court for issue of the writ and its service out of jurisdiction is necessary. The procedure to follow for the plaintiff is contained in RSC Order 11 r 1(1). The jurisdiction under RSC Order 11 r 1(1) is discretionary and thus the plaintiff must convince the court to exercise its discretion in his favour. Since the application for leave is made *ex parte*, certain requirements must be satisfied in order to protect the defendant.

First, an English court must be cautious and careful and allow service out of jurisdiction only in proper cases. Any doubt as to the interpretation of RSC Order 11 r 1(1) must be resolved in favour of the defendant. The plaintiff must fully disclose all the facts of the case (*Societé Générale de Paris v Dreyfus Bros* (1885); *Metall und Rohstoff AG v Donaldson Lufkin and Jenrette Inc* (1990)). If the case is within the letter but outside the spirit of the rule the service will not be authorised (*Société Générale de Paris v Dreyfus Bros, ibid; Kroch v Rossell* (1937)).

Secondly, the plaintiff must show that he has a good, arguable case on the merits of his claim, that is, that he has more than a prima facie case but he is not required to convince the court beyond reasonable doubt since it is a preliminary stage of proceedings and thus the court will not hear and determine the case. In this area the guidelines have been laid down in *Seaconsar Far East v Bank Markazi Jomhouri Islami Iran* (1993).

Thirdly, in authorising service out of jurisdiction an English court applies the doctrine of *forum non conveniens*. However, the burden of proof is on the plaintiff. Consequently, he must show that England is clearly the 'natural forum'. Finally the claim may be within the scope of more than one of the sub-heads of RSC Order 11 r 1(1).

The technical side of service out of jurisdiction is contained in RSC Order 11 rr 5 and 6.

The regime set up by the Brussels Convention (as amended over the years) applies in cases where the defendant is domiciled in a contracting state. If he is domiciled in a non-contracting state, subject to Article 16 of the Convention (in cases of immovable property Article 16 confers exclusive jurisdiction to the courts of the contracting state in which the property is situated) the common law rules of jurisdiction are applicable. In cases within the scope of application of the Convention, that is, in civil and commercial matters, the leave is not required. The main ground of jurisdiction under the Convention is domicile. A person domiciled in a contracting state should be sued before courts of that state (Article 2).

The meaning of domicile is to be determined in conformity with national law of a contracting state. Special jurisdictional rules are contained in Articles 5–18. In some cases a court in a contracting state will have additional grounds of jurisdiction than the domicile of the defendant (Article 5 in relations to contract, tort, maintenance etc), in others its jurisdiction will be excluded (Article 16). These special rules correspond broadly to the grounds on which leave to serve out of jurisdiction may be authorised at present under RSC Order 11. Special rules are also established in cases regarding insurance and consumer contracts. Finally the doctrine of *forum non conveniens* is excluded in cases within the scope of the Convention, although some uncertainty lingers in this respect, which will certainly be decided conclusively by the Court of Justice in the future. Indeed, the role of the Court of Justice is essential to the uniform application of the Convention throughout the European Union.

Under the 1971 Protocol on the Interpretation of the Brussels Convention, a reference for a preliminary ruling may be made to the Court of Justice of the European Communities in a very similar manner to references under Article 177 of the EC Treaty. However, only appellate courts are authorised to refer to the court (Article 2 of the Protocol). Also national authorities may request a ruling from the Court 'in the interest of the law' when a conflict of interpretation results from different judgments without, however, affecting those judgments (Article 4 of the Protocol). Schedule 1 to the Civil Jurisdiction and Judgments Act 1982 gives effect to the Brussels Convention of 27 September 1968 on the Jurisdiction and Enforcement of Judgments in Civil and Commercial Matters and on the Protocol of 3 June 1971 on the interpretation of that Convention by the Court of Justice of the European Communities as amended by the Convention of 9 October 1978 providing for the accession of Denmark, Ireland and the United Kingdom to the European Community. The 1982 Act has been in force since 1 January 1987.

Checklist

In order to answer the questions contained in this chapter students should be familiar with the following:

- traditional common law rules on jurisdiction in action *in personam*: service of a writ on a defendant present within the jurisdiction
- RSC Order 11 r 1(1): service of a writ on a defendant out of the jurisdiction
- the doctrine of *forum non conveniens*
- the Arbitration Act 1975 which gives effect to the New York Convention on the Recognition and Enforcement of Arbitral Awards
- limitations on jurisdiction especially the Diplomatic Privileges Act 1964
- the Civil Jurisdiction and Judgments Act 1982 as amended (The Brussels Convention and the San Sebastian Convention)
- Schedule 1 to the Civil Jurisdiction and Judgments Act 1991 (The Lugano Convention)

* by Alina Kaczorowska

Question 12 *

The simplicity of the English rules on jurisdiction has been stripped away by the coming into force of the Brussels Convention on Jurisdiction and the Enforcement of Judgments in Civil and Commercial matters.

Discuss.

Answer plan

This is an essay question which requires comparing traditional common law rules on jurisdiction with the rules on jurisdiction set out by the 1968 Brussels Convention on Jurisdiction and the Enforcement of Judgments in Civil and Commercial matters as amended.

The main points that should be covered are:

- common law rules on jurisdiction an in action *in personam* when

the defendant is present within the jurisdiction and when the defendant is outside the jurisdiction
- the main features of the Brussels Convention
- the relationship between the Conventions and the common law rules on jurisdiction
- the role of the Court of Justice of the European Communities in interpreting the Brussels (San Sebastian Convention)

Answer

Under the Brussels Convention, the San Sebastian Convention, the Lugano Convention and the traditional common law rules on jurisdiction, the plaintiff commences the proceedings by summoning the defendant.

Traditional common law rules on jurisdiction in action *in personam* are simple: an English court has jurisdiction if a writ is properly served on the defendant present within the jurisdiction or if the defendant submits to the jurisdiction of an English court. If the defendant is outside the jurisdiction an English court will exercise its discretion based on RSC Order 11 r 1(1). In that case the plaintiff must apply for leave and, if granted, the plaintiff may serve the writ upon the defendant outside the jurisdiction.

In order to understand the complexity of rules on jurisdiction under the system of Brussels Convention it is necessary to examine:

- the various versions of the 1968 Brussels Convention
- its material scope of application
- the relationship with other conventions on jurisdiction ratified by the United Kingdom (Article 57 of the Convention)
- its application to the defendants domiciled in a non-contracting state

The various versions of the 1968 Brussels convention

The main objective of the 1968 Brussels Convention is to ensure the free circulation of judgments throughout the European Community. In order to achieve this objective it was necessary to unify the law on international jurisdiction in contracting states since a *sine qua non* of the enforcement of foreign judgments is the verification by the enforcing court of the jurisdictional competence of a decision – giving court. As a result the 1968 Brussels Convention is very ambitious and regulates two major issues: international jurisdiction of courts in contracting states and the recognition and enforcement of judgments rendered in other contracting states.

As the free circulation of judgments within the European Community greatly contributes to a European integration, the condition of membership of the European Community is the ratification by a new Member State of the 1968 Brussels Convention and the Protocol on its interpretation by the Court of Justice of the European Communities. The original Brussels Convention on the Jurisdiction and Enforcement of Judgments in Civil and Commercial Matters was concluded between France, Germany, Italy, Belgium, the Netherlands and Luxembourg on 27 September 1968.

Each enlargement of the European Community has necessitated changes to the original 1968 Brussels Convention and provided an opportunity for revising the existing rules. As a result, over the years the original 1968 Brussels Convention has undergone substantial modifications. At present, we have five versions of the 1968 Brussels Convention.

The first enlargement of the European Community has substantially modified the original 1968 Brussels Convention which for that reason is now of little importance. The second version of the 1968 Brussels Convention (Brussels Convention) is contained in the Convention of 9 October 1978 providing for the accession of Denmark, Ireland and the United Kingdom to the European Community.

In the UK Schedule 1 to the Civil Jurisdiction and Judgments Act 1982 gives effect to the Brussels Convention of 27 September 1968 on the Jurisdiction and Enforcement of Judgments in Civil and Commercial Matters and the Protocol of 3 June 1971 on the interpretation of that Convention by the Court of Justice of the European Communities as amended by the Convention of 9 October 1978 providing for the accession of Denmark, Ireland and the United Kingdom to the European Community. The Civil Jurisdiction and Judgments Act 1982 came into force on 1 January 1987.

The third version of the Brussels Convention which is incorporated into the Civil Jurisdiction and Judgments Act 1982 (Amendment) Order 1991 takes into account the accession of Greece to the European Community. No substantial changes were made to the Brussels Convention. Only its geographical scope of application was extended to Greece.

The fourth version of the Brussels Convention is known as the San Sebastian Convention. This Convention not only incorporated Portugal and Spain into the existing scheme but also made substantive changes to the Brussels Convention. The Civil Jurisdiction and Judgments Act 1982 (Amendment) Order 1991 which came into force on 1 December 1991 gives effect to the San Sebastian Convention.

The fifth version of the Brussels Convention is contained in the Lugano Convention which is a parallel Convention to the Brussels Convention. The Lugano Convention was concluded between the European Community and the European Free Trade Association countries (the EFTA countries: Norway, Iceland, Lichtenstein, Switzerland). The Lugano Convention is very similar to the San Sebastian Convention but gives no interpretive jurisdiction to the Court of Justice of the European Communities. The Lugano Convention appears as Schedule 1 to the Civil Jurisdiction and Judgments Act 1991 and came into effect in the United Kingdom on 1 May 1992.

The first difficulty in applying the Brussels Convention is to determine which of its many versions is relevant to the dispute. For that reason, it is always necessary to verify the date on which the proceedings have been commenced in order to select the version which, at that time, was in force in England (Article 54 of the Brussels Convention: its scope of application *ratione temporis*). The next step consists of determining whether the selected version was in force, at that date, in the other contracting states.

The material scope of application of the Brussels Convention

The scope of the application of the Brussels Convention ratione materiae is defined in Article 1. It provides that the Convention applies in civil and commercial matters. However, the concept of civil and commercial matters should have an 'autonomous meaning'. As a result, a community definition applies and thus what constitutes civil and commercial matters under the Brussels Convention does not necessarily correspond to what is understood under this concept by English law. The Court of Justice has clarified the meaning of 'civil and commercial matters' in *Netherlands v Ruffer* (1980); *LTU Lufttransport v Eurocontrol* (1976) and *Sonntag v Waidmann* (1993). In *LTU Luftttransport v Eurocontrol* the Court of Justice held that the Convention did not apply where a public authority acted in the exercise of its powers.

The second difficulty in applying the Brussels Convention is to determine whether the dispute is within its material scope of application. Matters excluded from its ambit are to be governed by traditional common law rules. The Brussels Convention expressly excludes:

- revenue, customs or administrative matters (Article 1)
- the status or legal capacity of natural persons, rights in property arising out of a matrimonial relationship, wills and succession (Article 1(1)). However, while maintenance is within its scope of application (Article 5(2)), divorce is not. Also, these matters are not excluded if they are incidental to the main action
- bankruptcy, proceedings relating to the winding up of insolvent companies or other legal persons, juridical arrangements, compositions and analogous proceedings (Article 1(2))
- social security (Article 1(3))
- arbitration (Article 1(4))

Brussels Convention in relation to other conventions on jurisdiction – Article 57

Article 57(1) of the Brussels Convention states:

> 'this convention shall not affect any conventions to which the contracting states are or will be parties and which in relation to particular matters, govern jurisdiction ...'

This provision further complicates rules on jurisdiction in England and Wales. It means that if the subject matter is within the scope of application of the Brussels Convention and an English court exercises its jurisdiction over the parties it may happen that another convention on jurisdiction will also apply to the dispute. In that case the Brussels Convention does not override the other convention. However, in Case C-406/92 *The Tatry* (1995) the Court of Justice held that the specialised convention prevailed over the Brussels Convention in matters not governed by the latter. Thus if the specialised convention contains no provision on *lis alibis pendens* or related matters then Article 21 (*lis alibis pendens*) and Article 22 of the Brussels Convention apply. The conventions within Article 57 are for example, the 1952 Arrest Convention, the 1952 Collusion Convention of Maritime Law, the 1929 Warsaw Convention Relating to the Unification of Certain Rules Relating to International Air Carriage.

The application of the Brussels Convention when the defendant is not domiciled in a contracting state

The fundamental principle of the Brussels Convention on international jurisdiction of courts in contracting states is *actor sequitur forum rei* which means that when the defendant is domiciled in a contracting state, he or she is subject to the jurisdiction of the courts of that state and the nationality of the defendant is irrelevant. This simple rule is subject to many exceptions. Under Article 5 which refers to special jurisdiction in seven specific situations the plaintiff may sue the defendant in a different contacting state from the one in which the defendant is domiciled. However, the Brussels Convention will apply in certain circumstances to the defendants who are not domiciled in a contracting state, and in so doing, creates an additional difficulty. In this respect it is necessary to examine two situations.

The Brussels Convention delegates jurisdiction to an English court and authorises the application of common law rules on jurisdiction regardless of the place of domicile of the defendant (Article 4) or assigns exclusive jurisdiction to a contracting state (Article 16) or permits to enforce: the agreement on jurisdiction (Article 17); the agreement in a matter relating to insurance (Article 12); the agreement in a consumer contract (Article 15) or accepts the submission to the jurisdiction by the defendant not domiciled in a contracting state (Article 18).

The second situation arises once the proceedings have been commenced in a contracting state on the basis of traditional national rules on jurisdiction (*The Nordglint* (1988)) or the Brussels Convention. Under Article 21 *(lis alibis pendens)* where proceedings involve the same cause of action between the same parties, the courts first seised, once its jurisdiction is established, shall try the dispute and the court seised second must decline jurisdiction in favour of that court. In *Gubisch Maschinenfabrik KG v Palumbo* (1987), the Court of Justice held that Article 21 should be interpreted broadly. In *Overseas Union Insurance Ltd v New Hampshire Insurance Co* (1991) it was stated that it was not necessary for either party to be domiciled in a contracting state.

This means in practice that if the proceedings are commenced in another contracting state, an English court (although it is authorised under Common law rules to exercise jurisdiction) must decline it on its own motion in favour of the first seised court. Secondly, if the proceedings are commenced in a contracting state, the plaintiff is entitled to seek provisional or protective relief from the courts of other contracting states. Article 24 would include, for example, the *Mareva* injunction. In this regard it is observed that the Court of Justice held in *CHW v GJH* (1982) that Article 24 applies only to provisional measures which concern the matters within the scope of the application of the Brussels Convention. In the United Kingdom s 25 of the 1982 Act governs this question.

It is submitted that the simplicity of the common law rules on jurisdiction has been largely displaced by the Brussels Convention. An elaborate statutory scheme is now in force in the United Kingdom. As a result, when a question of jurisdiction is at issue, the preliminary consideration of the possible applicability of the Brussels Convention is necessary. Furthermore, once it is decided that the Convention applies, the case law of the Court of Justice relevant to the dispute must be consulted. Although the Brussels Convention governs civil and commercial matters, its impact on common law rules in areas outside its scope of application is considerable. In addition the doctrine of *forum non conveniens* does not apply and thus, once the Convention allocates jurisdiction to an English court, it has no discretion but to try the case. However, the advantages offered by the Brussels Convention prevail over the disadvantages. The rules on jurisdiction are identical in all contracting states, and the enforcement of judgments which prior to the entry into force of the Brussels Convention were burdened by excessive procedural formalities is now speedy and inexpensive. Finally, the controversies, the difficulties as to the interpretation of the Brussels Convention, and the risk of divergent interpretation in contracting states have been minimised since the Court of Justice is competent to make preliminary rulings on the interpretation of the Brussels Convention at the request of courts in contracting states.

* by Alina Kaczorowska

Question 13 *

James, domiciled in England, was injured in a car accident while crossing the Champs Elysées. The driver was a French national. He was driving very carefully but was unable to stop the car in time because the brakes were faulty. Although the car was manufactured in Germany, the faulty part was made in Belgium.

At first, James merely felt dizzy. He found no visible injury on himself so he decided to join his fiancée in Amsterdam. While visiting his fiancée he collapsed and was taken to hospital where he underwent a serious operation. His illness prevents him from returning to his previous work in England. He wants to sue for damages.

Advise James as to the jurisdictional issues.

Answer plan

The question involves the application of Article 5(3) of the Brussels Convention. The problem with Article 5(3) is that almost every word requires interpretation. Therefore, it is necessary to examine the concept of tort, delict or quasi-delict under the Convention and also to try to clarify the meaning of the second limb of Article 5(3) which refers to the 'place where the harmful event occurred'. Indeed, it is sometimes difficult to establish the place of commission of the tort for jurisdictional purposes as the essential elements of the tort (the act and the damage) may be of a multifarious and complex nature. Thus the sequence of events giving rise to the tortious liability may embrace two or more events taking place in different countries. The damage may also be suffered in more than one country. Our case illustrates this kind of problem.

Answer

The fundamental principle of the Convention on international jurisdiction of courts in contracting states is *actor sequitur forum rei* which means that where the defendant is domiciled in a contracting state, he or she is subject to the jurisdiction of the courts of that state. Special jurisdiction is provided in Article 5(3) which states:

> 'A person domiciled in a contracting state may, in another states, be sued ... (3) in matters relating to tort, delict or quasi-delict, in the courts for the place where the harmful event occurred ...'

The Court of Justice acknowledged this necessity for independent interpretation of the expression 'tort, delict or quasi-delict' in the *Netherlands v Rüffer* (1980). However, the claim in Rüffer fell outside the scope of application of Article 1(1) of the Convention and the opinion of the Court on the subject of independent meaning was provided in *Kalfelis v Schroder, Munchmeyer, Heuqst & Co* (1988) where it was stated that the concept of matters relating to tort, delict and quasi-delict must be regarded as an independent concept. In this case it was held that:

> 'The term "matters relating to tort, delict or quasi-delict" used in Article 5(3) of the Convention must be regarded as an independent concept covering all actions which seek to establish the liability of a defendant and which are not related to a "contract" within the meaning of Article 5(1).'

Thus the Court of Justice has stated that in an action which seeks to establish a defendant's liability is necessary to determine whether the claim is contractual and, if not, it is *prima facie* within the scope of application of Article 5(3) of the Convention. The mutual exclusivity of claims in tort and contract is based on the French doctrine of non-cumulation of remedies according to which a claim in contract precludes parallel remedy in tort. However, the distinction is not obvious. Article 5(1) and 5(3) of the Convention are interrelated. Indeed, an action may be framed as a claim either in contract or in tort but for the jurisdictional purposes the choice must be made.

The decisions of the Court of Justice regarding the autonomous meaning of 'tort, delict or quasi-delicts' in Article 5(3) suggest that when an action arises from the agreement of the parties, an agreement they have freely entered into, it is within the scope of application of Article 5(1). However, an action which arises from the law attaching legal consequences to the act of a party is within Article 5(3).

Our case is simple as it involves an action in tort. However, the determination of 'the place where the harmful event occurred' which is necessary in order to ascertain the appropriate forum under Article 5(3) is more difficult.

In the light of the second limb of Article 5(3) it seems extremely difficult to define or determine the place of occurrence of the harmful event since this may be understood as the place where the wrongful event giving rise to the damage occurred. Here we have a choice between the place where the accident took place (France), the place where the car was manufactured (Germany) and the place where the faulty part was made (Belgium). It is thus difficult to decide which event in the series of events constituting the tort is determinative from the point of view of the application of Article 5(3).

As to the place where the damage occurred, we have a choice between the place where the damage first occurred (France), the place where the damage became apparent (Holland) and the place where the effect of the injury continues to be suffered (England).

The leading decision of the Court of Justice as to the meaning of the second limb of Article 5(3) was given in *Handelskwekerij GJ Bier BV v Mines de Potasse d'Alsace SA* (1976) where it was stated that:

> 'Where the place of the happening of the event which may give rise to liability in tort, delict or quasi-delict and the place where that event results in damage are not identical, the expression "place where the harmful event occurred", in Article 5(3) ..., must be understood as being intended to cover both the place where the damage occurred and the place of the event giving rise to it.'

As a result, the defendant may be sued, at the plaintiff's option, either in the courts for the place where the damage occurred or in the courts for the place of the event which gives rise to and is at the origin of that damage.

Does this decision solve our problem? The answer seems obvious. However, in *Bier,* the Court of Justice did not have to solve such problems since there was *ab initio* a single *forum damni* (Holland) and a single *locus delicti* (France). Thus the question remains as to what happens in the case of multiple *fora damni* or a multiplicity of places where the wrongful act was done.

In *Kalfelis v Schroder* the Court of Justice has shed new light on the matter. It held that Article 5(3) should be given a restrictive interpretation since it constitutes the exception to the general rule *actor sequitur forum rei.* It is a general rule of interpretation that exceptions to a principle should be interpreted restrictively, so as not to undermine the principle. In *Kafelis* the Court decided that a court in a contracting state should be prevented from exercising jurisdiction over a claim as a whole when it has the jurisdiction over only a part of a claim. In *Kafelis* the national court had competence to deal only with the tortious part of a claim.

In the more recent decision of the Court of Justice in *Dumez France SA v Hessische Landesbank* (1990) it was held that where a parent company was injured as a result of losses suffered by its subsidiary (ricochet damage), it could not bring an action in the courts of the place where the parent company discovered that it had sustained damage to its assets.

Furthermore, the restrictive interpretation of Article 5(3) has been confirmed in two recent cases: *Shevill v Presse Alliance* (1995) and *Marinari v Lloyd's Bank* (1995). In *Marinari* the plaintiff, an Italian domiciliary, lodged promissory notes of an exchange value of US$752,500 with a branch of Lloyd's Bank in England. The promissory notes were issued by the Negros Oriental province of the Republic of the Philippines in favour of a company located in Beirut. The Lloyd's Bank staff refused to return the promissory notes and advised the police of their existence and uncertain origin. As a result, the plaintiff was arrested and the promissory notes were sequestrated. The plaintiff, after being released by the English authorities, brought an action against Lloyd's Bank in Italy. He sought compensation for refusal to pay the exchange value of the promissory notes, compensation for damage he had suffered as a result of his arrest, compensation for breach of several contracts and damage to his reputation. Lloyd's Bank challenged the jurisdiction of the Italian court by claiming that the damage had occurred in England.

The Court of Justice held that the term 'place where the harmful event occurred':

> 'must be interpreted as not referring to the place where the victim claims to have suffered financial loss consequential upon initial damage arising and suffered by him in another contracting state.'

The fact that the Court of Justice favours a restrictive interpretation of Article 5(3) combined with the following passage from *Bier*: '... the defendant may be sued, either in the court for the place where damage occurred or in the courts for the place of the event which gives rise to and is at the origin of that damage ...', provoke a number of observations in relation to multiplicity of places where the wrongful act was done and multiplicity of *forum damni*.

It seems that the place of origin of that damage is relevant for jurisdictional purposes. In our example it is the place where the defective part was made (Belgium). Similarly, the place where the damage occurred at an earlier point in time constitutes a second option for the plaintiff. In our example the damage first occurred in France.

It is submitted that Article 5(3) of the Convention should be construed restrictively in relation to the determination of the place where a tort has been committed for jurisdictional purposes. As far as the first element of the tort is concerned, the place where the event which originally started the sequence of events which eventually resulted in the damage and without which the damage could not have occurred is relevant for jurisdictional purposes. As to the second element, a forum is an appropriate place for the trial only if the person or his property first became affected by the damage within the territory of that state. The Court of Justice offered a wider choice of jurisdiction to the plaintiff in *Bier* only for convenience of litigation. It means that in cases where the damage continues to be suffered by the victim for a long time in a state other than the state where the damage first occurred or if the plaintiff commences proceedings in a court located in a state other than the state where the damage occurred at an earlier point in time, the court of that place must decline jurisdiction.

It is submitted that James can sue the defendant, regardless of the nationality of the defendant in the place of his domicile under Article 2 of the Convention (France). Under Article 5(3) James can sue the defendant in the place where the defective part was made (Belgium). Similarly, the place where the damage occurred at an earlier point in time constitutes a second option for the plaintiff (France). However, he cannot sue in England the place where the damage continues to be suffered as the Court of Justice clearly favours the restrictive interpretation of Article 5(3).

* by Alina Kaczorowska

Question 14 *

Plum Corporation, a multi-national with its headquarters in New York, a manufacturer of computers entered into a contract with Robotex Sarl, a French company based in Paris. The 'contract' was agreed over the telephone. Under the terms of the contract Plum Corporation promised to supply Robotex Sarl with a new revolutionary computer which could be used in telecommunication. The contract provided that English law would apply if any disputes arose.

Robotex Sarl was dissatisfied with the subsequent delivery of the computers. According to Robotex Sarl the computers did not live up to contract specification as there was nothing revolutionary about them. Plum Corporations argued that the computers were built according to a new revolutionary technology in the USA. In France, though, this technology had been in use for many years. Robotex Sarl has commenced proceedings in Paris alleging that the exclusive jurisdiction agreement is invalid. It claims that there was only an oral agreement between them on jurisdiction in England and although Plum Corporation sent a telefax confirming the oral agreement and stating: 'competent forum – London.' The telex has never been answered in writing by Robotex Sarl. The legal adviser to Plum Corporation contests the jurisdiction of the French Court.

Advise Robotex Sarl as to the jurisdictional issues.

Answer plan

The question concerns prorogation of jurisdiction founded under Article 17 or Article 18 of the Brussels Convention. Article 17 confers exclusive jurisdiction in cases where there is an agreement on jurisdiction between the parties. Article 18 deals with the implied jurisdiction from submission as a result of the defendant's entering an appearance. In order to answer the question it is necessary to determine the application of Article 17 to a dispute where one of the parties is from a non-contracting state. Secondly the formal requirements of Article 17 should be examined. Finally the question of what a court in a contracting state can do if a court in another contracting state exercises jurisdiction in breach of an express clause conferring jurisdiction upon that court should be discussed.

Answer

Parties to an international contract are usually from different states and from different legal backgrounds. For that reason it is preferable to leave the choice of the law applicable to their contract and the selection of a court which will have exclusive jurisdiction to settle any disputes which have arisen or which may arise in connection with their agreement to the parties themselves. This principle implies that parties have equal bargaining power and thus the terms of a contract are negotiated by them rather then imposed by the party with greater bargaining power.

At the outset, it is necessary to examine whether the Brussels Convention applies to their agreement on jurisdiction. In this respect, Article 17 of the Convention stipulates that if at least one of the parties is domiciled in a contracting state and the parties have conferred jurisdiction upon a court in a contracting state, that court shall have exclusive jurisdiction. When both parties are domiciled in non-contracting states then according to Article 17 the court selected by the parties would have jurisdiction over the dispute and the courts in a contracting state may exercise jurisdiction only if the chosen court has declined jurisdiction. In our case Robotex Sarl is domiciled in a contracting state – France – and a selected court is situated in a contracting state – England. Therefore the English court has exclusive jurisdiction and Article 17 applies.

Secondly it is necessary to examine the formal requirements under Article 17 since its substantive requirements are not contested by the plaintiffs. Indeed, Article 17 lays down some formal and substantive requirements which an agreement conferring jurisdiction must meet in order to be effective. Robotex Sarl claims that the formal requirement has not been satisfied and thus the exclusive jurisdiction agreement is void. Indeed Article 17 of the Brussels Convention as amended by the San Sebastian Convention states that an agreement on jurisdiction must be in writing or evidenced in writing (Article 17(a)), or be in a form which accords with the practices which the parties have established between themselves (Article 17(b)) or in a form which conforms with a usage in international trade of which the parties are or ought to have been aware and which is widely known and regularly observed by parties to similar contracts in a particular trade or commerce (Article 17(c)).

In our case the question is whether a telefax sent to the plaintiff subsequent to an oral agreement which has not been confirmed by the plaintiff in writing satisfies the requirements of Article 17. In this respect the Court of Justice has stated in many cases that the formal requirements of Article 17 are necessary in order to establish without doubt the existence of a consensus between the parties as to the exclusive jurisdiction agreement (*Salotti v RUWA* (1976); *Segoura v Bonakdarian* (1976); *Custom Made Commercial v Stawa Metallbau* (1994)). It is interesting to mention that the Court of Justice has considerably changed its approach toward the formal validity of exclusive jurisdiction agreements. In the early cases the formal requirement were strictly interpreted. In *Salotti v RUWA* the court held that a choice of jurisdiction clauses printed upon the reverse of a contract did not amount to an agreement under Article 17 (see also *Galeries Segoura Sprl v Firma Rahim Bonakdarian* (1976)). However, later on the court has acknowledged that the formal requirements should not be so onerous as to hinder normal commercial practices. Thus in *Partenreederi MS 'Tilly Russ' v Nova NV* (1985) a clause printed upon the bill of lading was considered to be written confirmation of an earlier communicated oral agreement between the parties. For our purposes the important case is *F Berghoefer GmbH and Co KG v ASA SA* (1985). In this case the Court of Justice held that an oral agreement later confirmed in writing by one party and accepted by another although not confirmed in writing by that party satisfied the formal requirements of Article 17. Recently in *IP Metal Ltd v Route OZ SpA* (1993) it was held that a telefax subsequent to an oral agreement stating that 'law-England competent forum London', amounted to a valid agreement within the scope of Article 17 evidenced by the writing of the telex. Thus the agreement between Robotex Sarl and Plum Corporation would be considered as valid. This conclusion is clearly based on the principle of good faith. Indeed, Robotex Sarl should have contested the telefax immediately had it disagreed with Plum Corporation on the exclusive jurisdiction agreement.

Finally, in the context of our case it is important to examine whether the French court is entitled to determine the formal validity of an exclusive jurisdiction agreement. According to the Schlosser Report the court seised must decide of its own motion whether Article 17 allows it to have jurisdiction when a party challenges the clause of jurisdiction on the basis of lack of compliance with formal requirements. In the light of recent cases few conclusions can be drawn.

First, in *Elefanten Schuh GmbH v Pierre Jacqmain* (1981) it was held that contracting states are not free to lay down formal requirements as to the validity of an agreement on jurisdiction other than those contained in Article 17. As a result, a French court or an English court should reach exactly the same decision as to the validity of the agreement between our parties. If the agreement is valid, as it is in our case, then a French court should decline jurisdiction of its own motion. However, if, in breach of a valid agreement on jurisdiction, a French court decides to pursue the proceedings the aggravated party will still have some options. In *Kloeckner & Co AG v Gatoil Overseas Inc* (1990) (followed in *Denby v Hellenic Mediterranean Lines Co Ltd* (1994)) it was held that when proceedings are commenced in another contracting state in breach of an exclusive jurisdiction clause the Article 21 of the Convention (*lis alibis pendens*) would not apply even if a court in another contracting state has been seised first. It means in practice that when the requirements of Article 17 are satisfied a court in a contracting state has no discretionary power to override Article 17. Thus a French court must decline jurisdiction. If not, in *Continental Bank NA v Aeakos Cia Naviers SA* (1994) it was held that when proceedings have been commenced in breach of a jurisdiction clause before a Greek court instead of an English court, the later had jurisdiction to enjoin the plaintiff from continuing proceedings in Greece although the Greek court has been the first seised. The Court of Appeal stated that the construction of the jurisdiction agreement was governed by English law (the proper law was selected by the parties) and decided that the contested jurisdiction clause had conferred exclusive jurisdiction upon an English court. Consequently, the Greek court should have declined jurisdiction of its own motion. Obviously, if the party pursues proceedings notwithstanding an injunction he is in contempt of an English court and a judgment obtained abroad will not be recognised in England.

It is submitted that Article 17 of the Brussels Convention as amended by the San Sebastian Convention applies to the agreement on jurisdiction between Plum Corporation and Robotex Sarl although Plum Corporation is not domiciled in a contracting state. The formal requirements of an agreement on jurisdiction are also satisfied. Finally, a French court should decline jurisdiction of its own motion. If it decides not to do so then Plum Corporation may apply for an injunction to an English court restraining Robotex Sarl from continuing proceedings in France.

* by Alina Kaczorowska

Question 15 *

General Oil Corporation, a multi-national with its headquarters in New York entered into a contract with Polar Airlines, a French air cargo company based in Paris, to supply jet fuel to Polar's fleet in all European airports. The contract specified that English courts would have exclusive jurisdiction to settle any dispute which might arise in connection with the contract. Furthermore, it stated that should any dispute arise, the law in force in the State of California would apply.

Recently, the price of oil on the international market increased dramatically. At the time of contracting the parties agreed on the price of $8 per barrel. Now the price per barrel has reached $25. General Oil Corporation has claimed force majeure and refuses to supply oil to Polar Airlines. Polar has commenced proceedings in Paris. The legal adviser to General Oil Corporation claimed before a French court that under UCC section 2–615 General Oil Corporation is allowed to terminate the contract.

As the dispute proceeded General Oil Corporation relied upon the exclusive jurisdiction clause and contested the jurisdiction of the French court.

Advise Polar Airlines as to the jurisdictional issues.

Answer plan

Three issues are involved: first, whether Article 18 applies to a defendant not domiciled in a contracting state; secondly, whether General Star has submitted to the jurisdiction of a French court by arguing in alternative as it has raised not only the issue of jurisdiction but has also made a submission as to the substance of the action. Thirdly, whether Article 18 overrides Article 17. The judgment of the Court of Justice in *Elefanten Schuh GmbH v Pierre Jacqmain* (1981) and the decision of the Court of Appeal in *Continental Bank NA v Aeakos Cia Naviera SA* (1994) should be discussed.

Answer

Article 18 of the Brussels Convention deals with the submission to jurisdiction. Article 18 stipulates that 'a court of a contracting state before whom a defendant enters an appearance shall have jurisdiction'. However, when a defendant enters an appearance solely to contest the jurisdiction of the court, by doing so, he does not submit to the jurisdiction. Finally, if a court has exclusive jurisdiction by virtue of Article 16 the entry of appearance of the defendant before a court in another contracting state has no effect on the exclusive competence of that court. The idea behind Article 18 is that the defendant's entry of an appearance shall not prejudice his rights to defence.

The first question concerns the application of Article 18 to a defendant domiciled in a non-contracting state. Some scholars consider that Article 18 should be examined in the light of Articles 3 and 4 of the Convention. According to Article 4 when a defendant is not domiciled in a contracting state, subject to Article 16, the jurisdiction of a court in a contracting state should be determined by the law of that state and consequently the question whether the defendant has submitted to the jurisdiction of that court should be governed by national rules. In favour of that solution it may be said that nothing in the wording of Article 18 suggests that it applies regardless of the domicile of the defendant. Also, it is submitted that the defendant not domiciled in a contracting state is better protected if his submission is governed by national rules. For example, in England a defendant challenging the jurisdiction of an English court takes no chances that his action would amount to submission. If he contests jurisdiction he follows the procedure set up in RSC Order 12 r 8(6). Accordingly, he gives notice of intention to defend and applies to set aside the proceedings (1).

On the other hand, it is considered that both Articles 17 and 18 concern the prorogation of jurisdiction and thus should be construed in the same way. Also, the non-distinction between a defendant domiciled in a contacting state and a defendant domiciled in a non-contracting state for the purposes of Article 18 should ensure the uniform application of the Convention and thus the objectives of the Convention will be achieved.

It is submitted that Article 18 should be applied regardless of the domicile of the defendant. As Article 18 overrides Article 17 it seems logical that both provisions should apply regardless of the domicile of the defendant. Finally, the uniformity of solutions in all contracting states should prevail over temporary uncertainties as to the exact meaning of the entry of an appearance under Article 18.

As to the question whether General Star has submitted to jurisdiction, it seems that the defendant must be very careful while challenging the jurisdiction. When the defendant enters an appearance and fights the action on its merits, he submits to the jurisdiction. However, if as in our case, the defendant argues in alternative, it is clear that he does not solely contest the jurisdiction. Thus the strict interpretation of Article 18 may suggest that he would be considered as submitting to the jurisdiction. This problem has been clarified by the Court of Justice. In *Elefanten Schuh GmbH v Piere Jacqmain* (1981) it was held that the objective and spirit of the Convention required a liberal interpretation of Article 18. Thus when a defendant argues in alternative, that is makes submission as to the jurisdiction of the court and the substance of the action, it is not considered as making submission to the jurisdiction 'only if the plaintiff and the court seised of the matter are able to ascertain from the time of the defendant's first defence that it is intended to contest the jurisdiction '(2) (at p 1685).

Hence, if the challenge to the jurisdiction is not preliminary to any defences as to the substance and does not occur after making of submission, the defendant does not submit to jurisdiction. The decision of the Court of Justice is justified on the basis that under some national laws the defendant who raises only the issue of jurisdiction might be barred from making submission as to the substance if the court rejects his challenge regarding jurisdiction. In *Continental Bank NA v Aeakos Cia Naviera SA* (1994) the defendant had to follow Greek rules of civil procedure which obliged him to fight the action on its merits while contesting the jurisdiction of the Greek court. Thus it would be unjust and contrary to the right of the defendant to defend himself to decide that the defendant submits to the jurisdiction under those circumstances. In our case Star International has clearly submitted to the jurisdiction of the French court as it first made submission on the substance and it was only later that it contested the jurisdiction.

In this context the question whether Article 18 overrides Article 17 is of utmost importance. The Court of Justice in *Elefanten Schuh GmbH v Pierre Jacqmain* has defined the relationship between both provisions. It held that Article 18 applies even where another court has exclusive jurisdiction as a result of an agreement between parties. Indeed, as parties to an international contract are allowed to select the court which will be competent in case of a dispute they are also allowed to change their agreement. The entry of an appearance within the meaning of Article 18 constitutes a voluntary act on the part of a defendant and thus there is no reason why a new agreement between parties should not be respected by a court in a contracting state.

It is submitted that Article 18 applies although Star International is not domiciled in a contracting state. By contesting jurisdiction of a French court subsequent to filing a detailed defence on the merits to the plaintiff's complaint, Star International has entered an appearance and thus submitted to the jurisdiction of a French court. Since Article 18 overrides Article 17 the French court has jurisdiction to hear and determine the dispute between Star International and Robotex Sarl.

Notes

1 It was held that when the defendant acknowledges service and applies to set aside the proceedings he does not submit to the jurisdiction (RSC Order 12 r 8, *The Sydney Express* (1988)).
2 See p 1685 of judgment.

* by Alina Kaczorowska

Question 16 *

Sheik Andvac, one of the richest men in the world was the President of Richland for 20 years. Three years ago a military *coup d'état* took place in Richland and Sheik Andvac escaped to Italy. He was tried *in absentia* by a military tribunal in Richland which found him guilty of genocide and crimes against humanity. He was declared a traitor to the nation and his property both at home and abroad was confiscated. During his years in power, Sheik Andvac had accumulated enormous wealth. He has numerous bank accounts in his name throughout the world, *inter alia,* at the Floyd Bank in England.

The military government of Richland has started proceedings against Sheik Andvac in Italy in order to recover his wealth. It has applied for a worldwide *Mareva* injunction in the English High Court.

Discuss, citing relevant authority, whether the application by the military government of Richland for the worldwide *Mareva* injunction will be successful?

Answer plan

The following points should be examined:

- The *Mareva* injunction under s 37 of the Supreme Court Act 1981
- Article 24 of the Brussels Convention: *De Cavel v De Cavel*
- s 25 of the Civil Jurisdiction and Judgments Act 1982
- Order 11 r 1(2); *Republic of Haiti v Duvalier; Balkanbank v Taher*

Answer

The list of interim measures which an English court may grant appears to be unlimited. Any interim measures necessary and reasonable in the context of a particular dispute falling within the court duty of doing justice will be granted (*Astro Excito Navegacion SA v Southland Enterprise Co Ltd* (1982)). The main categories of interim measures encompass:

- an order addressed to the plaintiff to foreign proceedings restraining him from continuing to prosecute in another country
- an order against a defendant freezing his assets – the *Mareva* injunction
- an order against a defendant requiring that he allows his premises to be searched and property to be removed from his premises – the *Anton Piller* order
- an order for the preservation of property (ss 33 and 34 of the Supreme Court Act 1981 and RSC Order 29)
- an order in relation to the obtaining of evidence
- interlocutory injunctions in general (*American Cyanamid v Ethicon Ltd* (1975))

However, interim measures are granted at the discretion of the court. Thus even if an English court has jurisdiction to make a particular order it may consider inappropriate to do so.

In our case the plaintiff applies for a *Mareva* injunction. This interim measure has been named after the case *Mareva Compania Naviera SA v International Bulk Carriers SA* (1975). Now it is contained in s 37 of the Supreme Court Act 1981, although s 37(3) refers to 'assets located within [the] jurisdiction' it has been established that overseas assets are included and that the *Mareva* injunction may be granted even though there are no assets in England (*Babanaft v Bassatne* (1990)). The explanation is that the *Mareva* injunction is personal, that is over the defendant, and not proprietary in character. The *Mareva* injunction includes an order to disclose the location of the defendant's assets, to freeze some or all of his assets for the indefinite period of time (*PCW (Underwriting Agency) v Dixon* (1983)) or even to move his assets from one jurisdiction to another (*Derby v Weldon (No 6)* (1990)). To render the *Mareva* injunction effective the court is empowered to order appropriate measures such as the discovery of documents and even to administer interrogations (*A v C* (1980)). If the defendant refuses to comply with the order he will be in contempt of the English court. Furthermore, a third party (a person not mention by the injunction) who consciously interferes with the assets contemplated in the injunction will also be considered in contempt of an English court. The *Mareva* injunction neither affects the ownership of the assets (the effect of dispute regarding the ownership of assets within the scope of the injunction has been discussed in *SCF Finance v Masri* (1985)) nor improves the position of the plaintiff as against other creditors of the defendant by giving him the priority over the assets. The *Mareva* may be granted both before and after judgment.

In the present case the plaintiff applies for a worldwide *Mareva* injunction. In order to succeed he must have a good arguable case and must show that the English assets are not sufficient to satisfy the likely judgment and that there are assets abroad; finally he must demonstrate that there is a risk that those assets will be dissipated or secreted and thus may render any judgment which he might obtain nugatory. Even though these criteria are fulfilled an English court will grant a worldwide *Mareva* injunction only in exceptional cases (*Babanaft*).

In our case the proceedings have been commenced in another contracting state to the Brussels Convention. Provided that the subject matter of the dispute is within the material scope of application of the Convention, Article 24 will apply (*De Cavel v De Cavel* (1979)). It was held in *Republic of Haiti v Duvalier* (1989) that a claim regarding tracing and recovering of stolen property falls within the ambit of the Convention. Furthermore in *Denilauler v SNC Couchet Frères* (1980) the Court of Justice emphasised that the court of the place where the assets are located is the best place to decide whether to grant the measure and also to decide what conditions and procedural requirements are necessary to ensure the effectiveness of the measure. In this context, it is necessary to examine Article 24 of the Convention which stipulates that:

> 'Application may be made to the courts of a contracting state for such provisional, including protective, measures as may be available under the law of that state, even if, under this Convention the courts of another state have jurisdiction as to the substance of the matter.'

It is clear that Article 24 does not require the court in another contracting state to grant this remedy and emphasises the national law as a source of the interim measures. Under the traditional rules the *Mareva* injunction was considered as an ancillary order which could only be granted if the English courts had jurisdiction over the main action (*The Siskina* (1971)) (1). Thus the application of the traditional approach would deprive Article 24 of the Convention of any practical importance. However, s 25(1) of the Civil Jurisdiction and Judgments Act 1982 remedies this situation as it provides that English courts may grant interim measures where proceedings have been or are to be commenced in another contracting state and that the subject matter of the dispute is within the scope of application of the Convention. The jurisdiction of an Italian court over the substantive dispute will therefore not prevent an English court from granting the *Mareva* injunction.

Both Article 24 of the Convention and s 25 of the Civil Jurisdiction and Judgments Act 1982 allow an English court to grant interim measures. However, the *sine qua non* for making such an order is that the defendant is subject to the jurisdiction of an English court. It means that the defendant for the purposes of the application for interim relief must be present within the jurisdiction and thus the service of the writ poses no problems or if he is outside the jurisdiction he must be liable to be served with the writ under RSC Order 11. In our case the defendant is outside the jurisdiction but he is domiciled in a contracting state. This is an important factor in relation to a worldwide *Mareva* injunction. It was held in *Republic of Haiti v Duvalier* (1989) that where a defendant is domiciled in a contracting state, on the basis that Article 24 gave the court jurisdiction to deal with the application, Order 11 r 1(2) (2) allowed the defendant to be served with the proceedings outside the jurisdiction without the leave of the court. Thus, the service of the writ is available as of right if the defendant is domiciled in a contracting state. In *Republic of Haiti v Duvalier* the plaintiff succeeded in his application for a worldwide *Mareva* injunction only because the defendant was domiciled in a contracting state. Also in *Balkanbank v Taher (No 3)* (1994) a worldwide *Mareva* injunction was granted in aid of Irish proceedings. Although the domicile of the defendant in a contacting state is fundamental for obtaining the relief in England, it seems that even more important is the fact that the proceedings are in a contracting state. In *X v Y* (1990), where a French court had jurisdiction over the main action and the defendant was not domiciled in a contracting state as he was a Saudi Arabian, the Court of Appeal granted the leave to serve out on the ground of RSC Order r (1)(b).

As a principle, English courts are very reluctant to grant a worldwide *Mareva* injunction outside the scope of s 25(1) of the 1982 Act. In *Rosseel NV v Oriental Commercial Shipping (UK) Ltd* (1990) the Court of Appeal refused to grant a worldwide *Mareva* injunction when the plaintiffs were seeking to enforce an arbitral award under s 3 of the Arbitration Act 1975 rendered in New York but granted a *Mareva* injunction in respect of assets of the defendants within the jurisdiction.

It is submitted that according to the decision of the Court of Appeal in *Republic of Haiti v Duvalier* the application by the Military government of Richland for the worldwide *Mareva* injunction in the English High Court will be successful. However, in *Republic of Haiti v Duvalier* , the French court held that it had no jurisdiction over the claim since claims made by a state against its present or former leaders were considered to be relating to public law and thus outside the competence of the French courts (Cass civ 1, 29 May 1990).

Notes

1 Section 25(3), (4) and (6) extends the jurisdiction of English courts to grant interim measures in cases outside the Convention. In *Channel Tunnel Group Ltd v Balfour Beatty Construction Ltd* it was decided that an English court may grant interim measures if it has personal jurisdiction over the defendant, and the plaintiff has a cause of action which he may pursue in England or elsewhere even though the court may try the dispute.

2 Order 11 r 1(2) states: 'Service of a writ out of the jurisdiction is permissible without the leave of the court provided that each claim made by the writ is ... a claim which by virtue of the Civil Jurisdiction and Judgments Act 1982 the court has power to hear and determine.'

* by Alina Kaczorowska

Question 17 *

Critically examine the application of the doctrine of *forum non conveniens* in England.

Answer plan

The doctrine of *forum non conveniens*, its gradual recognition in England and its objectives should be discussed. The guidelines laid down by the House of Lord in *Spiliada* as to the discretion with regard to stays of English proceedings should be examined. Finally, the application of the doctrine of *forum non conveniens* and the controversies it raises should be evaluated. The following cases are relevant to the question:

- *St Pierre v South American Stores (Gath and Chaves) Ltd*
- *The Atlantic Star*
- *MacShannon v Rockware Glass Ltd*
- *The Abidin Daver*
- *The Spiliada Maritime Corporation v Cansultex Ltd*

Answer

The fundamental objective of stays of English proceedings and restraining the plaintiff from commencing or continuing foreign proceedings is to prevent the forum shopping, that is, allowing the plaintiff to choose the forum which is most advantageous to him when he has a choice of one or more *fora*. Lord Pearson in *Boys v Chaplin* (1968) defined forum shopping in the following terms: 'a plaintiff by-passing his natural forum and bringing his action in some alien forum which gives him relief or benefits which would not be available to him.'

In England, the traditional common law rules on jurisdiction offer the plaintiff easy access to courts since their jurisdiction depends upon service. If the defendant is present within the jurisdiction he may be served with a writ, provided he is not fraudulently induced to come to England. No nexus between England and the actual subject matter of the dispute or parties to the dispute is required. On the other hand, if the court authorises service of a writ out of jurisdiction under RSC Order 11, the defendant is amenable to English jurisdiction regardless of where he is. Proceedings in England may be very advantageous to the plaintiff for many reasons depending upon the facts of the dispute. Some of these reasons include the higher level of damages in England than on the continent, the fact that English courts are known for their impartiality, expertise and fairness, and that the procedure offers the plaintiff an opportunity to bring his own experts witnesses etc. In this context the recognition of the doctrine of *forum non conveniens* as developed in Scotland *(Credit Chimique v James Scott Engineering Group Ltd* (1979)) or in the USA (*Gulf Oil Corporation v Gilbert* (1947)), was very controversial. On one hand the advantage to the plaintiff results in the disadvantage to the defendant and thus when an English court has jurisdiction on the basis of some procedural rules but English forum is not the most appropriate for trial, the requirements of natural justice are undermined.

On the other hand, the reputation of the English court has been achieved over centuries and there is no reason to believe that proceedings in England would cause an injustice to the defendant. Furthermore, international litigation constitutes a valuable export and if two foreigners litigate in England the financial advantage to the Crown and to the legal profession is obvious. Finally, non-recognition of the doctrine of *forum non conveniens* did not mean that English courts could not stay of proceedings or restrain the plaintiff from institution or continuance of proceedings in a foreign country. Under the test formulated in *St Pierre v South American Stores (Gath and Chaves) Ltd* (1936) if the plaintiff had 'set out deliberately to harass the defendant' the stay was granted provided it did not cause an injustice to the plaintiff and that his action was oppressive or vexatious to the defendant (1). This approach, in my opinion has been wrongly criticised, for demonstrating legal chauvinism. Be that as it may, the rule has gradually been relaxed. In *The Atlantic Star* (1974) the House of Lords held that the words 'oppressive and vexatious' should be interpreted more liberally and that the advantage to the plaintiff and the disadvantage to the defendant should be taken into consideration in granting a stay. Thus, a stay could be granted even where the plaintiff had not acted in bad faith.

In *MacShannon v Rockware Glass Ltd* (1978) Lord Diplock reformulated the test in order to make it even more liberal. He stated that two conditions must be satisfied to justify a stay: one positive – the defendant must convince the court that there is another forum available to him in which proceedings can be conducted at substantially less inconvenience and expense, and a negative one – the stay must not deprive the plaintiff of a legitimate personal or judicial advantage which would be available to him if he invoked the jurisdiction of the English court.

The doctrine of *forum non conveniens* was unequivocally accepted in *The Abidin Daver* (1984). In that case a Cuban vessel collided with a Turkish vessel in Turkish waters. The Turkish owner had commenced proceeding in Istanbul and the Cuban owner began an action in the English Admiralty Court. The Turkish owner applied for a stay. The House of Lords decided that the Turkish court was the natural and more appropriate forum and granted the stay. However, in *The Abidin Daver* and subsequent cases the difficulties arose as to the meaning of the plaintiff's 'legitimate personal or judicial advantages'. Thus, for example, the question of whether the prospect of recovering higher damages in one country than another amounted to a legitimate advantage had received conflicting views. In *Castanho v Brown & Root Ltd* (1981) it was held that the prospect of higher damages in Texas constituted a legitimate advantage while in *Smith, Kline & French Laboratories Ltd v Bloch* (1983) the Court of Appeal decided to the contrary as to higher damages in New York. In order to clarify the matter in *Spiliada Maritime Corporation v Cansulex Ltd (The Spiliada)* (1987) the House of Lords laid down guidelines as to the application of the doctrine of *forum non conveniens*. It held that in order to stay proceedings in England:

- There must be some other available forum in which the case may be heard and determined more suitably in the interest of all parties and of justice. In international litigation there are usually two or more available fora. Only when there is clearly a more appropriate forum abroad the stay will be granted (MacShannon, at 477; *European Asian Bank v Punjab & Sind Bank* (1982); *The Coral Isis* (1986); *Re Harrods (Buenos Aires) Ltd* (1992)). Consequently an English court will not stay proceedings if there is no clearly more appropriate forum abroad (*The Spiliada* – the collision took place on the high seas). However, when there is a more appropriate forum but justice requires the continuance of proceedings in England, no stay will be granted (in *The Abidin Daver*, for example, it was shown that the judiciary was not independent, in *Vishva Ajay, The Oinoussian, Pride* (1991) there was an inordinate delay of 10 years before trial; in *The Adhiguna Meranti* (1988) there was a derisorily low limit on damages). However, the plaintiff is not allowed to make general or unproven allegation about the inferiority of a foreign court and its procedural rules (*The El Amria* (1981)). Furthermore, it places the plaintiff in a dangerous situation: if the stay is not granted he has to return to the court criticised previously. Recent decision on this point are quite controversial. For example in *Roneleigh v MII Exports* (1989) the court did not stay proceedings in England on the basis that higher costs in New Jersey which was clearly a more appropriate forum would deprive the plaintiff of the results of his successful action in New Jersey although its judgment would certainly be recognised in England. In *Banco Atlantico v British Bank of the Middle East* (1990), the fact that the court of Sharjah would ignore the conflict of law rules or apply them is a way so different from the English as to be patently wrong resulted in refusing the stay. It was quite clear that the plaintiff would lose in Sharjah but win in England. This approach raises an objection. It is not the task of an English court to assess the conflict of law rules of a foreign state or its procedural rules. It should not be important whether the plaintiff wins or loses before a foreign court. The important consideration is whether the judgment of a foreign court will be recognised in England, and if so, there is no reason to refuse a stay.

- The burden of proof is on the defendant. He must show not only that England is not an appropriate forum but that there is clearly a more appropriate forum abroad. If he succeeds the burden of proof passes to the plaintiff who then would have a difficult task. He must prove that although there is a more appropriate forum abroad nevertheless there are important reasons why the case should not be tried in that forum but in England. At this stage the fact that there is a more appropriate forum abroad will become only a factor to be taken into account and the main consideration will be whether it will be just or unjust to stay proceedings in England.
- The natural forum is the one with which the action has its closest and most real connection. In order to determine the

'natural forum' many factors should be taken into consideration. However, a 'legitimate or juridical advantage' to the plaintiff, such as the prospect of higher damages and a longer limitation period, etc are factors merely to be taken into account, but are not conclusive (2).

In this regard, the advantage to the plaintiff can be personal or juridical. The fact that the plaintiff is resident in England will be treated as a personal advantage. A juridical advantage may be the existence of a favourable substantive rule not available elsewhere. For example, in *Power Curber International Ltd v National Bank of Kuwait* (1981) an English conflict of law rule would lead to the application of a summary judgment. Procedural advantage include higher damages (*The Atlantic Star*), or more generous limitation period (*The Spiliada*). Furthermore the advantage must be legitimate which excludes any benefit to the plaintiff which he seeks to obtain by harassing the defendant. However, it was emphasised in *The Abidin Daver* that the courts should not be engaged in comparing the quality of justice available abroad and that the great experience of the English Admiralty and commercial courts should no longer be considered as a considerable advantage to the plaintiff.

In general, the factors that are to be taken into account in determining the most appropriate forum vary depending on circumstances of a particular case. The important development in *The Spiliada* is that weight attached to the advantages to the plaintiff have been reduced, and thus a more objective test is to be run in order to determine the 'natural forum'. The evaluation of the significance of a particular factor is a factual matter and thus should not be done automatically or in abstract (*The Spiliada; The Po* (1991)).

Some factors may be extracted from recent cases. For example, if both parties reside in a same country it seems that for the convenience of litigation the courts of that country have *prima facie* jurisdiction to hear and determine their dispute (however, not if the residence is acquired merely for tax reasons: *The Spiliada*, Lord Goff pp 481–82). Further, procedural questions relating to evidence may be of some importance. As to the law applicable to the dispute, especially in tort matters, the *lex loci delicti commissi* will be applied anyway thus it makes more sense for the court of that place to have jurisdiction (*The Abidin Daver, The Nile Rhapsody* (1994)) but it is not the decisive factor (*Charm Maritime Inc v Kyriakou* (1987); the decision to the contrary *Muduroglu Ltd v TC Ziraat Bankasi* (1986)). However, if the matter concerns English public policy, it will certainly be decided by an English court (*DuPont v Agnew (No 1)* (1987)). In general the applicable law is not a decisive factor since a foreign court may not share the opinion of an English court as to the applicable law and furthermore the United Kingdom is a party to the European Convention on Information on Foreign Law which was elaborated under the auspices of the Council of Europe and entered into force on 17 December 1969. As a result, if a foreign law is applicable, it is relatively easy for an English court to assess objectively its content. Indeed, the system set up by the Convention is impartial, simple, reliable, relatively prompt and most importantly – free of charges for the parties but unfortunately rarely used (3).

The existence of *lis alibi pendens*, especially if the plaintiff commences proceedings in two different courts, varies in importance. In *Australian Commercial Research & Development v ANZ* (1989) the plaintiff had to select one of them. However, he may also seek to stay one proceeding while pursuing the other (*AG v Arthur Andersen & Co* (1989)). Finally, the interest of other parties to the litigation may be important but not conclusive. For example it had been of preponderant importance in *New Hampshire Insurance v Strabag Bau AG* (1992) but of little significance in *First National Bank of Boston v Union Bank of Switzerland* (1990). In *Charm Maritime Inc v Minas Xenophon Kyriakou and David John Mathias* (1987) it was decided that if by a trial in England the defendant is able to continue proceedings against two separate defendants in the same dispute, this is a significant advantage to the plaintiff yet not to the detriment of the defendant. Thus if a plaintiff obtains a significant advantage from a trial in England which does not result in a corresponding disadvantage to the defendant, there may be injustice if a stay were to be granted.

It is submitted that the doctrine of *forum non conveniens*, has finally taken roots in English private international law. The doctrine as applied and formulated in *The Spiliada* takes into consideration the interests of both parties and the requirements of justice. Its application poses some delicate problems which are inherent in determining the most real and substantive connection regardless of the context in which the substantive link is placed.

Although the recognition of the doctrine of *forum non conveniens* has been welcomed by English scholars, the High Court of Australia in *Oceanic Sun Line v Fay* (1988) (also in *Voth v Manildra* (1991)) which has rejected it. If the plaintiff considers England as the most appropriate forum, the requirements of natural justice are not undermined and provided the proceedings are not vexatious and oppressive, there is no reason to prevent the plaintiff from commencing his action in England. Furthermore, in practice the application of the doctrine of *forum non conveniens* introduces new uncertainty to often complex international litigation. Instead of concentrating on the merits of the action, the parties have to fight over procedural matters. Also, the assumption of jurisdiction under the common law rules are no more outrageous then the exorbitant jurisdiction of courts in other countries. For example, in France under Article 14 and 15 of the French Civil Code, a French court has jurisdiction if one of the parties is a French national even though he resides abroad. It is the one and only connecting factor allowing French courts to exercise jurisdiction.

Notes

1 It is not considered as vexatious if the dispute has no connection with England or English law.

2 In Canadian case *Amchem Products Inc v British Columbia (Workers' Compensation Board)* (1993) it was held that the loss of juridical advantage is not a separate condition but only a factor to be taken into consideration. The same in *Frymer v Brettschneider* (1994).

3 On this subject see *International Trade Conventions and Their Effectiveness: Present and Future* (1995) The Hague: Kluwer Law International, pp 82–85.

* by Alina Kaczorowska

Question 18 *

John Smith is a Canadian national employed as a chauffeur by the Canadian Ambassador in London. He has been a collector of Victorian dolls since his childhood.

Recently, he entered into a contract to supply 20 Victorian dolls worth £2,000 to Anna. Anna is domiciled in England and is a keen collector of Victoriana. Anna paid the purchase price and took delivery of the dolls. She has since discovered that the dolls were not genuine antiques, but clever imitations from the 1960s. She wishes to sue John Smith in London, but since she has little income she is concerned about the procedural aspect of commencing proceedings against him.

Advise Anna on all these issues.

Answer plan

Three issues should be discussed in relation to our case. First, it is necessary to examine whether John Smith is entitled to claim exemption from the jurisdiction of an English court. He works as a chauffeur for the Canadian High Commissioner in England and thus is a member of his diplomatic mission. If he enjoys absolute diplomatic immunity from civil proceedings in the United Kingdom under the Diplomatic Privileges Act 1964 Anna will be barred from commencing proceedings against him. On the other hand, if John cannot invoke the diplomatic immunity then it is necessary to examine common law rules on jurisdiction and to determine the mode and manner of service of process upon him. The following point should be examined:

- The Diplomatic Privileges Act of 1964 and especially the extent of immunity granted to a personal chauffeur of a High Commissioner
- common law rules of jurisdiction particularly when the defendant is present within the jurisdiction
- procedural rules regarding service of writs upon a defendant present within the jurisdiction

Answer

An English court cannot exercise jurisdiction over certain categories of persons and bodies which under international law are immune from the jurisdiction of municipal courts. First, foreign states enjoy sovereign immunity. In the United Kingdom the State Immunity Act 1978 which gives effect to the European Convention on State Immunity 1972 regulates the extent of sovereign immunity and makes provision for various exceptions from it. Secondly, diplomatic agents of a foreign state in the United Kingdom enjoy diplomatic immunity. Furthermore, the International Organisations Acts 1969 and 1981 regulate the extent of exemptions from jurisdiction of English courts of representatives of such organisations (*Standard Chartered Bank v International Tin Council* (1987)). Although consular officers of a foreign state are not diplomatic representatives they also enjoy the immunity from jurisdiction in England. This is governed by the Consular Relations Act 1968 which implements the Vienna Convention on Consular Relations 1963. Finally, special statutory limitations on jurisdiction are provided by international conventions such as, *inter alia*, the Rhine Navigation Convention, the Nuclear Installations Act 1965.

With respect to the first question it is necessary to emphasise that diplomatic immunity is 'essential for the maintenance of relations between states and [is] accepted throughout the world by nations of all creeds, cultures and political complexions' (*USA v Iran* (1980)). Indeed, diplomatic relations are based on mutual consent between the sending state and the receiving state. Since a state is both a receiving and a sending state the rules on diplomatic immunity are universally respected and rarely breached (for example during the Iran-USA crises where US diplomats were held hostages from 1979–81 no country supported Iran's actions). The protection of the representatives of another state is necessary to ensure that they perform their international political functions without fear of prosecution. In England the first statutory instrument in this area, the Diplomatic Privileges Act of 1708 was passed as a result of the arrest and detention of the Russian Ambassador and his coach by English authorities in order 'to prevent like insolence for the future (*Empson v Smith* (1965) discussing the case law on this subject). In the United Kingdom rules in force on diplomatic immunity are embodied in the Diplomatic Privileges Act of 1964. The Act is based on the Vienna

Convention on Diplomatic Relations which was approved by the UN Conference on Diplomatic Intercourse and Immunities held in 1961. The Vienna Convention on Diplomatic Relations came into force on 24 April 1964 and in January 1992 was ratified by 158 states. Under the Diplomatic Privileges Act 1964 the common law rule of absolute immunity is abolished and qualified immunity applies even to the head of the diplomatic mission. The Act of 1964 divides the staff of a diplomatic mission into three categories as to the extent of immunity they enjoy. The first category comprises 'diplomatic agents' such as the head of the mission or chargé d'affaires, members of his diplomatic staff: counsellors, attachés, secretaries. Provided they are not nationals or permanent residents of a receiving state they are entitled to complete immunity from (in both official and private acts) criminal, civil (including divorce petition: *Shaw v Shaw* (1979)), and administrative jurisdiction and from execution except in three cases:

- in a real action relating to private immovable propriety located in the United Kingdom, provided it is not held on behalf of the sending state for the purposes of the mission (State Immunity Act 1978, s 16(1)(b));
- in an action relating to succession in which the diplomatic representative is an executor, administrator, heir or legatee as a private person;
- in an action relating to any professional or commercial activity exercised by the diplomatic representative in the United Kingdom outside his official functions (Diplomatic Privileges Act 1964, Schedule 1, Article 31).

This immunity is also granted to the family of a diplomatic agent which form part of his household unless they are nationals of a receiving state *(ibid*, Article 37(1); *Re C* (1959); *R v Guildhall Magistrates' Court, ex p Jarren-Thorpe* (1977)).

The second category encompasses the members of the administrative and technical staff of the mission which includes clerks, typists, translators, radio and telephone operators etc and their families which form part of their household provided they are neither nationals nor permanent residents of the receiving state. The second category does not enjoy immunity from civil and administrative jurisdiction in relation to acts performed outside the course of their duties (Schedule 1 Article 37(2)). Finally, the third group comprises members of the service staff such as butlers, maids, cooks, chauffeurs, porters, cleaners. Provided they are not nationals or permanent residents of a receiving state, they only enjoy immunity from the civil jurisdiction in respect of acts performed in the course of their duties.

John Smith is employed by the Canadian government and thus not a private servant (1) of the Canadian High Commissioner. As such he belongs to the third category. Since his transaction was performed outside his duty he cannot claim exemption from the jurisdiction of an English court. Although he is a national of Canada and not a permanent resident in the United Kingdom, the fact that he is present within the jurisdiction is sufficient for an English court to assume jurisdiction. According to common law rules on jurisdiction the presence of the defendant, however short it may be, within the jurisdiction makes him liable to be served with a writ. In *Maharanee of Baroda v Wildenstein* (1972) a writ was served on the defendant who was on a fleeting visit to England in order to attend the Ascot races. The defendant was an art dealer domiciled in France, the plaintiff was an Indian princess, a resident of France, and their dispute was over the sale of a painting performed in France. Although the only connection with England was the presence of the defendant within the jurisdiction as he was served a writ at the race course, it was held that an English court had jurisdiction.

Proceedings are commenced with the issue of a writ by the High Court. According to RSC Order 6 r 8 a writ is generally valid for four months from the date of issue. During that time Anna or her agent have to serve, personally, the writ upon the defendant. Contrary to popular belief, it is not necessary to actually touch the defendant. The service is effected if Anna leaves a copy of the document with John. If John refuses to receive the copy, then Anna must explain to him what the document is and must leave it as near his possession as practicable. Alternatively, according to RSC Order 10 r 1(2) service may also be effected by first class post to the usual or last known address of the defendant. Anna may also put a copy of the writ into an envelope, seal it and insert it through the letter box at the defendant's address. Furthermore, if John's solicitor endorses upon the writ a statement that he accepts service on behalf of his client or if John himself acknowledges service then the writ is legally served upon the defendant. Finally, if all attempts fail, Anna may submit an application to the High Court for an order for substituted service (RSC Order 65 r 4). In this case, the court may order service of the writ in any way that appears to be just (*Porter v Freudenberg* (1915)). The substituted service is available not only when the defendant is present within the jurisdiction and cannot be served personally, but also when, after the issue of the writ, he leaves the jurisdiction in order to escape service.

Note

1 According to the Diplomatic Privileges Act 1964, Schedule 1, Article 37(4), Article 1(h), private servants of members of the diplomatic mission enjoy immunity only to the extent admitted by the receiving state.

* by Alina Kaczorowska

Question 19

Britten, a businessman living in Luton, England enters into a franchise agreement with Cimarosa, a producer of vodka in Moscow, Russia to develop the product in the United Kingdom. Cimarosa refuses to provide certain trade secrets to Britten and Britten alleges that Cimarosa has breached the franchise agreement. The agreement provides *inter alia* that 'any dispute arising under the agreement shall be determined and resolved in Russia'.

On 1 June Cimarosa boards a flight to New York from Moscow. As a result of bad weather the plane makes an emergency landing at Luton Airport. As the plane undergoes repairs, passengers stay at the Hotel Lut-On. Britten obtains a writ and serves it on Cimarosa whilst the latter eats his dinner at the hotel.

Britten then discovers that Cimarosa had in fact instituted action against him in Russia. It is common knowledge that the Russian judiciary is undergoing serious reform at the moment and any commercial litigation may take years to settle. Cimarosa believes that since the issue of trade secret has a strong cultural element it is best heard by Russian judges. Britten is also concerned that the Russian judiciary may be biased against foreigners.

Discuss the options available to either party as to the question of jurisdiction.

Answer plan

This question focuses primarily on jurisdiction and the principle of *forum non conveniens*. The student should keep this focus in the answer. There should be an introduction to the question of presence in jurisdiction and the finding of jurisdiction on the courts. What does presence mean? Are there any exceptions to the rule? Do these exceptions apply in Britten's case?

Once jurisdiction is established, are there any grounds to apply for stay of proceedings by the defendant? How does the principle of *forum non conveniens* fit into the picture?

From the facts it is clear that there are two concurrent actions involving the parties, one in Russia and the other in England. Is it advisable for the plaintiff to apply for an injunction restraining the defendant from proceeding with the action in Russia?

Answer

The first issue is whether by serving a writ on Cimarosa when he was in Luton it is sufficient to found jurisdiction in the English courts. In *Maharanee of Baroda v Wildenstein* (1972), it is immaterial how short the duration the defendant was in the country or what caused his arrival or stay. The mere fact of his presence in the country will suffice regardless of whether he was deemed by immigration authorities as having lawfully entered the country. It is the defendant's *de facto* entry which mattered not his entry as recognised by immigration laws. In *John Russell & Co Ltd v Cayzer, Irvine & Co Ltd* (1916) it was observed that at common law, the overriding rule is that service of the writ is based on presence within jurisdiction and once service has been properly made, the courts may exercise jurisdiction. The exception is that where the defendant has been lured into jurisdiction by the plaintiff's fraud and deceit, the court will not let itself be privy to the unconscionable conduct (*Watkins v North American & Timber Co* (1904)). In all other cases how the plaintiff discovered the presence of the defendant or the former's intention and motives, however incompatible with morality, will not be relevant to the jurisdiction issue.

For the purposes of this discussion it will be assumed that the High Court is where the action by Britten will be instituted. In order to prevent Britten from proceeding with the action in England any further, Cimarosa may apply to the court to stay the action. Section 44(3) of the Supreme Court Act 1981 provides the High Court may stay an action that is frivolous, vexatious or an abuse of the process of the court. This enablement is also found in the court's inherent jurisdiction.

Following an application from Cimarosa, the court may apply the doctrine of *forum non conveniens* as elaborated on in *Spiliada Maritime v Cansulex Ltd* (1987). The House of Lords in that case held that the principle of *forum non conveniens* applies to actions to stay proceedings in the same way as it applied to applications to serve out of jurisdiction under Order 11 RSC. In staying an action, the court should first of all be satisfied that there is another forum having competent jurisdiction which in its opinion is the appropriate forum for the hearing. To this end the court must assess the parties' interests and the justice of the action being heard by that other forum. In this regard the person applying to stay proceedings will bear the burden of showing that the other forum is the *forum conveniens*. As far as Cimarosa is concerned he will do well to rely on the 'jurisdiction' clause in the franchise agreement. The fact of the matter is that as the clause is representative of the parties' intention that Russia should be the appropriate forum, it should not be departed from lightly.

Taking the jurisdiction clause as it stands it may be argued that it does not evince clearly the parties' intention – it simply referred to 'all disputes ... to be determined and resolved in Russia'. There is no indication that the Russian courts were the appropriate forum. It may be contended that all the parties intended was that they should be free to use other means of dispute resolution methods, albeit to be based in Russia. This does not operate as an exclusion of the jurisdiction of the English courts. A jurisdiction clause if exclusive holds tremendous sway in the determination of the forum. In *The Eleftheria* (1970) the exclusive jurisdiction clause would prevail unless the plaintiff could show a strong case that based on the overall circumstances the more appropriate and natural forum is England.

In determining this issue the courts will consider the existence of all connecting factors, that is to say, elements that point to a real and substantial connection between the dispute and the forum in question. Such factors include convenience, expense, proximity of connection of the parties to the relevant jurisdictions, evidence, the applicable law of the contract and the justice and enforceability of any potential judgment. The court would also consider whether the defendant seeks adjudication in a foreign country with *bona fides* or simply to gain a procedural advantage. In Cimarosa's case for instance, where the adoption of Russia as the forum is simply a delaying strategy, then the court will not entertain his claim that the *forum conveniens* is Russia.

A marginal note of some degree of importance is that not only must Cimarosa show that England is not the appropriate forum but that Russia is in fact the more appropriate. It is submitted that if the courts are not convinced by the exclusive jurisdiction clause in the franchise agreement the onus on Cimarosa to rebut the applicant's case is exceedingly heavy. The proclivity of the English courts is to found jurisdiction when it is not too unjust so to do.

Once Cimarosa has discharged his burden, the onus then shifts to the plaintiff (Britten) to show that England is the more appropriate forum based on the factors as indicated. These are questions of fact which the party concerned will have to prove to the satisfaction of the court upon a balance of probabilities. In view of the difficulties that surround the Russian judicial system, it will be immensely hard for Cimarosa to succeed in showing that Russia is the more appropriate forum unless he can prove to the contentment of the court that the dispute is best resolved in Russian in the interest of both parties. In *The Nile Rhapsody* (1992), for example, Hirst J held that the case was best heard by the Egyptian courts because the contract was expressed to be governed by Egyptian law and there was also a choice of jurisdiction clause properly entrusting jurisdiction to the Egyptian courts. However, the problem of translating the documents into Egyptian from English is of minor concern, so is the fact that the parties are both British companies.

While Britten can effectively show that delays under the Russian legal process are a moral certainty, it remains the court's discretion to make the assessment of *forum conveniens*. In *Jeyaretnam v Mahmood & Others* (1992) the court held that the ordinary rules of *forum conveniens* are objective and hence there was no need to express any comment on the quality of justice obtainable from the Singaporean courts. Further it is within the requirement of judicial comity not to pass any judgment on the quality of justice from another jurisdiction. The consideration of quality of justice will be made on an objective basis rather than a subjective one. Hence factors like 'delays' will be relevant but not allegations of bias.

At this juncture it is noteworthy that a likely argument to be raised by the applicant is that the applicable law to the franchise contract is most probably English law making the case best heard and resolved by the English courts. Under the Contracts (Applicable Law) Act 1990, where the contract is to be performed in England, English law will apply where there is no choice of law clause (Article 4(2) Rome Convention). The franchise agreement is in effect a licensing agreement whereby the franchiser agrees to allow the franchisee to operate under his corporate image. The characteristic of the agreement that is alleged to have been breached in Britten's case is the transfer of technology. The transfer was to have taken place in England so that the franchisee may apply the information to the trade. It is apparent that the performance was due to be performed in England, hence the operation of Article 4 Rome Convention commences.

It is interesting to note that following two important commonwealth cases (*The Waylink* (1988) and *The Adhiguna Meranti* (1988)), *The Spiliada* may be said to have removed some weight off the deprivation of an advantage to one or the other party as a relevant factor and to have introduced more objective factors in the issue of *forum non conveniens*. It will not be open to Cimarosa to argue that the cultural element would have acted in his favour if the court had stayed proceedings and had allowed him to pursue the action in Russia. The courts will only consider objective factors and unless the cultural element is proved to be essential to the contract it is not a consideration at the preliminary stage of an action to stay proceedings.

The likelihood that a stay of action will not be granted leads to the unfortunate event where there are in existence two actions relating to the same subject matter, one in England and the other in Russia. According to the House of Lords in *The Abidin Daver* (1984), the position where the defendant is suing the plaintiff in a foreign court is that the English courts are disinclined to stay proceedings unless the defendant can show that the English court is not a *forum conveniens* according to the principles and criteria as enunciated above (1).

In the present context, Britten is advised to apply for an injunction restraining Cimarosa from proceeding with the action in Russia. In *SNI Aerospatial v Lee Kui Jak* (1987) the Judicial Committee of the Privy Council held that the applicant must show that the English court is a *forum conveniens* where justice could be done at less expense and inconvenience than the foreign court. It must also be shown that the grant of an injunction would not deprive Cimarosa of a legitimate personal or juridical advantage. It would appear from *Arab Monetary Fund v Hashim (No 6)* (1993), that this is nothing short of showing that pursuit of an action in Russia is vexatious and oppressive. It is difficult to say if Cimarosa will be deprived these advantages under English law from the facts but it may be suggested that the courts in this country will be slow to acknowledge any form of disadvantage (at least of a juridical nature) that the system may inflict upon the defendant. The granting of an injunction is a matter of the court's discretion (*Tracomin SA v Sudan OPil Seeds Ltd (No 2)* (1983) and *American Cynamid v Ethicon Ltd* (1975)) but subject to the limited facts, it would appear that Britten has a strong case.

Notes

1 Where the plaintiff is suing the same defendant abroad, the defendant must show that the two actions are identical and that there is no difference between the remedies available from the English court and the foreign court (*Ionian Bank v Couvreur* (1969)).

Question 20

Dvorak, domiciled in Italy has contracted to act as Elgar's financial advisor. Elgar lives in Birmingham, England. Dvorak was requested by Elgar to advise him on his prospective investment in a multi-national company. Dvorak sent his written advice to Faure for confirmation before he would dispatch it to Elgar. Faure who is domiciled in France added his approval to the advice.

Elgar then invested heavily in the company based on the advice given. The company subsequently collapsed and Elgar lost £1.2 million. It is Elgar's contention that both advisors had acted negligently in dispensing the advice.

On 1 March Elgar commences proceedings in England against Dvorak. The writ is issued on 25 March and served on Dvorak whilst he was in London for his sister's wedding. Meanwhile on 20 March Dvorak commences action in Italy against Elgar for non-payment under the financial consultancy agreement. The writ is served on Elgar on 31 March.

Elgar wishes to take action in England against Faure.

Advise Elagar on the jurisdictional issues in relation to his grievances against Dvorak and Faure.

Answer plan

The student will need to know when the Brussels Convention is applicable and should point out the general rule that the defendant must be sued in the state of his domicile. The properly structured answer should discuss the two possible defendants separately.

The case concerning Dvorak involves a question of contractual liability and one in tort. Recalling the exceptions of special jurisdiction to the general rule in Article 2, the likelihood of Elgar succeeding in relying on these exceptions (for example Article 5(1) and Article 5(3)) should be raised in the discussion. The issue of determining the connecting factor in tort should be assessed in the light of *Bier v Mines de Potasse* (1976).

Article 21 needs to be discussed next. This involves the concept of *lis pendens* (but note how the concept is applied differently in the Convention as against the common law). On this note it is important to determine which court was seised with jurisdiction first. How is this to be determined? There are some important cases in association with this issue including *Kloeckner v Gatoil* (1990), *Dresser UK Ltd v Falcongate Freight Management* (1992).

Finally the relationship between Elgar and Faure, who appears to be outside the contractual relationship, should be discussed. If this is the case the possible cause of action under English law would be tort. Thus, it will necessitate a brief re-application of the principles under Article 5(3).

Answer

Elgar wishes to take action against Dvorak and Faure both of whom are domiciled in states privy to the Brussels Convention on Jurisdiction and Enforcement of Judgments. The general rule in the Convention as contained in the Civil Jurisdiction and Judgments Act 1982 is found in Article 2. Article 2 provides that persons domiciled in a contracting state shall, whatever their nationality be sued in the courts of that state. This rule is however subject to other provisions of the Convention which permit concurrent or special jurisdictional powers to be exercised by the courts of another state. It is proposed to consider first the case against Dvorak.

In this cause of action Elgar alleges that he has suffered a loss as a result of a breach of contract and perhaps, a tort committed by Dvorak by dispensing him bad advice. Under Article 2 of the Convention which applies to all civil and commercial matters, Elgar should have sued in Italy. Italy is where Dvorak has his domicile. However Elgar has instituted action in England. The question is whether he had acted within the rubric of the Brussels Convention. The Brussels Convention allows for special jurisdiction where persons domiciled in one contracting state may be sued in another.

If the matter upon which Elgar wishes to place his claim is that of the contract he may rely on Article 5(1) of the Convention. Under Article 5(1) a person domiciled in a contracting state may in another contracting state be sued in the courts of the place of performance of the obligation in question. This means that Elgar may sue Dvorak in England if it is proved that the obligation to provide financial advice is to be performed in England. It appears from the facts that the intention of the parties was that Elgar would receive the advice in England and it was Dvorak's duty to ensure that this advice which was to be delivered to Elgar in Birmingham be proper advice. The place of performance of the contact is likely to be in England.

As far as the tort issue is concerned, Article 5(3) provides that a person in a contracting state may be sued in another contracting state where that other contracting state is the place where the harmful event occurred. Following the European Court of Justice ruling in *Bier v Mines de Potasse* (1976), this refers not only to the place of the tortious act but also the place of the damage. In our case the alleged negligent act was committed in Italy but the damage (ie the financial loss caused in reliance on the advice) may be said to have taken place in England. It is uncertain though as to where the funds for the investment actually emanated or have been transferred to.

Under the common law, in identifying the place of a tort it is important to apply the *lex fori* to determine the connecting factor. In *Re Martin* (1900) it was held that to determine the connecting factor of domicile the law of the seat of the forum has to be relied on. In *Distillers Co (Biochemicals) Ltd v Thompson* (1971) the Privy Council held that the right approach was to look back over the series of events constituting the tort and ask where in substance did the cause of action arise. This has been applied by the Court of Appeal in *Castree v ER Squibb* (1980) where the substance of the tort was held to have taken place in England even though the machine had been manufactured in Germany negligently because it was in England where the machine was sold and the plaintiff was injured as a result. It would not be too tenuous to argue that the substance of the tort was in England since the advice was expected to be delivered to Elgar in England and was to be acted on in a transaction emanating from England. Returning to the Convention these common law cases should be read in line with the European Court's pronouncement in *Bier v Mines de Potasse* (1978). In that case the French defendant was alleged to have polluted the waters of the Rhine in France. The Rhine also flows into Holland where the damage was caused to the Dutch plaintiff's property. The European Court of Justice held that both the French and Dutch courts had jurisdiction. Taking this ruling it is open therefore to Elgar to take action in England.

The next important question is whether Article 21 will apply compelling either the Italian court or the English court (but not both together) to stay proceedings until such time as the jurisdiction of the court first seised with jurisdiction is established. Before Article 21 may be used a few preliminary points must be satisfied. The first is that both sets of proceedings must involve the same cause of action and are between the same parties. In the present case, it may be assumed that the cause of action is the same, that is to say, entitlement and compensation under the contract to provide financial advice. It does not appear to be relevant that under the two *lex fori*, the actual labels of the cause of action are different as long as the subject matter of the dispute is the same. Under Article 21 neither court has any discretion in the matter unlike in a situation of *lis pendens* under common law (*S & W Berisford plc v New Hampshire Insurance* (1990)).

The second and final question for consideration is which court is first seised? In *Zelgar v Salinitri* (1984) the court that is first seised is the court before which the proceedings first become 'definitely pending'. To determine when the proceedings were definitely pending, the law of the seat of that particular court must be referred to. The original position was stated in *Kloeckner v Gatoil* (1990) where it was held that proceedings on an *in personam* action were 'definitely pending' following the issue of the writ and not when it was finally served. The case was not followed by the Court of Appeal in *Dresser UK Ltd v Falcongate Freight Management* (1992) where it was decided that an action is, as a general rule, only definitely pending after the writ has been served. The exceptions to the general rule do not apply to Elgar and hence as far as he is concerned, the action before the English court will only be treated as definitely pending on 25 March. This means that unless Italian laws take the same stance, it may be that the Italian court was first seised with jurisdiction.

Where this is the case, the only way Elgar may insist on action in England is to show to the satisfaction of the Italian court that they do not have jurisdiction and once this issue has been established successfully, the original action in England can proceed (Article 21).

Moving on to consider the situation between Elgar and Faure, it may be assumed that since there is no contract between Elgar and Faure, the possible cause of action is therefore in tort. Under the general rule Elgar could sue Faure in France. But it may be possible to rely on Article 5(3). In this instance, it will have to be the place where the harmful event took place. Using the same guidelines and principles outlined earlier, it is reasonable to say that the place where the harm occurred is England while the place where the breach of duty took place is France. This essentially means that it is open to Elgar to sue Faure in England provided he is able to obtain leave to serve a writ abroad.

In conclusion it should be added that the joinder of defendants provision in Article 6(1) does not apply. This is because the relevant court, namely the English court is not a court of either Dvorak's or Faure's domicile.

Question 21

Mark wishes to institute proceedings against Najata, a defaulting buyer. Najata lives in Cuba and has his place of domicile in Cuba. Mark believes that Najata is absolutely unscrupulous and will do anything to avoid settling the debt.

Najata has substantial savings in the Old Age Building Society in London and two other accounts in France and Italy respectively. He also has a small bi-plane which is held by Porky Aviations as a result of Neil not settling the repairs bill. It has also come to light that Najata has convictions in France, Ireland and the United States for fraud, conspiracy, money laundering and theft.

How would you advise Mark who resides in England?

How will your advice differ if Najata is domiciled in France?

Answer plan

The *Mareva* injunction is a very important interim relief which is frequently relied on by plaintiffs needing some protection from unscrupulous defendants who would dissipate their assets so as to make themselves 'judgment proof'. The law however recognises the significance of the defendant's rights over his assets until judgment for the plaintiff is given. The student's advice to Mark should therefore make this balance clear. The ingredients that must be satisfied before the *Mareva* injunction is granted are stringent. They are provided for in s 37 Supreme Court Act 1981. The good answer will demonstrate and discuss how these elements have been applied by the courts. Pay attention to the meaning of *The Siskina* (1979).

There is also the need to consider which asset/s may be attached and under what conditions. Here too the good essay will take into account case law on the subject including competing interests between the plaintiff and third parties, money kept in bank accounts and a worldwide *Mareva.*

The advancement brought about by the Brussels Convention should not be neglected, albeit forming only a small segment of the full answer.

Answer

Part 1

The solution to Mark's problems may be found in the 'nuclear weapon' of English law; the *Mareva* Injunction. Until 1975, it has been long settled that English law does not permit an injunction to restrain a person who is alleged to be a debtor from parting with his property in avoidance of the debt (*Robinson v Pickering* (1881)). Under the traditional rule the plaintiff must obtain judgment first (whether summarily or after trial) and then attempt execution of the judgment and where the situation warrants institute bankruptcy or winding-up proceedings. This honourable way of execution opens itself to the dishonourable and quite unscrupulous practice of transferring assets elsewhere so as to deny the plaintiff the justice of the judgment.

The law was changed in *Mareva Compania Naviera SA v International Bulk Carriers SA* (1975) by the Court of Appeal. In that case where the plaintiff can show a good arguable claim to be entitled to money from a defendant and that there is a real risk of the defendant removing the assets from jurisdiction or disposing of them so as to render them unavailable or untraceable, an injunction may be issued to prevent the defendant from doing so. This discretionary power is now contained in s 37(1) Supreme Court Act 1981.

As far as Mark is concerned, he must prove the following elements:

- a cause of action justiciable in England and Wales
- a good arguable case
- assets of the defendant are in jurisdiction
- a real risk of removal and disposal of the assets

A justiciable cause of action

The *Mareva* injunction as an injunction must be ancillary to a substantive claim within the jurisdiction of the court. Mark must show in his affidavit the exact and relevant cause of action including all material facts of the case (*Bank Mellat v Nikpour* (1985)). Although the urgency of the application may allow for some variance in establishing his cause of action in finite detail and precision, the general rule is that the application is always ancillary to the main substantive claim and hence the cause of action should be clearly identified (*The Kapetan Markos* (1986)).

In the present case as Najata lives in Cuba, service out of jurisdiction is needed. In this respect Order 11 r 1(1) RSC will apply apart from Order 11 r 1(1)(b) RSC. In *The Siskina* (1979) the cargo owners plaintiffs in Saudi Arabia sued the defendant ship owners, Panamanian company. The bill of lading issued on shipment conferred exclusive jurisdiction on the courts of Genoa. The ship was registered in Panama and the claim was in respect of discharge of the cargo in Cyprus. The subject matter had therefore no connection with England but *The Siskina*, the defendant's sole asset had sunk and the insurance money was to be paid in London. The House of Lords held that Order 11 r 1(1)(b), which provides for service abroad for an injunction being sought to ordering the defendants to do or not to do anything within the jurisdiction, could not be relied on. There was no cause of action triable in jurisdiction and the grant of the *Mareva* must hinch on a substantive cause of action. It has no axle of its own.

From *The Siskina*, it is clear that Mark must succeed in bringing his action within jurisdiction. If from the facts there is some connection between the contractual obligation and the jurisdiction falling within the guidelines set out in *Amin Rasheed v Kuwait Insurance* (1984), service abroad will be allowed.

A good arguable case

While Mark's claim need not be so strong as to succeed in an Order 14 judgment, it must be shown that he has a good arguable case according to *Rasu Maritima SA v Pertamina* (1978). This means that it must not only be capable of serious argument, but that there is a real chance of success (*Ninemia Maritime Corpn v Travel etc, The Niedersachsen* (1983)).

From the given facts there is insufficient evidence as to the strength of Mark's case against Najata. Mark is advised to take this factor into account before making an application for the *Mareva*, his chances of success on the substantive claim must be above the bare probability.

Assets in the jurisdiction

As was held in *Rasu Maritima SA v Pentamina*, the plaintiff must show a *prima facie* case that the defendant has assets in jurisdiction although allowance is given on the basis that the defendant is *ex hypothesi* a somewhat elusive character and it will not be entirely practicable to establish exactly what he has available in the jurisdiction.

In the case of bank accounts the plaintiff should make every effort to identify the locations of the accounts and if possible the exact account number for each. Once the *Mareva* is issued, assets coming into those accounts will also be attached by the injunction (*TDK Tape Distributors Ltd v Videohouse Ltd* (1986)). For the purposes of the *Mareva* the account in the building society will be treated as a bank account and may be seizable.

It is clear that Najat not only has assets in England but that he has bank accounts in Italy and France. It will not normally be possible to apply the *Mareva* to these accounts overseas, but where Mark succeeds in showing a case for a worldwide *Mareva* these monies may be attached. In *Babanaft International v Bassatne* (1990), the plaintiff must not only show that he has a good arguable case for the grant of the *Mareva*, but that the assets in jurisdiction are not sufficient to meet any likely judgment and that there is evidence of assets of the defendant abroad. Even then it is an exceptional case where the court will grant the injunction for the fact that the element of extra territoriality is involved. As to whether it may be raised against Mark's application that the Babanaft judgment must be distinguished on the premise that in that case judgment had already been ordered when the application for the worldwide injunction was made. This may be answered by reference to *Republic of Haiti v Duvalier* (1990), *Derby v Weldon (Nos 1, 3 and 4)*

(1990) where the courts did not see this as a distinguishing factor of any materiality. Mark will have to satisfy the court that the money in the Old Age Building Society and possibly the aeroplane (subject to discussion below) will not be sufficient to meet the possible judgment debt.

On the issue of the aeroplane being held by Porky Aviations, the law according to *Allen v Jambo Holdings Ltd* (1980) is that movable property could be made the subject of the *Mareva*. The issue becomes a bit more awkward for Mark because of the repairers' competing interest. It would appear that the repairers are exercising their lien over the plane for non-payment. In *The Angel Bell* (1981), a *Mareva* injunction must be subject to the rules of insolvency. The plaintiff does not hold a proprietary interest in the assets enjoined. Further he is not to be preferred over the other creditors in the event of the defendant's insolvency. This being the case, the plane is open to the enjoinder but in the event of Najata's bankruptcy, subject to the rules of insolvency, it would appear that Porky Aviations would take priority over Mark. In short the dissolution and distribution of the property will be determined according to the law of competing priorities in insolvency.

A real risk of removal and disposal

Under s 37(3) Supreme Court Act 1981, the power to grant the *Mareva* shall be exercised in cases where the defendant is, as well as in cases where he is not, domiciled, resident or present within that jurisdiction. There is therefore no requirement that the defendant be a foreign resident or have any geographic connection with a foreign country. All that is needed is that there was a risk of the assets being, or that they would be removed from jurisdiction (*Z Ltd v A & Others* (1982)). The injunction will be refused if there is no real danger of the defendant dissipating the assets to make himself 'judgment proof'. On this matter the courts appear to take account of character evidence to a certain extent. In *Montecchi v Shimco (UK) Ltd* (1979) where the defendants were found to be Italian resident of good financial standing and any English judgment against them could be enforceable without much difficulty through the agency of the Italian courts, the *Mareva* was not suitable. It is uncertain from Montecchi how far evidence of general character may be taken into account as it is clear that in Montecchi the court considered only the question of financial standing. It is submitted however that where the evidence of general character points towards the risk of the dissipation of the assets then there is no reason why it should be refused. *A fortiori* unlike Italy, the Cuban judiciary do not operate reciprocal recognition of English judgments.

In conclusion Mark should bear in mnd that the *Mareva* like any other injunctive reliefs, is subject to variation and discharge. As an ex parte order it is also liable to be discharged for material non-disclosure (*Brints-MAT Ltd v Elcombe* (1988)). The plaintiff is obliged to make full and fair disclosure of all material facts known to him and the issue of materiality is to be determined by the court on an objective level. The *bona fides* of the action appears to carry considerable weight. Should there be a material change in circumstances it is incumbent on Mark to inform the court accordingly (*Commercial Bank of the Near East v A* (1989)). This element of *bona fides* is also reflected in the requirement of the plaintiff to give an undertaking in damages (*Allen v Jambo*).

Part 2

Where Najata is in fact domiciled in France, a Brussels Convention Member State, variation from the rule in *The Siskina* is permitted. Section 25 Civil Jurisdiction and Judgments Act 1982 provides that an English court may grant interim relief, including the *Mareva* if the proceedings are, or will be, proceedings whose subject matter is within the scope of the Convention and this view was adopted in *X v Y & Y Establishment* (1990). This solves the difficulty placed by *The Siskina* where the House of Lords held that the English courts had no power to grant a *Mareva* over assets within the jurisdiction in the absence of a cause of action justiciable here. Section 25 does not however apply in a non-contracting state unless it has so been extended by an Order in Council. A further point for consideration is that Mark need not apply for leave to serve a writ on Najata who is domiciled in a contracting state, unlike the first situation (Order 11 r 1(2) RSC). Other considerations will apply *mutatis mutandis*.

Chapter 4

Recognition and Enforcement of Foreign Judgments and Arbitral Awards

Introduction

The main issue in this chapter is to what extent is a successful plaintiff in a foreign judicial or arbitral proceedings entitled to enforce that award in England and Wales. Enforcement is frequently connected with the act of judicial recognition of the award by the English courts.

At common law the plaintiff has but one recourse to 'enforce' the foreign award. He has to serve a writ on the defendant instituting an action based on the judgment debt in the English court against the latter. Where the judgment debt is entitled to recognition and/or enforcement under the Civil Jurisdiction and Judgments Act 1982 (incorporating the Brussels Convention and the Lugano Convention), the Foreign (Reciprocal Enforcement) Act 1933 or the Administration of Justice Act 1920, recourse to the old common law rule is unnecessary.

In respect of the enforcement and recognition of an international arbitral award, regard must be had to the New York Convention on the Recognition and Enforcement of Foreign Arbitral Awards 1958 (which has been given effect to by the Arbitration Act 1975) and the Geneva Convention 1927.

The general rule on recognition and enforcement of foreign awards is that the English court will enforce a foreign judgment if that court was a competent court so to do under the rules of competency in English law. On the elements of jurisdiction, see Chapter 3.

Once the foreign tribunal's jurisdiction or international competence has been established, it is important to examine if the defendant is entitled to raise any of the defences recognised by English law. These defences include public policy considerations, the taint of fraud in the judgment obtained, failure of natural justice and the application of the Protection of Trading Interests Act 1980. These defences are similar whether the enforcement and recognition exercise is carried out via the statutory framework, the common law or the Brussels Convention. Similar considerations apply with respect of international arbitral awards.

Checklist

- enforcement of a judgment debt at common law
- recognition and enforcement under the Brussels Convention
- recognition and enforcement under the Administration of Justice Act 1920 and the Foreign (Reciprocal Enforcement) Act 1933
- rules of jurisdiction and the international competency of the foreign court
- defences to the recognition and enforcement of foreign judgments and international arbitral awards
- stay of proceedings under Article 30 Brussels Convention
- operation of the New York Convention on the Recognition and Enforcement of Foreign Arbitral Awards 1958

Question 22

Quek who used to live in Atlantis had entered into a contract with Ray to build a factory in Mireland where Ray resides.

In 1993, Ray brought an action for breach of contract against Quek in Mireland. The Mirish court gave leave to serve the writ on Quek who was then on holiday in Spain. Quek's lawyer appeared before a Mirish judge to contest the court's jurisdiction. The judge overruled the lawyer's contention and proceeded to give judgment for Ray.

Damages of £100,000 were ordered. Also, in accordance with a Mirish statute, a charge of £1,000 payable to the plaintiff was imposed on Quek as a litigant who, in the court's opinion vexatiously challenged its jurisdiction. Quek intends to appeal against the decision and the appeal is to be heard by the Mirish High Court soon.

In the meantime Ray wishes to enforce the Mirish judgment in England against Quek who now lives in London. Ray believes that Quek has considerable assets in England.

Advise Ray.

Answer plan

In order to address this question effectively the student must highlight the following matters:

- the different regimes within which recognition and enforcement may be executed
- the treatment of jurisdiction of the foreign court under English law
- the interaction of public policy *vis-à-vis* penal damages on the enforcement and recognition procedure
- the enforceability of damages equivalent to exemplary damages
- whether the penal award may be severed from the enforceable damages

Answer

In determining the applicable regime to the resolution of this problem, the first question is whether Mireland, where the judicial award was made is a contracting state to the Brussels Convention 1968 or not. Since it is clear that Mireland not being an EC Member State, is not privy to the Convention, the issue will have to be dealt with under the common law as may be qualified by the Administration of Justice Act 1920 or the Foreign Judgments (Reciprocal Enforcement) Act 1933. It should perhaps be noted that since Mireland is not part of the commonwealth, it is unlikely that the 1920 Act has any application. Be that as it may, the rules contained in the statutes and in the common law are similar in substance.

At common law, in *Grant v Easton* (1853) the procedure appears to be this. The judgment creditor intending to enforce the judgment debt may not do so by direct execution of the debt. He must bring an action on the foreign judgment, normally in reliance on Order 14 Rules of the Supreme Court on the ground that the defendant has no defence to the debt.

Where on the other hand the Foreign Judgments (Reciprocal Enforcement) Act 1933 is to be applied, for example when it has been established that an Order in Council has extended the application of the Act to Mireland (usually as a result of an agreement from the foreign state to recognise and enforce a judgment of the English court, s 1), the plaintiff is then entitled to register the Mirish judgment as of right. He could then enforce the judgment without further need of proof.

Whether the rules of the common law or the 1933 Act are used, the English court must satisfy itself that the foreign court has jurisdiction according to English rules of private international law. In *Buchanan v Rucker* (1808) the plaintiff attempted to enforce the judgment of the court in Tobago. The defendant had never been in the territory, nor had he submitted to its jurisdiction. Substituted service was executed by way of nailing the writ on the court house door. It was held by Lord Ellenborough that such assumed jurisdiction cannot bind the rights of the English courts. Jurisdiction of the foreign court must be proper, in the eyes of English law.

The bases for jurisdiction are classed by Buckley LJ in *Emanuel v Symon* (1908) as follows:

- the defendant is a subject of the foreign country where the judgment has been obtained;
- the defendant was resident in the foreign country when the action was commenced;
- the defendant had selected the forum as the one in which he would sue should a cause of action accrue to him;
- the defendant has made voluntary appearance before the foreign court;
- the defendant has contracted to submit himself to the jurisdiction of the foreign court.

These rules with the exception of the first may be broadly channelled into two heads of jurisdiction: residence and submission (1).

On the given facts, it is observed that Quek was not resident in Mireland when the writ was served. Although the temporary presence of the defendant in the forum concerned would have been sufficient to confer that court jurisdiction under the rule in *Adam v Cape Industries plc* (1990), it is clear that this is not the case here. Quek was no longer a resident in Mireland when the writ was served.

The next issue is therefore whether his counsel by appearing before the Mirish judge to contest the jurisdiction of the court had entered appearance as required by the head of jurisdiction in *Emanuel v Symon*. According to some older authority like *Harris v Taylor* (1951), the court had indicated that an appearance to argue that the court did not have jurisdiction was to be treated as submission. This position has now been replaced by s 33 Civil Jurisdiction and Judgments Act 1982. Section 33 provides that the defendant should not be regarded as having submitted to the jurisdiction of a foreign court if he appeared simply to do one of the following:

- to contest the jurisdiction of the court; or
- to ask the court to dismiss or stay proceedings on the ground that the dispute should be submitted to arbitration or to determination of the courts of another country; or
- to protect or obtain the release of property seised or threatened with seizure in the proceedings.

In this light then Quek could not be said to have submitted to jurisdiction when his counsel appeared to contest the court's jurisdiction over him. It may be argued, however, that by appealing to the Mirish High Court against the lower court's decision Quek is submitting to Mirish jurisdiction. This argument is tenable only if the appeal is on the merits of the first instance judgment. If Quek is appealing only on the basis that the Mirish lower court lacked the jurisdictional power to hear his case, it is unlikely that the appeal will be treated differently to the original contest of jurisdiction.

If it is indeed established that Quek had submitted to the Mirish court's jurisdiction, the ensuing issue is whether Ray could institute proceedings in England for the enforcement of the two judgment awards or debts pending an appeal. It was held in *Nouvion v Freeman* (1889) that the foreign judgment must be 'final and conclusive' before the English courts have power to entertain an action for recognition and/or enforcement. In Lord Herschell's words, the existence of the judgment debt must be *res judicata* between the parties at the court in which the debt was established. The principle of *res judicata* however still applies even though the matter is subject to an appeal (*Colt Industries Inc v Sarlie (No 2)* (1966)). In s 1(3), of the Foreign Judgments (Reciprocal Enforcement) Act 1933 a judgment shall be deemed to be final and conclusive notwithstanding that an appeal may be pending against it or that it may still be subject to appeal, in the courts of the country of the original court. This being the state of the law, if it is successfully proved that Quek had submitted to the Mirish court's jurisdiction, Ray may seek to enforce the judgment in England subject to the following considerations.

The first consideration is whether Quek may raise any valid defence at common law against the claim lodged by Ray to enforce the judgment. The entrenched rule at common law as stated in *Sadler v Robins* (1808) and *Russell v Smyth* (1842) is that the judgment to be enforced must be for a debt or a definite sum of money including damages and costs. On this authority, it is quite pellucid that the £100,000 would be in *gremio legis* and be successfully enforced. On the other hand, unless it is shown that the £1,000 is a true reflection of costs and not simply a penalty or tax, then its purported enforcement may be rejected.

It is for the English court to determine whether the foreign statutory provision is penal in nature (*Huntingdon v Attrill* (1893)). The rationale as stated by the Privy Council in that case is that all breaches of public law punishable by pecuniary penalties or otherwise, at the instance of the foreign government, are local in the sense that they are only cognisable and punishable in the country where they were committed. Any enforcement of these penal provisions by the *lex fori* would be an unwarranted interference with the foreign state's sovereignty. It is submitted that since the £1,000 is levied as a punishment, it would be penal in nature and thus, could not be enforced at English law. Accordingly in s 1(2) of the 1933 Act, it is stated that a sum payable in respect of taxes or other charges of a like nature or in respect of a fine or other penalty may be enforced.

On the other hand where the damages awarded are equivalent to the English law award of exemplary damages, they can be enforced. By the rule laid down in *SA Consortium General Textiles v Sun and Sand Agencies Ltd* (1978) it would be necessary to enquire as to the nature of the £1,000 under Mirish law.

The final question is whether this unenforceable sum (assuming that it is penal) may be severed from the judgment and consequently Ray would still be entitled to the £100,000. The position in *Raulin v Fischer* (1911) is that it is not *contra bonos mores* to allow the enforcement of the damages where it is clearly severable from the penalty. In our case, the two awards are quite distinct from each other making it possible for the court to remove one from the other without affecting the overall effect of the awards.

Notes

1 See the judgments of the High Court in *Blohn v Desser* (1962); *Rossano v Manufacturers' Life Insurance Co Ltd (1963)* and *Vogel v RA Kohnstamm Ltd* (1973).

Question 23

Critically examine the circumstances in which an English court would refuse to recognise and subsequently, to enforce a judgment of a foreign court under the Convention on Jurisdiction and Enforcement of Judgments in Civil and Commercial Matters 1968.

Answer plan

This is a relatively straightforward question. There are also very few English cases on the application of the s 1 (Articles 26–30) of the Brussels Convention. There are however some European cases on the matter which the student should take cognisance of.

A comprehensive understanding of the ambit of Article 27 is essential; it is also useful to indicate how the rules are different (if at all and to what extent) from the position at common law. Do not simply reproduce the provisions of Article 27 *et seq*. Some commentary is imperative; the question requires that a critical examination be carried out. This is not easy when there are so few cases on the subject.

Answer

The scope of the English court's power to refuse to recognise a judgment of a foreign court is dependent on the applicable framework of recognition and enforcement of foreign judicial awards. The recognition and enforcement of foreign judgments is generally covered by the three distinct regimes; the common law rules on enforcing the judgment as a debt, the Civil Jurisdiction and Judgments Act 1982 (incorporating the Brussels Convention 1968 and the Lugano Convention 1988) and the two statutes applicable to non-contracting states, the Foreign Judgments (Reciprocal Enforcement) Act 1933 and the Administration of Justice Act 1920.

The position of the Brussels Convention is founded on the general principle in Article 26 which provides that a 'judgment given in a contracting state shall be recognised in the other contracting states without any special procedure being required'. This is quite distinct from the common law process whereby the defendant has to bring an action on the foreign judgment as a debt against the judgment debtor. There is no right of direct execution.

The Convention is also wider in ambit as it permits the recognition and enforcement of reliefs other than money judgments, eg specific performance and injunctions.

Article 26 is however not unqualified. Article 34 states that an application for recognition (and subsequently enforcement) may be refused as long as one of the circumstances in Article 27 exists. Article 27 catalogues six grounds on which a foreign judgment could be denied enforcement and recognition legitimately:

- Article 27(1) provides that where the recognition of such a judgment is contrary to pubic policy in England, that judgment may be refused. The precise compass of this defence is not clear as there is little judicial authority based on Article 27(1). Some assistance could perhaps be derived from a common law case where the court refused to enforce a maintenance order made by the Maltese court because it was contrary to the public policy of England to enforce an affiliation order not limited to the child's minority (*Re Macartney* (1921)). It is obvious from the court's judgment in *SA Consortium General Textiles v Sun and Sand Agencies Ltd* (1978) that the courts will be deliberately slow in finding a rule of public policy for the purposes of private international law.
- If the judgment was given in default of appearance and the defendant was not duly served with the writ in sufficient time to enable him to arrange for his defence (Article 27(2)), this judgment given in defiance of natural justice cannot be enforced in England. It has been held in *Pendy Plastic Products BV v Pluspunkt* (1982) that the notion and meaning of 'duly served' should follow the definition adopted by the law of the original court (ie the court that issued the judgment) but what constitutes sufficient time is to be construed according to the law of the state in which recognition is sought.
- If the judgment is irreconcilable with a judgment given in a dispute between the same parties in the state where recognition

is sought (Article 27(3)). In *Hoffman v Krieg* (1988) the attempt to enforce a maintenance order failed because the order would have been inconsistent with the divorce granted in the state where recognition was sought.

- Specifically relevant to the enforcement of maintenance claims, if the original court has decided a preliminary question on the status or legal capacity of any natural persons, rights arising out of a matrimonial relationship, wills or succession in a way which conflicts with a rule of English private international law, recognition may be refused. The exception is where the same result would have been reached by the application of the rules of private international law of that state.
- Under Article 27(5) if the judgment is irreconcilable with an earlier judgment given in a non-contracting state involving the same cause of action and between the same parties, again enforcement may be denied provided that the earlier judgment concerned is entitled to recognition (and enforcement) in England.

Besides Article 27, the English court may also refuse to enforce and/or recognise a foreign judgment which conflicts with the jurisdictional provisions of Articles 7–12A (insurance), 13–15 (consumer contracts) or 16 (exclusive jurisdiction). However, according to the European Court of Justice in *LTU v Eurocontrol* (1976), the English court is not entitled to question the findings of fact arrived at by the court of the contracting state.

An important provision is Article 16 which provides that the courts of a particular contracting state are to have exclusive jurisdiction based on the nature of the subject matter of the dispute. Where the court of a contracting state exercises jurisdiction contrary to Article 16, then the judgment it issues could not be enforced in England. The cases in this context where exclusive jurisdiction accrues are proceedings relating to immovable property and rights *in rem*, the status and validity of corporations, the validity of entries in public registers and the validity and recognition of intellectual property rights.

On whether fraud is a ground for negating enforcement of a foreign judgment under the Convention as is the case at common law, it is common agreement that this defence falls within the remit of Article 27(1) on public policy. In *Kendall v Kendall* (1977), for example, it was expressly stated by the court that a foreign divorce obtained by fraud need not be recognised because to do so would be contrary to public policy.

A less patent defence is that found in Article 59. Where to enforce the foreign judgment is contrary to an existing agreement or undertaking to a non-contracting third state, the courts may decline to effect that judgment.

It could perhaps be said that the two additional defences in the Lugano Convention could go some way to enhance and improve the operation of the Brussels Convention. Under Article 54B(3) of the Lugano Convention the recognising court has the discretion to refuse enforcement or recognition if the grounds of jurisdiction on which the judgment has been made differ from that resulting from the Lugano Convention and the recognition or enforcement is sought against a party who is domiciled in a contracting state which is not a member of the EC, unless the judgment may otherwise be recognised or enforced under any rule of law in the state addressed. The second specific defence is found in Article 57(4) which grants that where the jurisdiction was assumed under some other international convention (eg the Warsaw Convention on International Carriage by Air 1929), enforcement of the judgment must be refused where to do so would be to go against the convention in question.

Question 24

In 1993 when Bach was living in Philistia, he entered into a contractual arrangement with Chopin to promote and market Chopin's handmade musical instruments in Philistia. Chopin was then living in Musika, a neighbouring country. The contract was signed at Bach's home.

Early 1994 Chopin instituted action against Bach for breach of contract but before a writ was served on Bach, Bach left Philistia for England with his British wife, Delia. Chopin also alleges that Bach had taken with him some money which was set aside by Chopin for advertising.

Under Philistian law, a plaintiff may not be served a writ when he is abroad where there is an allegation of criminal conduct involved, unless leave is expressly given by the court. Chopin applied for leave at the Philistian Sessions Court.

But before leave was given, Bach's lawyer appeared before the Philistian court to contest the court's general jurisdiction over the matter. Dispensing with issue of leave, the Philistian court held that it had jurisdiction and proceeded to give judgment in default of appearance to Chopin. It also ordered that Bach pay compensation to the value of £12,000 and punitive damages to the value of £1,000.

The United Kingdom has extended the provisions of the Foreign Judgments (Reciprocal Enforcement) Act 1933 to Philistia.

Chopin wishes to enforce the judgment in England where Bach has substantial assets.

Discuss the requirements that an English court will demand before the Philistian judgment can be enforced.

Answer plan

This is a question which requires consideration of the various defences against enforcement of a foreign judgment. The main concern here is that jurisdiction of the foreign court for the purposes of enforcement can only be founded on submission (either by agreement or appearance) or presence. Other special rules be they Philistian or English will be irrelevant.

While the student may swiftly come to the conclusion that the Philistian court did not have jurisdiction, the discussion should not stop there. The question requires a discussion of the 'requirements' for enforcement. It is not confined to simply advising Chopin or Bach. The student should then offer to deal with the issues of natural justice and public policy as defences against enforcement.

Answer

The general framework for the recognition and enforcement of judgments delivered and issued by a foreign court may be subclassified into two main categories – judgments obtained within the EC and judgments obtained without. The fact that Chopin's judgment was obtained from a state under which the Foreign Judgments (Reciprocal Enforcement) Act 1933 (hereafter to be referred to as the 1933 Act) indicates that this falls within the latter category.

Under the 1933 Act, a judgment may be registered first and then the applicant may apply to have it enforced in this country. Section 4 provides however that the registration may be set aside if certain conditions are not met.

In particular under s 4(1)(ii) the court will set the registration aside if it is proved that the courts of the country of the original court had no jurisdiction in the circumstances of the case. The determination of whether the foreign court has jurisdiction over the subject matter is to be assessed based on English law and not the foreign court's own rules (*Buchanan v Rucker* (1809)). By the same token however English courts will not simply recognise the foreign court's competence because the English courts would have had jurisdiction under the same circumstances (*Schibsby v Westenholtz* (1870)). They will not recognise jurisdiction founded on rules similar to the Rules of the Supreme Court, Order 11 r (1) for example. This is particularly relevant because it might be suggested by Chopin that under Order 11 r 1(1)(d)(i) the Russian court would have jurisdiction over contracts made within its jurisdiction. International competence can only be assessed on two grounds: presence in jurisdiction (*Adam v Cape Industries plc* (1990)) or submission to jurisdiction (*Emanuel v Symon* (1908)).

Applying this rule to Chopin's claim, it is evident that the Philistian court did not have jurisdiction on the basis of presence since Bach had already left the country at the material time. Limited therefore to the second limb, it may be raised in argument that Bach by instructing his lawyer to appear before the court has in fact submitted to the court's jurisdiction, assuming that there is no choice of jurisdiction clause between Bach and Chopin.

Where the Civil Jurisdiction and Judgments Act 1982 applies, a distinction must be made between appearance to challenge the jurisdiction of the courts and appearance to challenge the merits of the case. If it were the former, s 33 provides that such an act will not be deemed to be submission to the jurisdiction of that court. Under the old rule of the common law the position is quite the contrary. In *Henry v Geoprosco International Ltd* (1976), the court held that a challenge on the grounds of *forum non conveniens* was in fact submission to jurisdiction. This rule has been superseded by the Civil Jurisdiction and Judgments Act 1982. Bach by merely contesting the jurisdiction of the Philistian court falls neatly on the spread of s 33(1)(a) which provides clearly that there has been no submission to jurisdiction on his part.

While it is safe to assume that under English law the Philistian court has no international competence, it warrants discussion as to whether there is a case for claiming that the Philistian court was in excess of jurisdiction under Philistian law and how this may affect enforcement in an English court. The position as set out in *Vanguelin v Bouard* (1863) is that this is a matter for the foreign legal system and as a matter of judicial comity it is not open to the English court to discuss the merits of the case, albeit under the foreign law. Any recourse open to the claimant aggrieved by the 'lack of internal competence' must be restricted to claims and appeals within that domestic structure. This would mean that if Bach is not satisfied with the Philistian court acting without serving on him a properly executed writ (there being no mention of a writ actually served on him), he cannot take this issue up within the English court. It is of no relevance unless it goes to show failure of natural justice which will be discussed later.

In *Castrique v Imrie* (1870) however, the court regarded it as material 'whether the sovereign authority of that state has conferred on the court of jurisdiction to decide as to the disposition of the thing and whether the court has acted within its jurisdiction'. While this case refers to an action *in rem*, it is not certain how far this difference should be taken. Further support for this position is seen in *Macalpine v Macalpine* (1958). In that case the distinction made between a foreign decree being void or simply voidable for fraud appeared to have held the hinges of the decision. This assessment relied on a consideration of the foreign power conferring law. Where the foreign judgment is irregular and simply voidable, *obiter dicta* in *SA Consortium General Textiles v Sun & Sand Agencies Ltd* (1978) suggest that the judgment will be held valid in England until it has been properly annulled in the foreign country. In Bach's case, the judgment entered in default of appearance under those circumstances and the failure to take cognizance of leave may be contrary to Philistian law but until the matter is properly addressed by Philistian law, it will be hard to apply this defence.

At common law as stated in *Adam v Cape Industries plc* (1990) the concept of natural justice may be pleaded to impeach a foreign judgment seeking enforcement in this country. The Court of Appeal in Adams found that if the defendant could have applied to the American court to have the judgment in default set aside then there was no breach of natural justice. In that case the defendant had no knowledge of the facts or the means to find out whether they could apply to set aside the judgment. This did not therefore prevent them from using the natural justice defence against enforcement. In this context, it may be possible for Bach to argue that he had been denied natural justice because it would appear from the facts that no leave to serve the writ was actually granted. Even if the leave had been granted his case was not heard since all his lawyer did was to contest jurisdiction and not the merits of the case.

Another defence which may be of relevance is that of public policy. Where the enforcement or recognition of a foreign judgment will contradict the public policy of this country, that foreign judgment may be impeached. In practice however this has not been very successfully applied because it is never easy to prove the existence of a principle of public policy. In Bach's situation though, Chopin may rely on the inclination of the courts as seen in *SA Consortium* to treat punitive or exemplary damages as a matter outside the public policy defence. Where unless the punitive order encroaches some rule of fundamental human rights, it is difficult to envisage the courts departing from this inclination to restrict the ambit of what constitutes public policy. This approach was taken by the Canadian court in *Burchell v Burchell* (1926).

Question 25

Comment on how the different regimes on the recognition and enforcement of foreign arbitral awards decide as to when an award will be recognised.

Answer plan

In order to answer this question effectively the student must have at least done some reading around the subject of enforcement of foreign awards. The treatment of this topic in an undergraduate course in private international law is not likely to be too deep. What is usually required would be a fair working knowledge of the two conventions, the New York Convention and the Geneva Convention and how they differ from each other.

The chief difficulty with this question is identifying which provisions of which of the three Arbitration Acts are applicable and how they interrelate. The emphasis is on the various grounds for non-enforcement. Concentrate on these grounds. It is not about the procedure involved in getting an award recognised, the student should omit this from the discussion as a matter of economics and relevance.

Answer

Foreign awards which may be enforced in England and Wales could be roughly sub-classified under Convention awards (ie awards covered by the Convention on the Recognition and Enforcement of Foreign Arbitral Awards, New York 1958, to be referred to as the New York Convention) and non-Convention awards. The New York Convention has been set into the legislative tablets of this country following the passage of the Arbitration Act 1975 (hereafter to be referred to as the AA 1975).

Convention awards

Section 7 AA 1975 defines a Convention award as an award pursuant to a written agreement which is made in any Member State of the New York Convention other than the United Kingdom. Under the provision of s 7, the award shall be treated as binding, to all intents and purposes, on persons between whom it was made and is enforceable as such in the country.

One preliminary point is that the time enforcement of the award is crucial. In *Kuwait Minister of Public Works v Sir Frederick Snow* (1984), the House of Lords held that although the award was made before Kuwait became a member to the Convention, the enforcement action could be expedited through the machinery of the New York Convention because the enforcement proceedings were fixed after it had ratified the Convention. This is a very important decision in that awards made before a state became a Member State will be enforceable provided the enforcement proceedings were started after that state has become a member.

Once the award is a properly constituted Convention award, s 3 AA 1975 provides that the award shall be enforceable in England and Wales either by action or in the same manner as the award of a locally made award. The latter is enforceable by means of s 2 AA 1950. Hence under the Convention there is to be no distinction between foreign and domestic awards in terms of enforcement and recognition.

A foreign award may however be refused recognition or enforcement if its enforcement would be contrary to public policy under s 5(3). Besides public policy grounds, the court may also refuse enforcement on the ground that a party to the arbitration agreement was under legal incapacity. The test of his incapacity is to be based on the law applicable to him. This raises the problem as to whether 'the law applicable to him' is his personal law or the law relating to the contract which he has entered into. The balance should perhaps be in favour of the former to prohibit the use of a commercial agreement to avoid the personal law restrictions on matters like infancy or mental incapacity.

Where the arbitration agreement was not valid under the applicable law, or if the parties have given no indication on the matter under the law of the country where the award was made, there is no question of enforcement because the law can only recognise an award that is legal. To enforce the contrary is to commit an act of self-contradiction. Not only is the agreement itself subject to such determination, the actual process shall be made likewise. The composition of the arbitral tribunal or the procedure must be in accordance with the agreement of the parties or the law of the seat of the arbitration. The consensual element here is complemented by the law of the country where the arbitration took place. The arbitration is connected with the law of the country where it is set.

The fact that the respondent or person against whom the enforcement is sought had not been given proper notice of the appointment of the arbitration proceedings or was otherwise unable to present his case will result in the courts not recognising that award. This is to ensure that the rules of natural justice are satisfied.

That the award contains decisions on matters outside the reference which cannot be severed from it is another ground for refusal of enforcement. This goes to show the main feature of an arbitration as envisaged under the Convention – *consensus ad idem*. The jurisdiction of the arbitrator stems from the agreement and where a matter dealt with is outside the intentions of the parties as evinced by the agreement, it may not be considered by the arbitrator at all.

Where the award has been set aside or suspended by a competent authority in the country where the arbitration took place, English courts would not intervene unless there is concrete evidence that that authority was not a competent authority. Pursuant to s 5(5) AA 1975, if proceedings to set aside the award are opening in the country where it was made, the court may adjourn the application to enforce the award but may require security from the other party . Under paragraph (f) of the sub-section, enforcement may be refused if it is proved that the award has not yet become binding.

Non-Convention awards

Where the New York Convention does not apply, an award may be implemented or enforced in accordance with the provisions of Part II AA 1950, which covers the duties and rights generated by the Geneva Convention 1927. Specifically the award must qualify as a 'foreign award' as described in Part II of the said Act. It must not be a New York Convention award and should have been made pursuant to a written arbitration agreement to which the Geneva Protocol of 1923 applies. Further, each party must have been subject to the jurisdiction of a Power which an Order in Council states is a parry to the Geneva Convention. These are states which have reciprocal provisions for the enforcement and recognition of arbitration awards made in this country.

Signatories to the 1923 Protocol bind themselves to recognising the validity of arbitration agreements made between parties of different states whatever the place of the arbitration. They also recognise that the procedure should be governed by the terms of the arbitration agreement and the *lex fori*. The implications of this recognition is the eventual preparedness to enforce such agreements by ensuring the disputes are referred to arbitration as intended and by seeing to it that awards made pursuant to them are properly recognised and enforced.

Section 37 AA 1950 provides that the award must have been made under a valid arbitration agreement by a properly constituted arbitral tribunal in conformity with local law and it must be final on an issue which could have been referred to arbitration by English law. Section 37(2) further states that awards will not be enforced if:

- the arbitration agreement was not adhered to;
- the other party was not given sufficient notice or was unable to present his side of the arguments;
- the award itself has been overruled;
- the award is against public policy in England or against English law.

It is readily seen that these grounds are similar to those set out by the New York Convention, the apparent exception being that the conditions under s 37(2) are couched in more general terms. How this will in practice lead to dissimilar implications from the New York Convention is probably negligible.

Further to s 37, besides the power to refuse enforcement the court may postpone enforcement of the award. Where, for example, the award does not deal with all the matters referred or under s 37(3) where the party resisting the enforcement could show other grounds (other than those mentioned in s 37(2)) that the award is not valid, the court may postpone enforcement to enable the arbitral tribunal to resolve the issues first. The power of postponement underpins the principle of finality of awards as stressed by the AAs in general.

Once these provisions are satisfied the foreign award may be enforced either by action or in the same manner as a domestic award. A domestic award according to s 26 AA 1950 is treated like a judgment of the court. Hence, the award could at the same time be relied on as a set off or defence in any proceedings in this country provided it is done in line with s 36.

The chief difference between a Convention award and a protocol award is that in the latter the claimant must prove to the satisfaction of the court that the agreement was valid and that the correct procedure has been adhered to. As regards the latter where the procedure was to be under the civil process of another state, expert evidence on the correctness of the procedure will have to be adduced. This will lead to higher costs and inconvenience. A Convention award on the other hand is governed by s 4 AA 1975 which simply requires that the claimant produce the authenticated original award or a certified copy before the court. The proof of any inconsistency in process is the burden of the defendant (s 5 AA 1975).

In conclusion where the award does not fall within the New York Convention or the Geneva Convention, enforcement may be pursued by suing the respondent under English law and relying on the summary judgment procedure (Order 14, Rules of the Supreme Court). This is not in fact enforcement but the fresh application in the courts of this country claiming settlement of a foreign judgment debt. This means that the plaintiff will have to prove the debt and shall not be allowed to rely on any statutory presumption as is the case under the two Conventions. The normal rules and problems in proving a debt will operate.

Chapter 5

Contract

Introduction

At common law, party autonomy means that the parties to the contract are entitled to make a selection of the system of law to govern their contract. This choice of law shall be recognised and enforced by the courts unless it is against public policy or the forum's mandatory rules. Where the parties have not expressed a choice of the law, the rule is that the law with which the contract is most closely connected shall be the proper law.

The Contracts (Applicable Law) Act 1990 which came into force on 1 April 1991 brings into English law, the Rome Convention 1980. The Convention recognises the principle of party autonomy in that the parties' express choice of law shall be taken to be the applicable law of the contract. Where there is no selection made, the rule in Article 4(1) is that the law with which the contract is most closely connected shall be the applicable law. Article 4(2) provides a presumption to the extent that the contract is most closely connected with the country where the party who is to effect the characteristic performance of the contract has his habitual residence at the time of the conclusion of the contract.

Where the subject matter is a right in immovable property, then the contract is presumed to be most closely connected with the *lex situs*.

The presumptions set out in Article 4(2)(3)(4) may be rebutted if it appears that the contract is more closely connected with another country and with reference to Article 4(2), where the obligation of which performance is characteristic of the contract is indeterminable.

It is also noteworthy that like the rules of common law, the applicable law must not derogate from mandatory rules of the forum and public policy considerations.

On issues of material and formal validity, the principles are as follow:

- The essential validity of a contract is to be determined by the law which would govern the contract, assuming that it had been validly made.

- Formal validity rules include:
  (a) in general the contract is formally valid if it meets the formalities of the law of the country where either or both the parties are resident, or the applicable law;
  (b) consumer contracts are subject to the formalities of the law of the country where the consumer is resident;
  (c) contracts involving immovables and similar rights *in rem* are to be determined by the *lex situs* where the issue of formal validity is concerned.

Checklist

- the principle of party autonomy
- common law rules on proper law of the contract (*Amin Rasheed Shipping Corp v Kuwait Insurance Co* (1983))
- scope of the Rome Convention as regards party autonomy
- the rebuttable presumptions in the Rome Convention
- operation of Article 4(5) of the Rome Convention
- material and formal validity of contracts
- matters to be governed by the applicable law and Article 10

Question 26

Compare and contrast the regime under the Contracts (Applicable Law) Act 1990 with the framework as developed by English judges at common law.

Answer plan

The good answer should demonstrate a sound comprehension of the framework and application of the Contracts (Applicable Law) Act 1990. The principles of party autonomy and freedom of contract should be alluded, as they form the bases of the Rome Convention. The operation of these principles in the Convention should be contrasted against their application under common law.

The answer should further examine how the presumptions in Article 4 have resulted in some degree of confusion, and ultimately, as a consequence of Article 4(5), the common law factors applied by *Amin Rasheed Shipping Corp* (1984) may still be applicable under the Act.

There should also address the questions of material and formal validity of contracts, which was a matter of considerable debate at common law.

Answer

The Contracts (Applicable Law) Act 1990 brings into force the Rome Convention on the Law Applicable to Contractual Obligations 1980. The objective of the Rome Convention is to harmonise the choice of law rules in contract and, in so doing, discourage forum shopping. The common law, on the other hand, does not have as its express aim the harmonisation of choice of law rules being domestic in nature but, as will be demonstrated, the rules of the Convention are not entirely different from those developed by the English judges. The Convention invariably has to take into account rules of private international law relating to contracts from all Member States and has benefited from the wealth of the common law on this sector of concern. Having said that however, it is yet the intention of the Convention to replace the rules of the common law.

The Convention covers contractual obligations involving a foreign element or, in terms of Article 1(1), contractual obligations in any situation involving a choice between the laws of different countries. It is implicit from this Article that while there is full EC participation, membership to the Convention is not thence restricted. However, although membership to the Convention is open to any state, Article 1 of the Brussels Protocol states that the European Court of Justice shall have the final say in the interpretation of the Convention. This leads to an auxiliary question which must not be undervalued. If the European Court of Justice has the final say in matters of construction it is important to at least outline the methods of interpretation adopted by the European Court. The approach of the European Court entails several methods of interpretation which are fairly distinct from the norms applied by the common law courts. One method which stands out as individually marked is the teleological approach. The European Court in purporting to construe any rule of EC law will not only rely on the literal reading of the provision but will poise itself to apply the purpose of the rule as the guide to interpretation.

Returning to the Act, there are several contracts that are outside the purview of the Convention (Article 1(2)(3)(4)). Where this is the case the choice of law issue is to be determined by the common law or any other applicable law. Aside from this it should be mentioned that Article 2 provides that all other contracts are to be governed by the Convention regardless of the absence of any EC connection.

As a matter of contrast, the terminology in the Act is different from the common law. The term 'proper law' as applied in the common law has been replaced with 'applicable law'. The rules for determining what the applicable law is are not dissimilar to those embodied in the common law. The overriding provision is that where the parties have made a choice of applicable law to their contract that selection must prevail. Article 3 provides that the choice must be express or at least can be demonstrated with reasonable certainty by the terms of the contract or the circumstances of the case. Where the contract is severable, the choice of law could apply to certain parts of that contract. There is basically no restriction to the choice of applicable law – Article 2 enables the parties to select any law regardless of the absence of any connection with the contract.

At common law, the core of the judgments is very much the same; for instance, in *Vita Food Products Inc v Unus Shipping Co Ltd* (1939) it was held that where there is a valid choice of law clause, and there is no objection to that choice in terms of public policy, the court will not interfere. Enshrined in both the common law and the Convention rules is the principle of freedom of contract, subject to nothing but public policy.

Where there is no choice of law clause or agreement identifiable from the facts surrounding the contract, Article 4 provides that the court will have to ascertain the law of the country with which the contract is most closely connected. This, too, is not dissimilar to the approach of the common law. From *Amin Rasheed Shipping Corp v Kuwait Insurance Co* (1984), the contract is to be governed by the system of law which has the closest and most real connection with the contract. A point of departure found in Article 4 is the provision for rebuttable presumptions. These presumptions are intended to assist the courts in ascertaining the close connection. At common law it was expressly held that some of the old common law presumptions must be rejected. The court at common law has full discretion to determine if the burden of proof has been properly discharged (*Amin Rasheed*).

The more prominent presumption is that stipulated in Article 4(2). Article 4(2) presumes that the law of the party who has to effect 'the performance which is characteristic of the contract' will apply to the contract as the law having the closest connection. This is usually the place where the performer of that obligation in question resides habitually or has his place of business. While this would appear to be quite different from the common law position, it is submitted that the changes are purely architectural. The result following a common law analysis will probably be the same. Article 4(5), for example, removes the presumption (which in any event is rebuttable), where it is apparent from the circumstances of the circumstances as a whole, that the contract is in fact more closely connected with a different country than that which the presumption lead to. The proof of Article 4(5), that is to say, in order to establish that the country presumed is not in fact most closely connected with the contract, the party would still have to rely on criteria set out by the common law.

Another novelty in the Convention is the provision that consumer and employment contracts are automatically protected by any mandatory rules of the place of the consumer's habitual residence (Article 5(2)) or where the employee habitually carries out his duties (Article 6) whatever the terms of the contract are. It may be argued that this is one instance where there is a difference with the common law.

A further element of protection of the private individual who is not given the same regard at common law is found in Article 8. This Article permits any party claiming the lack of consent when making a contract to rely on the law of the country in which he has his place of habitual residence. At common law, this is not addressed simply because the common law's primary concern is with the domestic situation. Also, the common law's provision for the putative proper law of the contract makes it impossible to deal with issue of consent in this way.

The Convention refers to 'rules which cannot be derogated from by contract (Article 3(3)) or mandatory rules which the party cannot attempt to avoid by a choice of law agreement. Article 7(1) goes on to provide that effect may be given to the mandatory rules of another country with which the contract has a close connection. The impact of this provision has somewhat been diminished by permitting Member States to opt-out of. The UK, for example, has exercised its right to opt-out under Article 22. However, while Article 7(2) remains applicable, the courts may apply the mandatory rules of the forum in which the case is heard. In *The Hollandia* (1983) it was held that a clause in the bill of lading that provided for the application of Dutch law and hence the lower limit of compensation was ineffective against the discretion of the English court as the forum to apply the mandatory Hague-Visby limit. The case, which was not decided on the basis of Article 7(2), demonstrates how the common law has taken into account such deviant commercial practice.

An entrenched English law rule that prescribes that the court may refuse to enforce a contract which involves trading with the enemy or other dealings contrary to public policy has found its way into the Convention. Article 16 which refers to *ordre public* states that the application of a rule of any country specified by the Convention may be refused where the application is manifestly incompatible with the public policy of the forum. From this angle, it is difficult to see any real change in the Convention on the issue of illegality.

In terms of material validity of the contract (leaving aside the question of consent which had been dealt with), the provisions of Article 8 are not too far transposed from the common law 'putative proper law' approach. In *Albeko Schuhmaschinen v Kamborian Shoe Machine Co Ltd* (1961), the issue was whether the contract was properly concluded; under Swiss law it would not have been, where under English law it would have been, made the minute the letter of acceptance was posted. The putative proper law approach enables the court to refer to the law which would have been the proper law of the contract had it been concluded. Salmon J in that case held that there was no contract because there was no evidence that the letter had been posted. His Lordship however expressed the opinion that if it had been, Swiss law would govern, leading to the finding that there is no contract concluded (because if a contract had been concluded, Swiss law would have been the proper law). The position lodged in Article 8 does not take into account the suggestion that, where reliance on the putative proper law of the contract leads to grave injustices, a party must be able to rely on the law of business or residence.

As for formal validity, Article 9 is slightly more generous than the common law prescription. Article 9 sets out a number of situations which, if complied with, will lend formal validity to the contract for the purposes of the conflict of laws. At common law, such validity is derived from either the place of the contracting parties or by the proper law.

There is some degree of variance as a result of Article 10. Article 10(2) appears to make it imperative that the court is to apply the law of the country in which performance takes place in matters covering the manner of performance. On the other hand, Article 10(1)(b) specifically refers to the use and application of the applicable law to decide questions of performance. The Giuliano-Lagarde Report, in commenting on the dichotomy, suggests that the court has a discretion but the Report does not proceed to explain how this discretion is to be exercised. At common law, it is mandatory that the judge applies the law of the place where performance is to take place.

In passing, the operation of the *renvoi* is expressly excluded as with the common law when dealing with questions of conflict of laws (Article 15).

It is vital that the rules and methodology of the common law not be totally disregarded when applying the Convention. Although the position is very much to be determined according to the interpretative methods of the European Court of Justice where there is a lacuna, the traditional rules should assist in filling it. It must, however, be conceded that there are some irreconcilable differences between the two legal orders especially where the provisions in the Convention leave some room for doubt as to their meaning.

Question 27

When Joe was living in Xenon he agreed to buy some shares from King Kong Corp, a Xenon registered company. Joe made part payment of 30% of the full purchase price. Joe was then 20 years old.

Under the contract it is provided that 'King Kong Corp and/or its agents are expressly exempt from liability arising from any pre-contractual representation concerning the state of the company'. The contract further states that it is to be governed by Portuguese law, Portugal being the place where the holding company is situated.

According to the law of Xenon, persons under the age of 21 cannot transact or deal in shares. The position on the other hand is not clear under Portuguese law.

Joe has now returned to England. He has discovered that one of the representations made to him by King Kong about the financial state of the company was untrue. If he had known the true position he would never have purchased the shares. He now refuses to pay the remainder of the purchase price.

Xenon law provides that misrepresentations made to induce a person to enter into a contractual relationship are unlawful and any contract entered into on the basis of a misrepresentation is void *ab initio*.

King Kong Corp has instituted proceedings in England against Joe for full payment of the purchase price.

Discuss the parties' legal position under the Contracts (Applicable Law) Act 1990.

Answer plan

A good answer should include the following points:

- capacity to contract under the relevant regime
- Article 1(2)(a) and Article 11 Rome Convention
- Article 3 and Article 7 on mandatory rules
- Article 10(1)(e) Rome Convention on the consequences of nullity of contracts

Answer

Under Article 1(1) of the Rome Convention which is enforceable in England by virtue of the Contracts (Applicable Law) Act 1990, all contractual obligations in any situation involving a choice between the laws of different countries are governed by the Convention.

This is regardless of the fact that the other countries involved in the dispute are not contracting parties to the Convention.

The first question that befaces King Kong Corp is whether Joe has the capacity to contract. The starting point is perhaps Article 1(2)(a) which provides that the rules of the Convention are inapplicable to questions involving the status and legal capacity of natural persons. From this perspective the Rome Convention may not have an impact on the determination of Joe's status or capacity to contract. However this view must be subject to the qualifier in Article 11.

Article 11 provides that in a contract concluded between persons who are in the same country, a natural person who would have capacity under the law of that country may invoke his incapacity resulting from another law only if the other party to the contract was aware of his incapacity at the time of the conclusion of the contract and was not aware thereof as a result of negligence. Fortunately or unfortunately for the parties, Joe's status will still have to be assessed at common law. At English law Joe does not lack capacity. His lack of capacity is only found in Xenon law.

At common law the general principle is that capacity to contract being a matter of personal law, must be assessed by the *lex domicilii* (*Sottomayor v De Barros (No 1)* (1877)). The *lex domicilii* should indicate what the personal law is or should be. If Joe is domiciled in England, this would mean that following this rule Joe's capacity should be measured by English law. Under English law he would have the capacity to contract, the age of majority being 18.

According to Professor McClean, while the dearth of authorities have not been consistent, the proposition that the putative proper law of the contract should be applied is probably the most practical approach. This does not mean the law that the parties themselves have chosen for the governance of the contract (*Cooper v Cooper* (1888)). The reason is perhaps best illustrated by Lord Macnaghten in the following terms, '[i]t is difficult to suppose that Mrs Cooper could confer capacity on herself by contemplating a different country as the place where the contract was to be fulfilled'. Consequently the courts will have to determine the proper law of the contract with the selective ignorance of the parties' choice of law.

At this stratum of the facts, it may be suggested that Xenon law is probably the objective proper law. The reasons are that the contract was to be performed in Xenon where the shares are transacted and transferred to Joe. Even though the holding company has its place of business in Portugal, it is a perfectly conceivable and credible proposition that the shares are those of the Xenon based company and not those of the holding company. Under Xenon law, Joe does not have the capacity to contract; which means the contract is void *ab initio* and King Kong will not be able to demand full payment. Incidentally it could also be raised that, as could be derived from *Male v Roberts* (1800), the *lex loci contractus* could be used to determine the issue of capacity. If this approach is taken, the same result will be arrived at since the contract was entered into in Xenon.

The second issue is whether the exclusion of liability clause written into the contract has any legal effect under the choice of law rules in the Rome Convention if the contract is valid. Article 3(1) of the Convention states that the party may choose the applicable law of their contract. On this basis, the selected Portuguese law will take priority and be applied, regardless of the fact that the contract may have no connection with the place chosen. This is the oft-quoted rule of party autonomy.

Article 3(1) however must be read subject to Article 3(3) which provides that where all the other relevant elements to the situation when the choice was made are connected with one country only, then the mandatory rules of that country may not be derogated from in the application of the chosen law.

Whether or not all the factors relevant to the situation at the time of the choice are connected with one country, and in the present case, Xenon, is a question of fact. In the Australian case of *Golden Acres Ltd v Queensland Estates Pty Ltd* (1969), the operation of 'all elements relevant to the situation' while explored, does not seem capable of any decisive and consistent definition. In that case the place where the estate agency was based and indeed, the domicile of the purchasers were deemed to be elements relevant to the situation, even though in a business context, they were of little materiality. If this type of an approach is recommended then it is likely that since Joe is (presumably) domiciled in England, not all the elements relevant to the case are connected with one country alone. Whether the seat of the holding company is a relevant factor when it does not seem to be involved at all must be left as a matter for speculation.

Joe may wish to rely on Article 7(1) which specifies that effect may be given to the mandatory rules of the law of a country other than that of a chosen law with which the situation has a close connection with in so far as those rules must be applied whatever the law applicable to the contract. This would entitle Joe to rely on Xenon law since Xenon is the country very closely connected with the contract. Unfortunately for Joe, the opt out spelt out in s 2(2) of the 1990 Act is to the effect that Article 7(1) has no application in the United Kingdom.

On the issue of whether Joe will be able to recover his part payment, the rules on restitution at common law shall be applicable. Article 10(1)(e) which allows the applicable law to determine the consequence of nullity of the contract does not apply since the United Kingdom has entered a reservation to the provision. In this context there is a view, on the other hand, that the proper law at common law should determine the issue of the consequences of nullity of the contract. This would mean that Portuguese law will govern, that being the law expressed in the choice of law clause.

Question 28

Over the last 20 years Mark and Jason Co Ltd, a company based in Luton, England have conducted various business dealings with each other. In many of these contracts they have adopted various American statutory provisions and forms as their contractual terms.

Last month Mark telephoned Jason Co Ltd from Essexia offering to sell a consignment of rubber balls. Jason Co Ltd accepted the offer. The goods were to be delivered to Jason Co Ltd's subsidiary company in Ireland. It was agreed that payment was to be made in three instalments, the first two to be made in Sterling and deposited in Mark's bank account in London and the third, in US dollars to be entered into Mark's account in Essexia.

The shipment of the cargo has been substantially delayed as a result of the Essexian authorities not granting a certificate of quality. Mark contends that the contract has been frustrated.

Discuss how the Contracts (Applicable Law) Act 1990 will determine the applicable law of the issues.

Answer

The general rule under the Contracts (Applicable Law) Act 1990 is that if it has been expressly agreed between Mark and Jason that a particular system of law is to govern the contract, that chosen system shall prevail. This is the case even though the contract may have little or no connection at all with that country.

Where there is no express selection, the courts will have to decide whether there is an implied choice of law from the facts. Article 3(1) provides that the choice must be demonstrated with reasonable certainty by the terms of the contract or the circumstances of the case. It has been suggested that this entails the difficult issue of construction. The Giuliano-Lagarde Report appears to suggest that this is not necessary, all that the court has to do is to construe the wording of the contract in the light of the circumstances of the case. The courts in this regard will analyse relevant trade practice, previous course of dealings between the parties and whether the parties in the course of their dealings have indicated a selection which can be treated as such with reasonable certainty.

In our case, Mark and Jason have for a number of years relied on American statutory forms and provisions as terms for their business transactions. Before any inference may be drawn following the rules in the Rome Convention, it must be mentioned that where these previous dealings are similar to the transaction in question, the stronger that inference may be made. This goes some distance in showing the consistency of practice so vital to reasonable certainty. Assuming that this element is met, the second point for determination is whether the use of American forms and precedents is an implied selection of American law as the choice of law or simply as a set of terms without that effect. In *Adamastos Shipping Co Ltd v Anglo-Saxon Petroleum Co* (1959), the contract in question was simply a restatement of the statute verbatim. The provisions operated as a set of agreed terms between the parties and not as a statute. The acid test is whether the contract will still be bound by those provisions in question when the statutes have been repealed or amended.

If there is no choice of law between the parties either by express selection or by implication, Article 4(1) shall apply affiliating the contract with the law of the country with which it is most closely connected. Article 4(2) then comes in with a presumption of the country with which the contract is most closely connected.

Article 4(2) makes reference to the party who is to effect the performance which is characteristic of the contract. According to the Giuliano-Lagarde Report, the obligation characteristic of the contract is that for which monetary consideration is given in exchange, usually that which is linked with the socio-economic environment of the transaction. From the facts, this would be the obligation to deliver the rubber balls. Hence, Mark is the relevant party for the purposes of the presumption.

Subsequent to this, the courts will have to determine whether that party (namely Mark) is to perform the contract in the course of his trade or profession. If he did so as the facts suggest, then the country most closely connected with the contract is Mark's principal place of business. Although Mark made the phone call from Essexia, without further information it is unsafe to conclude that Essexia is his principal place of business.

It may be the case that as the contract provides that performance is to be effected through Essexia, namely that the rubber balls are to be exported from Essexia, the location of *that* place of business becomes relevant and not the principal place of business. This means that even though Essexia is not Mark's principal place of business, it appears to be the place through which the contract is to be performed.

If Mark was not dealing in the course of his trade or profession, the place of his habitual residence at the time of conclusion of the contract shall be the presumed country having that close connection with the contract. From the facts the contract was concluded instantaneously over the telephone when Mark was in Essexia. However we are not told if Essexia at that time was the place Mark had his habitual residence.

The presumption in Article 4(2) is not irrebuttable. Article 4(5) in a rather oblique way spells out that where the circumstances as a whole reveal that the contract is more closely connected with another country then the presumption is to be ignored. In this regard, the court may have to resort to the text set out in the Pre Contracts (Applicable Law) Act 1990 case of *Amin Rasheed Shipping Corp v Kuwait Insurance Co* (1984). The factors the court will take into account according to that case include the place where the contract is to be performed, where the parties are situated, the currency the contract is expressed in, the language and form of the contract, the existence of a choice of forum clause and other circumstances indicating the parties' intention. In Marks' case the place of performance could be either Ireland or Essexia depending on the nature of contractual term. The place where the contract was made is the place where the acceptance was communicated to, namely Essexia (*Byrne v Van Tienhoven* (1880)). The language and form is similar to American statutory provisions. The currency is in both Sterling and US dollars, and part of the payment is to be made in England and the rest in Essexia. The factors seem to be quite split in either direction. It is difficult to place any extra emphasis on any of the factors mentioned. The paradigm is the presumed intention of the parties. This must be objectively ascertained by the court.

Another issue of particular importance is whether the question of frustration of the contract is to be determined by the applicable law. Article 10 of the Convention specifies that questions of performance, discharge and extinguishing of obligations are to be governed by the applicable law. This is however qualified by Article 10(2) which provides that in relation to the manner of performance and the steps to be taken in the event of defective performance regard shall be had to the law of the country in which performance takes place. This according to the Giuliano-Lagarde Report legitimises the displacement of the first general provision and allows the courts to apply the law of the place of performance where to do so would converge on the justice of the case.

At common law a similar position is reflected in the Court of Appeal's decision in *Jacobs v Credit Lyonnais* (1884). The court held that the law of the place of performance might regulate the method and manner of performance but this is not to be extended to matters of detail, especially those matters which do not affect the substance of the obligation. Juxtaposing this on the present case, the law of the place of performance which is most likely to be Ireland (where Mark is to deliver the goods) shall be applicable to determine the issue of frustration. On whether there is a requirement to obtain the certificate of quality, Essexian law is to apply but Irish law will be used to decide whether this duty is to be imposed on Mark or whether the failure to do so frustrates the contract.

Note

1 See Woolf, *Private International Law* (2nd edn, 1950) p 439.

Question 29

Isabelle Co, a Sociologian company entered into an agreement with Judith Co, a Teacherian company to purchase Teacherian artefacts. The contract states that the artefacts are to be shipped on Utopian ships. Payment was to be made in Utopian currency through a bank based in Utopia.

In the meantime, under international pressure, the Sociologian government passed a law banning the import of certain artefacts from states like Teacheria. In reliance on this intervening illegality, Isabelle Co refused to pay and take delivery of the artefacts.

Convinced that they will not get justice in Sociologia, Judith Co institutes action against Isabelle Co in England by serving a writ on Isabelle Co's office in London. The office is manned only by the typist and the documentation clerk. The office is responsible for collecting mail on behalf of the main offices in Western Europe.

Examine how English courts will determine the question of jurisdiction and the applicable law of the contract.

Answer plan

The first issue is that of jurisdiction where the defendant has only a slight presence in the country. The position in *South India Shipping Corp v The Import Export Bank of Korea* should provide the solution. Mention too the other grounds upon which jurisdiction is founded.

This question then tests the student's ability in applying the rules under the Contracts (Applicable Law) Act 1990 which incorporated the Rome Convention. The Rome Convention sets out in a systematic fashion the stages the court should go through to determine the applicable law.

The first stage is to locate a choice of law clause or agreement. This agreement may be express or implied, it would appear. The implication of the choice clause is probably based on the traditional common law rules. It should be noted that there are those who argue that the implication of a choice of law clause has no place under the Convention. Where the agreement is silent the court should move on to applying the presumptions in Article 4. Only where the presumptions fail under Article 4(5) should the court apply the traditional rules.

The question also expects some treatment of the issue of mandatory rules and material invalidity.

Answer

In determining whether English courts have jurisdiction to hear and entertain the dispute, the relevant set of rules on jurisdiction must first be identified. On matters of jurisdiction the courts are governed by three different regimes, the Brussels Convention, the Lugano Convention and the traditional Rules of the Supreme Court which purport to represent the common law. In the matter concerning Isabelle Co and Judith Co, the natural conclusion is that the two Conventions will not apply because none of the contracting states is involved.

The establishment of jurisdiction is dependent on the following conditions:

- the defendant is present in jurisdiction when the writ was served;
- the defendant has submitted to jurisdiction either through a choice of jurisdiction clause/agreement or by appearance before the court;
- where Order 11 r 1(1) RSC applies for the proper service of the writ abroad.

On the facts Isabelle Co has been served with the writ at their mail collection office in London. The question is whether this amounts to a valid service of the writ considering the fact that the office is only a publicity office. In *South India Shipping Corp v The Import Export Bank of Korea* (1985), the Court of Appeal held that the writ had been properly served on the Korean Bank's publicity office in the City of London. Although the office was not maintained for trading as is the case with Isabelle Co, the court held that the defendants had effectively established a place within jurisdiction which is capable of accepting service. On this basis Judith Co has lawfully instituted action in England against Isabelle Co.

The next question is what law will the courts apply to resolve the dispute as presented by the contract.

The court will have to rely on the Contracts (Applicable Law) Act 1990 to determine which law is applicable to the contract. The general rule is that if the parties, Isabelle Co and Judith Co had pre-agreed on a particular law to govern the contract, under Article 3 the court will apply that law. The choice of law agreement or clause must be demonstrated with reasonable certainty from the terms of the contract or the circumstances of the case. Where the clause is not expressed clearly, extraneous factors may be adduced to construe the ambiguous clause.

If there is no choice of law clause entered into between the parties, the question is whether it is possible to deduce from the facts that there is an implied agreement as to the choice of law. There is some doubt however as to whether an implied selection is to be applied before resorting to the presumptions in Article 4 Rome Convention. It is submitted that the problem is more apparent than real. This is because in the event where the party concerned is able to show that contrary to the presumption in Article 4(2)(3) the contract is more closely connected to another country, that presumption may be rebutted pursuant to Article 4(5). In the proof of Article 4(5), the general view is that the factors under the common law (as illustrated in *Amin Rasheed Shipping Corp v Kuwait Insurance Co* (1984)) are needful.

For the sake of orderliness it is proposed to deal with the presumptions in Article 4 first. Article 4(2) enables the court to presume that the law of the country with which the contract is most closely connected is the law of the party who has to effect 'the performance which is characteristic of the contract'. This would take the place of the party's place of habitual residence or business.

The preliminary issue is what does the 'performance which is characteristic of the contract' mean? The Giuliano-Lagarde Report offers some assistance. It describes the 'characteristic performance' as that which links the contract to the social and economic environment of which it will form a part'. The performance which is characteristic of the contract is the performance for which payment is due as this is that which usually constitutes the centre of gravity and the socio-economic function of the contractual transaction. In the present case, this must necessarily point at the delivery of the artefacts and since it is Judith Co that has to supply the goods, Judith Co's place of business will be presumed to be the place having the closest connection with the contract. If Judith Co has its place of business in Teacheria then Teacheria will be the place with which the contract is most closely connected. Where the dispute is about the carriage of goods, the presumption in Article 4(2) does not apply. Instead the court will under Article 4(4) hold the place of the carrier's principal business as the place with which the contract of carriage is most closely connected if that place is also any of the following:

- the place of loading;
- the place of discharge;
- the principal place where the consignor of the goods has his business. From the facts it is fairly certain that the claim that Judith Co has lodged against Isabelle Co is one based on the agreement of sale rather than that of carriage. Even if the agreement in question is that of the carriage obligation, it is unclear if any of the two named parties is the carrier.

Regardless, the court will not be able to rely on these presumptions where it is proved successfully that another country is more closely connected with the contract. The factors which the court will apply in exercising its powers under Article 4(5) to reject a presumption are similar to those espoused at common law.

The approach of the common law has been to assess the situation relying on circumstances surrounding the contract and the terms of the contract in question. In *Amin Rasheed Shipping Corp v Kuwait Insurance Co* (1983), the intention of the parties *vis-à-vis* the choice of law must be clear from the terms of the contract or from the circumstances surrounding the contract. In the latter issue, the courts may consider pre-contractual negotiations, representations and also the previous conduct of the parties. In general the courts will consider the following points:

- the existence of an exclusive jurisdiction or arbitration clause;
- while the language of the contract is generally not of much significance, it becomes pivotal when it employs certain terminology which is *sui generis* to a particular system of law

(*Whitworth Street Est v James Miller* (1970)). In *Amin Rasheed* the court inferred from the use of the English Marine Insurance Act 1906 that terms in the insurance policy must necessarily mean that the parties intended to interpret the contract of insurance using English law;

- the currency of payment may be useful where it forms one of several factors. As a lone factor it does not carry much weight but the court will not exclude its consideration where there are other factors. In *The Assunzione* (1954), the court concluded that the contract was intended to be governed by Italian law by taking the cumulative effect of the evidence that the contract was made in Italy and that freight and demurrage should be paid in Italian currency. It should be noted that in that case the facts were so nicely balanced between French and Italian law that the Court of Appeal placed the decisive factor on the place where performance was to be effected. Delivery and payment were to take place in Italy as indicated by the currency expressed, hence the decision.

The circumstances that the court will have to consider in Judith Co's application include the place where delivery of the artefacts was to take place. The delivery is probably to take place at Sociologia where the import ban was so relevant. The added aggravation is that the currency of payment and delivery of the goods appear to be more connected with Utopia than any of the two states involved. Upon the caveat in *Amin Rasheed*, these discrete factors must be accommodated with care, it is the task of the court to weigh all such matters together to assess their cumulative effect.

Once the selection of the applicable law has been made either through operation of the presumptions or not, it is important to determine if the Sociologian law banning the import of certain artefacts is protected by the Rome Convention. The Rome Convention recognises the importance of some national rules and provides that the relevant applicable law must not derogate from the mandatory rules as defined in the Convention. It suffices to say that Article 3(3) does not apply in Isabelle Co's situation because the parties have not made a selection of a foreign law. As for Article 7(1) the United Kingdom has opted out of its operation.

However it is pertinent to refer to Article 10(2) which provides that in relation to the manner of performance regard shall be had to the law of the country in which performance is to take place. The issue is whether the court while applying Teacherian law will have to consider Sociologian law. The Giuliano-Lagarde Report makes a somewhat perfunctory treatment of the issue by simply stating that the judge has discretion in every case but offered no guidelines as to how this discretion is to be exercised.

Another matter of doubt is found in the phrase 'manner of performance' which is nowhere defined in the Convention. This too is not offered any clarification in the Giuliano-Lagarde report.

The discretion of the judge in general is governed by Article 16. That article provides that a rule of the law of any country specified by the Convention may be referred only if such application is manifestly incompatible with the public policy of the forum. This too is yet anther element that the applicant should be wary of.

Finally it is not open to the party concerned to argue that the contract may be invalid under the applicable law, hence the selection process based on the contract is frustrated. Article 8 addresses the situation by stating that the existence and validity of the agreement shall be determined by the law which would govern it under the Convention if the contract or term were valid. The common law concern as reflected in rules on putative proper law is met.

Question 30 *

Assess the impact of Article 7(1) of the Rome Convention on the Law Applicable to Contractual Obligations on the Principle of Party Autonomy.

Answer plan

In the first part the traditional approaches to the limitations on the party autonomy should be examined: in England, the decision of the House of Lords in *Vita Food Products Inc v Unus Shipping Co Ltd*. As a comparative study, ss 1–105(1) of the Uniform Commercial Code of the USA and para 187 of the Restatement (Second) of Conflict of Laws could be considered. In the second part, the unlimited freedom of choice of applicable law and the limitations introduced by the internationally binding mandatory rules are to be discussed. In this respect, the decision of the Hoge Raad in *The Alnati* and Article 7(1) of the Rome Convention on the law Applicable to Contractual Obligations provide the illustration as to the meaning of the new approach. Article 7(1) should be analysed in detail.

Answer

Party autonomy is a rule of conflict of law according to which parties to international transactions are free to choose the law applicable to their contract. The extent of their freedom to select the applicable law is governed by the relevant national law. In England the House of Lords in *Vita Food Products Inc v Unus Shipping Co Ltd* (1939) recognised the unlimited freedom of choice, provided it is bona fide, legal and not contrary to the public policy. However, this liberal approach has not been followed in many countries. Several limitations have been imposed by national laws in order to restrain parties' choice: necessity of substantial links between the contract and the selected applicable law, the objective localisation of contract, the reasonable connection requirement, the mandatory application of the *lex fori* when the contract is to be performed in the territory of that state.

The Uniform Commercial Code of the USA provides in ss 1-105(1) that '... when a transaction bears a reasonable relation to this state and also to another state or nation the parties may agree that the law either of this state or of such other state or nation shall govern their rights and duties'. Thus the UCC allows the parties to choose between the law of the seller, the law of the buyer and law of a third state provided that it has a reasonable link with the transaction. The Restatement (Second) of Conflict of Laws para 187 (1971) endorses the UCC approach. Nowadays, such limitations on party autonomy are, however, not particularly favoured. Modern legislation or international conventions in this area prefer the unlimited freedom of choice. For example, the State of New York has rejected the substantial relationship approach advocated by the Restatement. The Assembly Bill 7307-A of 1984 which was implemented as Title 14 of the New York Law of General Obligations stipulates in ss 5–1401 that when a transaction involves $250,000 or more, no connection between the applicable law and the transaction is needed.

At the European level, Article 3(1) of the Rome Convention on the Law Applicable to Contractual Obligations recognises unlimited freedom of choice. Also the 1986 Hague Convention on the Law Applicable to Contract for the International Sale of Goods imposes no limits on party autonomy. The reason of the new approach is that new limitations have emerged: national and international mandatory rules. Article 7(1) of the Rome Convention provides the best example in this area. The antecedents of Article 7(1) are the judgment of the Hoge Raad in *The Alnati* (1966) and Article 15 of the Hague Convention on the Law Applicable to Agency of 14 March 1978. The judgments of the Hoge Raad in *The Alnati* concerns a contract of carriage of potatoes by a Dutch carrier from Antwerp to Rio de Janeiro under a bill of lading stipulating that Dutch law shall be applicable to the contract. The Supreme Court of the Netherlands decided that no mandatory rules of Dutch or Brazilian laws were applicable to the contract. However, it took into consideration the potential application of Article 91 of the Belgian Commercial Code which incorporated the Hague Rules and according to which, in cases involving the carriage of goods originating at a Belgian port, Article 91 is directly applicable. Although the Hoge Raad upheld Dutch law as the *lex contractus* it states that: 'it may happen that, for a foreign state, the observation of certain of these rules, even outside its own territory carries such importance that the courts must take them into account.'

Article 7(1) of the Rome Convention incorporates and broadens this idea. It provides that: 'When applying under this Convention the law of the country, effect may be given to the mandatory rules of the law of another country with which the situation has a close connection, if and in so far as, under the law of the latter country, those rules must be applied whatever the law applicable to the contract. In considering whether to give effect to these mandatory rules, regard shall be had to their nature and purposes and to the consequences of their application or non-application'. The definition of mandatory rules is provided in Article 3(3) of the Rome Convention. They are 'rules of the law of a country which cannot be derogated from by contract'.

Article 7(1) poses considerable practical difficulty. Indeed, a national judge is required to assess the interest of a foreign state (or foreign laws) which is neither the *lex fori* nor the *lex contractus*. Thus the question arises as to the criteria which should guide the judge in determination of the vital and essential priorities of a foreign state. One way of determining whether certain rules are mandatory is to follow the interpretation of the foreign courts of the potentially interested country as to the mandatory nature of the rules. Accordingly, if the foreign law itself has decided that the rule at issue is mandatory, then the forum should uphold its characterisation. However, it may happen that even a foreign court is uncertain as to whether the rule in question is mandatory if, for example, there is no case law or legislation in this respect. The obvious answer is that if a foreign law is unclear on the matter then the forum should reject the application of a rule of dubious mandatory nature. However, it is not that simple. For example what does a French judge know about essential and vital interests of the law of Venezuela? Logically, the forum can only assess the mandatory nature of foreign rules by reference to its own national law. In this respect, Article 19 of the Swiss private international law is more explicit. It provides that the mandatory rules of a law other than the applicable law may be taken into account if interests of a party which are at issue are considered worthy of protection and manifestly preponderant according to the standards of Swiss law.

Furthermore, under Article 7(1) more than one law may be closely connected with the situation. The Giuliano Report explains the necessity of giving wide latitude to the judge particularly in cases where there are contradictory mandatory rules of two different countries, both purporting to be applicable to the same situation and the judge must make a choice between them. In this context the question arises as to what it meant by 'close connection' as the very nature of an international contract implies that it has contacts with various legal systems. Thus almost any factor can be important: the nationality of the parties, the place of habitual residence of the parties, the place of business, the place of performance of contractual obligations of each party, the place of conclusion of a contract etc. The Report suggests that in the determination of the situation which has the close connection required thereunder, the contract 'as a whole' should be taken into consideration.

Kaye argues that this interpretation is unacceptable. He states that the connection between the point in dispute and a particular law applicable to it should prevail. For example, if the dispute concerns the seller's claim that the buyer failed to pay for delivered goods, the question at issue is the forthcoming payments and the country for payments mandatory rules would be the most appropriate to be taken into account, not the *lex contractus* which may be, for example, the law of the seller's place of business. He emphasised that the dismemberment of the contract is the inevitable consequence of Article 7(1). Although this view has some validity, it is submitted that the application of mandatory rules of closely connected laws should be kept within reasonable bounds. Thus where the applicable law has been chosen by the parties, the search for a closely connected law is justified. However, where the court determines the applicable law on the basis of the choice of law rules set out in the Rome Convention, it seems ludicrous to allow the court to keep looking for another law which is also closely connected with the situation but not as closely as the previously selected law. Only the closest connection should be taken into account. There must be a limit to potentially applicable laws, especially in the absence of choice by the parties. Furthermore, as the Rome Convention recognises the depeçage, in some cases, a judge will already have several laws to consider, as well as the potential application of several mandatory rules. For example, when parties have selected the *lex contractus*, the judge will have to examine the following laws and their mandatory rules:

- public policy requirements of the forum and its mandatory rules par excellence envisaged by Article 16 of the Rome Convention;
- mandatory rules of the *lex contractus* since they form an intrinsic part of that law;
- mandatory rules of the closely connected law or laws under Article 7(1) of the Rome Convention;
- mandatory rules of the *lex fori* under Article 7(2) of the Rome Convention;
- in the case of *depeçage*, mandatory rules of the laws applicable to the contract;
- if Article 3(3) of the Rome Convention applies, the mandatory rules of the law with which the contract is entirely connected.

The complexity of Article 7(1) has prompted many countries to refuse its application. As a result, Article 7(1) is inapplicable in the United Kingdom, Germany, Ireland and Luxembourg.

It is submitted that mandatory rules of a third country should be taken into consideration only if the parties have selected the *lex contractus* and provided that the selected law is not the one which would be normally applicable in the absence of choice by the parties.

Article 7(1) introduces a new approach as to the meaning of the party autonomy. Indeed, the traditional restrictions on party autonomy have given way to new ones, the directly applicable mandatory rules of the forum and the internationally binding mandatory rules of third countries closely connected with the contract.

* by Alina Kaczorowska

Question 31 *

Marlex Sarl, a Italian manufacturer of under-water equipment, and Vartex GmbH, a German company specialising in production of computerised, heavy duty machinery, have entered into a contract for the purchase of a custom-made under-water digging machine.

The contract was negotiated in Germany, written in German and the price was fixed in Deutsche Mark. The parties neither discussed the question of jurisdiction nor the applicable law to their contract. Under the terms of the contract Marlex Sarl was to deliver and install the under-water digging machine at the buyer's place of business. Marlex Sarl performed his contractual obligation. However, Vartex GmbH refused to pay the agreed price. When Marlex Sarl commenced proceedings before an Italian court in Rome, Vartex GmbH contested the jurisdiction of the Italian court.

Advise Marlex Sarl taking into consideration the Brussels Convention on Jurisdiction and the Enforcement of Judgments in Civil and Commercial Matters and the Rome Convention on the Law Applicable to Contractual Obligations.

Answer plan

The relationship between Article 5(1) of the 1968 Brussels Convention on Jurisdiction and the Enforcement of Judgments in Civil and Commercial Matters (as amended) and Article 4 of the Rome Convention on the Law Applicable to Contractual Obligations should be examined.

If the jurisdiction of a court in a contracting state is challenged the court must determine the place of performance of the obligation to pay on the basis of Article 4 of the Rome Convention in order to ascertain the law applicable to the contract. Article 4 of the Rome Convention is crucial to the determination of the law applicable to a contract when the parties have not chosen the *lex contractus* by virtue of Article 3(1). Article 4(1) addresses the choice of law issue for contracts in the absence of the choice by the parties. Under Article 4(1) the contract is governed by the law of the country with which it is most closely connected. The following case law should be examined:

- *De Bloos Sprl v Bouyer SA* (1976)
- *Custom Made Commercial Ltd v Stawa Metallbau GmbH* (1994)
- *Société Nouvelle des Papéteries de L'Aa SA v BV Machinefabriek BOA* (Hoge Raad, 25 September 1992, 1992 Nederlandse Jurisprudentie, No 750).

Answer

Article 5(1) of the Brussels Convention and Article 4 of the Rome Convention are interrelated. Article 5 confers special jurisdiction on courts in a contracting states when there is a close connection between the court and the individual case. It constitutes an exception to Article 2 of the Brussels Convention which provides that a person domiciled in a contracting state should be sued in the court of the contracting state where he is domiciled. Article 5(1) confers jurisdiction 'in matters relating to a contract, in the courts for the place of performance of the obligation in question'. Thus Article 5(1) applies to contractual matters.

The Court of Justice held in *Peters v Zuid Nederlandse Aannemers Vereniging* (1983) and also *Powell Duffryn v Petereit* (1992) that the concept of contractual matters must have a community meaning. A sort of definition was provided in (*Handtle v TMCS* (1992)).

The phrase 'the obligation in question' also has an autonomous meaning under EC law. What constitutes 'the obligation in question' was defined by the Court of Justice in *De Bloos Sprl v Bouyer SA* (1976) as one which formed the basis of the legal proceedings, the obligation on which the claim of the plaintiff is based. In our case the obligation for the purposes of Article 5(1) is the defendant's obligation to pay. This is a simple and single obligation. Where a dispute arises in relation to numerous obligations the principle is *accessorium sequitur principale*, that is, the principal obligation must be identified and the court of the place which has jurisdiction over the principal obligation, also has jurisdiction to deal with other obligations (*Medway Packaging Ltd v Meurer Masschinen GmbH* (1992); *Union Transport plc v Continental Lines SA* (1992)).

The next question is to determine the place of performance of the obligation since Article 5(1) confers jurisdiction on that court. In *Tessili v Dunlop* (1976) the Court of Justice held that the court of the place where the dispute had arisen must determine the law applicable to the obligation in question in conformity with the rules of private international law and on the basis of that law identify the place of the performance of the relevant obligation. This approach has been recently confirmed in *Custom Made Commercial Ltd v Stawa Metallbau GmbH* (1994). In this case the Advocate General suggested introducing an autonomous concept of the place of performance of the obligation in question. He stated that 'as regards each type of contract, the place of performance should be identified according to the factual realities, rather than according to legal niceties' (at 2934 (para 82)). Indeed, the reference to national rules of conflict of law has been strongly criticised. However, with the entry into force of the Rome Convention on the Law Applicable to Contractual Obligation and especially the fact that it applies *erga omnes* and replaces the existing choice of law rules in this area, the risk of divergencies and discrepancy has considerably diminished.

The Rome Convention, has been enacted into the Contract (Applicable Law) Act 1990 and came into effect in the United Kingdom on 1 April 1991. Its basic rule is set out in Article 3 which enshrines unlimited freedom of choice of the applicable law by the parties to their contract. However, in the absence of choice Article 4(1) provides for application of 'the law of the country with which [the contract] is most closely connected'. That country is presumed to be the place of residence or place of business of the party who is to effect the performance which is characteristic for the contract (Article 4(2)). The concept of characteristic performance is not defined in the Convention. In the context of the international sale of goods the place where the party is to effect the characteristic performance is where the seller has his place of business. The concept of characteristic performance indicates the centre of gravity of the transaction. The presumption of characteristic performance has not as it objective the determination of the place of the characteristic performance but the residence or a place of business of the party who is to effect the characteristic performance. However, Article 4(5) provides that this presumption is rebuttable and may be displaced when the characteristic performance cannot be identified or if it appears that the contract is more closely connected with another country than the one where the seller has his place of business.

In our case an Italian court has to determine according to Article 4 of the Convention (Italy being a contracting state to the Rome Convention) the law which governs the contract between Martex and Vatex. In this respect two possibilities arise: the court may apply Article 4(2) or disregard the presumption of characteristic performance on the basis of Article 4(5). In the first option, according to the Report on the Convention by Professor Giuliano and Lagarde, when goods are exchanged for money, the supplying of goods is the characteristic performance, not the payment. Furthermore, under Italian law the place of payment of money is, contrary to the English law, the place of the creditor's residence. Accordingly, Italian law would be indicated by the presumption as the applicable law.

However, the second option appears quite persuasive in the light of the many factors that point to German law as applicable to the contract: the contract was negotiated in Germany, written in German, the currency in which the price was expressed was Deutsche Mark. Furthermore, under German law the place of payment of money is the place of the debtor's residence. If the Italian court disregards Article 4(2) in favour of Article 4(5) the plaintiff will have to sue under Article 2 of the Brussels Convention, that is at the place where the defendant has his place of business. Indeed, the main and only connection to Italian law is the place of business of the seller. In *Société Nouvelle des Papéteries de L'Aa SA v BV Machinefabriek BOA* (Hoge Raad, 25 September 1992, 1992 Nederlandse Jurisprudentie, No 750) the Supreme Court of the Netherlands (Hoge Raad) confronted with a similar choice decided to apply Article 4(2). It held that Article 4(1) contained a general rule and that Article 4(5) is an exception and as such should be interpreted restrictively in order to ensure uniformity in the application of the Convention. The presumption in Article 4(2), that is, the characteristic performance is the most important connecting factor. Finally, it was stated that the presumption in Article 4(2) should apply as a rule unless there is a real and significant connection between the contract and another country than that where the seller has his place of business. As a result, the application of Article 4(2) conferred jurisdiction on the Dutch court.

Following the Hoge Raad's reasoning, it may be submitted that the Italian court should have jurisdiction over the dispute.

* by Alina Kaczorowska

Chapter 6

Tort

Introduction *

Uncertainty and unpredictability in the choice of law are unfortunately the prevailing hallmarks in the area of multi-state torts. Indeed, it is uncertain whether the rule of double actionability by the *lex fori* and the *lex loci delicti commissi* still applied or whether the new doctrine of the proper law of tort prevails. The double actionability rule provides that a tort committed abroad is actionable in England if it satisfies two requirements: it is actionable as a tort in England, that is, an act, if done in England, would be a tort, and secondly it is actionable under the law of the foreign country where it was done. This rule originates from a judgment delivered over one hundred years ago in *Phillips v Eyre* (1870).

On the other hand, the doctrine of the proper law of tort introduces a more flexible approach. It provides that the applicable law to multi-state torts is the law of the country which has the most significant relationship to the occurrence of the event generating tortious liability and the parties. This doctrine has gained recognition in many states of the USA and has become a corner stone of the 'American revolution' in conflict of laws. A great deal of controversy had lingered since *Boys v Chaplin* (1971) was decided, a leading authority on multi-state torts in England. For some no *ratio decidendi* can be extracted from the case, for others the lower courts may select from five judgments delivered by their Lordships, the one which they considered appropriate to the dispute at hand.

What is certain is that the House of Lords in *Boys v Chaplin* had overruled *Machado v Fontes* (1897) and decided that the double actionability rule of *Phillips v Eyre* should be subject to a flexible exception without specifying upon what this exception should be based. According to Dicey and Morris (*Conflict of Laws*) it means that the proper law of tort applies in some 'exceptional circumstances' as a compliment to the traditional rule stated in *Phillips v Eyre*. In practice, English courts have applied the doctrine of proper law in numerous cases (*Church of Scientology of California v Commissioner of Police* (1976); *Johnson v Coventry Churchill*

International Ltd (1992)), and thus they seemed to accept Lord Wilberforce's judgment in *Boys v Chaplin* as a definite statement on English choice of law rules in multi-state torts. The complexity was compounded by the 'new' approach taken by the Privy Council in *Red Sea Insurance Co Ltd v Bouygues SA* (1994).

However, most of the uncertainties will be lifted by the Private International Law (Miscellaneous Provision) Act 1995 which gives effect to the recommendation of the Law Commission in the area of multi-state torts. The 1995 Act which is not yet in force, abolishes the common law rules on multi-state torts. The double actionability rule as modified in *Boys v Chaplin* is replaced by the *lex loci delicti commissi*: the law of the country in which the events constituting the tort occurs. This general rule is displaced if a more significant connection is established between a law of another country and the tort. It should be noted that the 1995 Act does not apply to, *inter alia*, the tort of defamation. As a result, the traditional common law rules retain their importance in this area.

Checklist

- traditional common law rules in tort: *Phillips v Eyre; Boys v Chaplin*
- the proper law of tort
- the implications of the judgment of the Privy Council in *Red Sea Insurance Co Ltd v Bouygues SA*
- The Private International Law (Miscellaneous Provisions) Act 1995
- rules relating to tort of defamation

* by Alina Kaczorowska

Question 32 *

John and James are both resident in Redland. John wanted to visit his friend Alfred in Blueland and invited James to travel with him to Blueland. Owing to John's negligent driving they met with an accident in Blueland. James was seriously injured. According to the law of Blueland a gratuitous passenger has no claim against a driver. Under the law of Redland, on the other hand, James can recover damages.

Analyse the situation of James in the light of English conflict of law rules in tort. Would his situation be different if James could recover damages under the *lex loci delicti* but had no claim under the *lex fori*?

Answer plan

In order to answer the question it is necessary to examine new developments in choice of law in tort. The rule as stated in *Phillips v Eyre* has been modified to the extent that it is no longer clear how it should be applied. Conflict of law in tort is in a state of great uncertainty. First, the decision of the House of Lords in *Boys v Chaplin* is far from being clear. The limit of the application of the proper law to multi-state torts by virtue of the exception introduced in *Boys v Chaplin* has to be discussed. Secondly, the revolutionary judgment of the Privy Council in *Red Sea Insurance Co Ltd v Bouygues SA* and its implications should be examined.

Answer

The fundamental rule of English private international law in tort was formulated over 126 years ago in *Phillips v Eyre* (1870). It is contained in the *dictum* of Willes J who stated:

> 'As a general rule, in order to found a suit in England for a wrong alleged to have been committed abroad, two conditions must be fulfilled. First, the wrong must be of such a character that it would have been actionable if committed in England ... secondly, the act must not have been justifiable by the law of the place where it was done' (at pp 28–29).

This double actionability rule implies that the wrong must be actionable in England and the act must not have been justifiable by the law of the place where it was committed. In practice the rule is very disadvantageous for the plaintiff as he has to prove that he has a claim under the law of the forum and the law of the place where the wrong occurred.

The double actionability rule was modified in *Boys v Chaplin* (1971). In this case both parties were British servicemen domiciled in England but temporarily stationed in Malta. They had a motor car accident in Malta. The plaintiff, through the admitted negligence of the defendant, was seriously injured. Both parties were off duty at the time of accident. By Maltese law the plaintiff could only recover £53 of special damages for expenses and loss of earnings. However, under English law he was entitled to recover £2,500 as general damages for pain and suffering.

Under the rule of double actionability the plaintiff could only recover £53 as a lowest common denominator of both English and Maltese law. The House of Lords held unanimously that the plaintiff should recover the greater amount under English law. However, it is almost impossible to extract the ratio decidendi from this case. Their Lordships justified the application of English law on different grounds. Consequently, the right to claim damages for pain and suffering was explained as follows.

Lord Guest and Lord Donovan decided that it was a procedural matter and as such the *lex fori* applied which was English law. According to Lord Hodson and others it was a substantive issue. Lord Hodson stated that the rule in *Phillips v Eyre* should be applied with flexibility taking into account public policy consideration as expressed in the American Restatement. Lord Pearson agreed that some flexibility should be allowed in the operation of the rule in *Phillips v Eyre* but not in the present case. Lord Wilberforce, who considered the issue as substantive, recommended flexibility in interpretation of the rule in *Phillips v Eyre*, especially in the context of important policy consideration. He emphasised that in this case Maltese public policy was not interested in denying the application of English law where both parties were so closely connected with England.

In addition, three judges rejected the approach of *Machado v Fontes* (1897) concerning the second limb of the rule in *Phillips v Eyre* which required non-justifiability of a wrongful act under the law of the place where it was done rather than actionability under the *lex loci delicti*. In *Machado v Fontes* the second limb of the rule in *Phillips v Eyre* led the judges to the conclusion that the requirements of the rule were satisfied where the defendant's conduct attracted criminal, but not civil liability under the *lex loci delicti*. Thus, now the actionability not the wrongfulness under the *lex loci delicti* is required. The decision in *Boys v Chaplin* has left English conflict of laws in foreign tort in a state of great uncertainty. Amongst the speeches of the Lords, that of Lord Wilberforce has been most frequently cited and applied as authoritative by academics and judges alike. It would be safe to say that the rule of double actionability still applies but is subject to a more flexible interpretation. Hence, the law of the forum can be applied by way of exception. This exception has been applied in some cases.

In *Johnson v Coventry Churchill International Ltd* (1992) an English employee working in Germany for an English company was allowed to sue his employer who failed to provide a safe means of access to his place of work although under German law he had no claim against his employer. Furthermore, as the plaintiff and the defendant were English they could not benefit from the German no fault insurance scheme which provided remedy in such circumstances. In this case the rule in *Phillips v Eyre* was applied with flexibility, the plaintiff was allowed to sue even though his claim was not actionable under German law, the *lex loci delicti*.

However until the *Red Sea Insurance Co Ltd v Bouygues SA* (1994) it was considered that the exception could not be applied to the whole of the cause of action but only to a particular issue. The *Red Sea* case was decided by the Privy Council in July 1994. In this case the 23 plaintiffs brought an action in Hong Kong against the Red Sea, an insurance company incorporated in Hong Kong with its headquarters in Saudi Arabia. The plaintiff claimed to be indemnified under an insurance policy issued by the defendant for loss and expenses incurred in relation to correction and repairs of some structural damage to construction work at the University of Riyadh in Saudi Arabia. Red Sea argued that the loss claimed by the plaintiff was not covered by the policy and counterclaimed against a Consortium PCG which according to them was in breach of its duty of care to the plaintiffs by supplying them faulty pre-cast concrete building units unfit for the project. Consequently, if Red Sea was liable under the policy they were entitled to recover the loss from PCG by subrogating to the others plaintiffs' rights. PCG applied to strike out the counterclaim. In response Red Sea applied for leave to amend the counterclaim. The Red Sea claimed that they were entitled under Saudi Arabia law to sue PCG directly, in negligence, for the damage caused to the other plaintiffs. The Court of Appeal of Hong Kong struck down this aspect of counterclaim on the ground that the direct action against PCG was not available since it was not part of Hong Kong law. The decision was reversed on appeal. The Privy Council endorsed the rule of double actionability and concentrated on the exception. It held that the exception was not limited to the application of the *lex fori* as in *Boys v Chaplin* but could also lead to the application of the *lex loci delicti* in cases where that law was more closely connected to the case as a whole or to a particular issue of the case even though under the *lex fori* the liability did not exist as it was not recognised by it. Since the case was more closely connected with the law of Saudi Arabia, the Privy Council decided that the exception to the double actionability rule should apply and consequently the defendant was allowed to rely exclusively on the *lex loci delicti.*

In the light of new developments in conflict of laws and especially the decision of the Privy Council in *Red Sea,* it seems that the situation of James should greatly improve. Previously under the strict application of a double actionability rule James' action against John would be dismissed, as the claim was not actionable under the law of Blueland although actionable under the *lex fori.* Now, James may rely on the exception in *Boys v Chaplin* (if it is in fact an exception and not a new rule) and commence proceedings against John.

On the hypothesis that James can recover damages only under the *lex loci delicti* but not under the *lex fori* until the *Red Sea* decision, his action would be dismissed. However, it was decided in Red Sea that the exception was not limited to the application of the *lex fori.* Thus the departure from the strict rule in *The Halley* (1868), according to the Privy Council, is justified otherwise it would contradict the flexibility allowed by the exception as stated by Lord Wilberforce in *Boys v Chaplin.* Furthermore, the exception is not only limited to a specific issue but can applied to the whole case. As a result, if all significant factors point in the direction of the *lex loci delicti,* the latter applies to the whole case.

* by Alina Kaczorowska

Question 33 *

Assess critically the situation of a plaintiff who commences proceedings in England in relation to a tort committed abroad.

Answer plan

The plaintiff who brings proceedings in England in relation to a tort committed abroad is disadvantaged by choice of law rules in a variety of ways. The following points should be examined: the double actionability rule and its impact on the position of the plaintiff, the principle of the lowest common denominator in respect of recovery of damages, the non-application of foreign law *ex officio* if the *lex loci* delict is a foreign law, the defences available to the defendant which allows him to escape the liability, the uncertainty of rules of conflict of laws in multi-state torts.

Answer

The position of the plaintiff to a dispute involving a wrongful act committed abroad which is tried and determined in England is particularly difficult. First, under the rule of double actionability which has been formulated in *Phillips v Eyre* he has to prove that the action is actionable under the law of the forum and under the law of the place where the wrong occurred. This solution imposes a heavy burden on the plaintiff and is unfair to him. Indeed, no matter where the tort was committed he has suffered damage and should obtain compensation. The actionability by the *lex fori* exaggerates the importance of the forum. This attitude particular to English law is nationalistic and parochial at the same time since it attributes to the English domestic law a special importance in matters which are primarily connected with foreign countries as they concern torts committed abroad. Furthermore, the *lex fori* claims its application regardless of the circumstances of a particular case and the situation of the parties. Also this approach produces astonishing results. It denies remedy when an action is not recognised by the *lex fori* and thus assigns to the *lex loci delicti* a subordinate role. Thus if a claim is actionable under the *lex loci delicti* but not the *lex fori* the plaintiff's claim will be dismissed by an English court. In *Def Lepp Music v Stuart-Brown* (1986) the plaintiff brought an action for infringement of a United Kingdom copyright which he alleged took place abroad. It was held that such acts were not actionable as a tort under the Copyright Act 1956 (now repealed by Copyright, Designs and Patents Act 1988) or at common law. As a result, his claim was dismissed. The same decision was reached in *Tyburn Productions Ltd v Conan Doyle* (1991).

Secondly, the *lex fori* sets up a maximum of damages that the plaintiff can recover. As a result when the *lex loci delicti* is more generous to the plaintiff, the *lex fori* ignores it. Conversely, if the *lex fori* is more generous, the *lex loci delicti* intervenes. As a result, the plaintiff can recover only the strict minimum under both laws. *M'Elroy v M'Allister* (1949) illustrates this point well. In this case the widow of a man killed in an accident in England brought proceedings in England. At the time of accident her husband was a passenger in a lorry owned by his employer. All parties, the man killed in the accident, his widow, the lorry driver and the defendant were resident in Scotland. If the accident had happened in Scotland under Scottish law the widow would have been entitled to substantial damages for *solarium*. If the accident had happened in England and the parties had been resident in England she would have been entitled to substantial damages under the Fatal Accidents Act and also loss of the deceased's expectation of life under the Law Reform (Miscellaneous Provisions) Act 1934. The Court of Session applied the double actionability rule and held that the widow was entitled to recover £40 in respect of funeral expenses as it was the only point on which both laws agreed. The application of a lowest common denominator in respect to damages creates gross injustice for the plaintiff.

Thirdly, the fact that foreign law is treated as a question of fact which must be pleaded and proved as any other fact further disadvantages the plaintiff. Judges are presumed to be technically ignorant of unproven foreign law, even though the foreign law is 'a question of fact of a peculiar kind' (*Parkasho v Singh* (1968); *Dalmaria Dairy Industries Ltd v National Bank of Pakistan* (1978)) it is still a question of fact and consequently a matter of procedure although a special status of foreign law is recognised by s 69(5) of the Supreme Court Act 1981. It provides that when '... it is necessary to ascertain the law of any other country which is applicable to the facts of the case, any question as to the effect of the evidence given with respect to that law shall, instead of being submitted to the jury, be decided by the judge alone'. Thus not only the cost of proving and pleading foreign law is important to the plaintiff but also the fact that judges assess the competence of the experts and are entitled to their own opinion as to the meaning of submitted evidence. A judge's perception of foreign law may come as a total surprise to the all parties concerned (*Dubai Bank Ltd v Galadari* (1990)). Although both parties are in the same position as to the application of foreign law, the plaintiff as a weaker party will be even more vulnerable. If, for financial reasons he is unable to prove the content of the foreign law in question, the judge will have only one version of the foreign law on a particular point. Uncontested foreign law may fortify the position of the defendant and thus disadvantage the plaintiff even more.

Fourthly, the defendant can easily escape the liability as every defence valid under English law is available to him. Similarly, he can plead any defence provided by the *lex loci delicti* unless it is a procedural defence. It is particularly unjust to the plaintiff if the defendant can defeat an action on the basis of a defence available under the *lex fori*. Indeed, the connection between a tort committed abroad and a defence provided by the *lex fori* but not *lex loci delicti* enhances the disadvantageous position of the plaintiff. The defences available to the defendant include the defences at common law. Also under the Foreign Limitation Periods Act 1984 the defendant can defeat the action if the limitation period expires under the *lex fori* or under the *lex loci delicti*, whichever is shorter. In this respect in *Metall und Rohstoff AG v Donaldson Lufkin & Jenrette Inc* (1990) the distinction between substantive and procedural defences under the *lex loci delicti* in relation to the limitation period was abolished. As to the contributory negligence it constitutes a valid defence which means that if a tort was committed in a county which considers it as a complete defence, the claim will fail.

Finally, uncertainty has been well rooted in English private international law in relation to multi-state torts. The rule in *Phillips v Eyre* has been modified but it is difficult to assess to what extent. The House of Lords in *Boys v Chaplin* delivered five different speeches and inconsistencies are apparent between aspects of those judgments. Thus we know that the double actionability rule should be applied with flexibility but its exact meaning and impact is difficult to determine. Its consequences are open to speculation. In practice the uncertainty constitutes an additional disadvantage to the plaintiff. After the judgments of the Privy Council in *Red Sea* it is impossible to predict the outcome of a particular dispute. Between flexibility and certainty a balance must be struck. Under present rules of conflict of laws in torts this objective is far from being achieved.

It is submitted that English conflict of laws rules in multi-state torts have been rightly criticised. The plaintiff is disadvantaged by many aspects of current solutions of private international law in multi-state torts. He must prove that both requirements of the double actionability rule as formulated 126 years ago are satisfied. Thus the alleged wrong must have been actionable as tort if committed in England although it was committed abroad. It had to be actionable in the *lex loci delicti* regardless of the circumstances of the case and the parties. Furthermore, the plaintiff gets the worst part of both laws: the *lex fori* and the *lex loci delicti*. He can only recover damages which are recoverable under both laws which means that the principle of the lowest common denominator is applied. Also the defendant can easily escape the liability as he is entitled to any defence available under the *lex fori* and the *lex loci delicti*. As a result gross injustice is done to the plaintiff in the situation when his claim is not recognised under the *lex fori* and thus it will be dismissed, but the defence, unknown to the forum, will be available to the defendant (*Lieff v Palmer* (1937)) and this will enable him to escape the liability. In general, English private international law overstates the importance of the *lex fori* to the detriment of foreign law but in multi-state torts this tendency is even more obvious. Finally, the uncertainty as to the choice of laws solutions under present rules does not contribute to improve the position of the plaintiff. The plaintiff who is usually a weaker party, a victim of a wrongful act is entitled under the *lex fori* and the *lex loci delicti* to the strict minimum. Whichever law is more generous to him the other one precludes its application.

* by Alina Kaczorowska

Question 34 *

Critically assess the solutions in conflict of laws in tort introduced by the Private International Law (Miscellaneous Provisions) Act 1995.

Answer plan

The most important features of the Private International Law (Miscellaneous Provision) Act 1995 should be examined. The main characteristic of the 1995 Act is that it abolishes the double actionability rule and the distinction between tort committed in England and foreign torts. The general rule under the 1995 Act provides that the law of the country in which the events constituting the tort or delict occur applies, that is, the *lex loci delicti commissi* governs the multi-state torts. However, the exception in favour of the application of the proper law of tort provides the basis for the critical assessment of the 1995 Act. In conclusions the following points should appear:

- whether the 1995 Act strikes the right balance between certainty and flexibility
- whether it treats equally the plaintiff and the defendant
- whether it leads to fair and just solutions
- whether the 1995 Act is preferable to the old common law rules in conflict of laws in tort.

Answer

The current rules in conflict of laws in tort have been strongly but rightly criticised. The Law Commission and Scottish Law Commission have recommended new solutions in order to provide rules of conflict of laws in tort appropriate to requirements of modern society and in line with solutions in other countries. A Working Paper was published in 1984 (1) which after consultations led the Law Commission to prepare recommendations which were accompanied by a Draft Bill in 1990. Part III of the Private International Law (Miscellaneous Provisions) Act 1995 (ss 9–15) implements the Law Commission's draft bill. However, the 1995 Act is not yet in force but will come into effect on such day as the Lord Chancellor and the Lord Advocate may by statutory instrument appoint. As to the territorial scope of the 1985 Act it applies to England, Wales, Scotland and Northern Ireland. Its structure is very simple. The 1995 Act establishes a general rule regarding the determination of the applicable law to torts and then states the exceptions to the rule. Finally the 1995 Act has no retrospective effect.

Excluded from its scope of application are the tort of defamation, torts committed on the high seas and the question of contractual defences in a tort action. As a result the current rules will apply to the torts of defamation and the uncertainty as to the possibility of contractual defences in a tort action remains (*Sayers v International Drilling Co* (1971)). As to the torts committed on the high seas they are still governed by the principles of maritime law.

The main innovation introduced by the 1995 Act is that the double actionability rule as modified in *Boys v Chaplin* is replaced by the *lex loci delicti commissi*: the law of the country in which the events constituting the tort occurs. In order to identify the *lex loci commissi* when significant elements of those events take place in different countries, according to s 11(2):

> 'the applicable law under the general rules is to be taken as being:
> (a) for a cause of action in respect of personal injury, caused to an individual or death resulting from personal injury, the law of the country where the individual was when he sustained the injury;
> (b) for a cause of action in respect of damage to property, the law of the country where the property was when it was damaged; and
> (c) in any other case, the law of the country in which the most significant element or elements of those events occurred.'

The application of *lex loci delicti* is in line with solutions in most countries. The rule discourages the forum shopping as the substantive law in most cases will be the same regardless of the country where the court is situated. Also, in most cases, it constitutes the best solution as the place of tort is usually in one country. Thus the new rule responds to the reasonable expectations of the parties. Furthermore, s 9(1) of the Act provides that the characterisation of issues relating to a tort or delict is to be determined by the forum. This provision precludes English courts from deciding actions for torts unknown to English law such as privacy, unfair competition or criminal compensation.

Finally, the general rule may be displaced and a law of another county may be applied if a more significant connection is established between it and the tort. In order to ascertain the law which is substantially more appropriate than the one selected by the general rule, a comparison of the significance, in all the circumstances, of factors which connect a tort with the law of the country which is *prima facie* applicable and the significance of any real and substantial factor connecting the tort with the law of another country must be made. If, as a result of this comparison, it appears that the law of another country is more substantially appropriate than the *prima facie* applicable law, the law of that country should be applied. In search of the law with which the tort has the closest and most real connection for the purposes of applying the rule of displacement, certain factors may be taken into consideration. Although, s 12 of the 1995 Act does not provide an exhaustive list, it specifies that such factors include those relating to the parties, to any of the events which constitute the tort or to any of the circumstances or consequences of those events. The proper law exception ensures the flexibility necessary in deciding multi-state torts. This exception will apply to cases where it is difficult to determine the place of wrong not only because the act and the damage may have been dissociated geographically but also the essential parts of those two elements of tort may be distributed over the territories of many states and the parties themselves may have no significant connection with the place of occurrence or the events leading to the tort. Secondly, the exception will apply in the situation where it would be substantially more appropriate to apply other law than the *lex loci delicti* commissi since all significant factors may point in the direction of one law as in *Boys v Chaplin* where the applicable law was clearly the English law or in *Red Sea* where the law of Saudi Arabia had the most real and substantial connection with the parties involved and the circumstances of the dispute. The exception causes some interpretation problems but it is necessary in order to ensure flexibility.

The Private International Law (Miscellaneous Provisions) Act 1995 stipulates that the application of a foreign law determined by virtue of above mentioned rules will be disregarded if it is contrary to the principles of English public policy, if it is penal in character and if it concerns foreign revenue or other public law. The 1995 Act gives also priority to mandatory provision of the forum and makes clear that any questions of procedure in any proceedings before an English court are to be determined in accordance with the *lex fori*. The *renvoi* is expressly rejected by s 9(3). Thus when an English court determines according to the rules contained in the 1995 Act that the applicable law is a foreign law, the substantive provisions of that law would be applied and its conflict of law would be excluded.

It is submitted that the Private International Law (Miscellaneous Provision) Act 1995 is a step in the right direction in relation to multi-state torts. It cannot be perfect as it is impossible to find an ideal solution in this area of law but it strikes a good balance between certainty and flexibility. Indeed the general rule is clear and poses no major interpretation problems. The exception, as any exception, is formulated in broad and imprecise terms. The Law Commission has indicated that it is against the application of different laws to different issues and favours the application of the exception to the whole of a tort or delict. Furthermore it recommends that in cases where there are three or more parties to same proceedings, the applicable law should be determined separately for each pair of opponents. In general the exception is not easy to apply and thus the nature of the issue in the case will dictate whether the general rule should be displaced. Furthermore, the exception should be applied restrictively so as not to undermine the general rule. It is submitted that whatever problems may arise under the 1995 Act, its solutions should certainly be preferred to the old common law rules. Even if the 1995 Act does not achieve a greater certainty it eliminates unfair and unjust solutions inherent in the old rules. The plaintiff and the defendant are treated equally. The manifest disadvantages to the plaintiff have been swept away by the 1995 Act.

Notes

1 Law Com Working Paper No 87. Private International Law: Choice of Law in Tort and Delict (1984).

* by Alina Kaczorowska

Question 35 *

Examine the jurisdiction of English courts under Article 5(3) of the Brussels Convention in tort of defamation and critically assess English conflict of laws rules in this area.

Answer plan

Under traditional conflict of laws rules in tort the question of jurisdiction has always been more important than the determination of the applicable law. For that reason it is necessary to focus on the question of jurisdiction. The decision of the Court of Justice in *Shevill v Presse Alliance SA* sheds new light on the interpretation of Article 5(3) in tort of defamation. Regarding the conflict of law rules, once the place of tort is determined, which very often has to be determined in the context of jurisdiction, the rule of double actionability as modified in *Boys v Chaplin* and interpreted by the Privy Council in *Red Sea* applies. It is also important to emphasise that the tort of defamation is excluded from the scope of application of Part III of the Private International Law (Miscellaneous Provisions) Act 1995.

Answer

Article 5(3) of the Brussels Convention covers many different kinds of tort. In cases of, *inter alia*, product liability, unfair competition, transnational pollution or defamation the determination of the place where the harmful event occurred from a jurisdictional standpoint can be extremely difficult. In particular, defamation cases give rise to confusion and uncertainty because the damage to reputation is of a non-physical nature and cannot be located physically except on a fictional basis.

In spite of the obvious attraction of granting a wider choice of jurisdiction to the plaintiff, the decision of the Court of Justice in *Bier v Mines de Potasse* (1976) gives rise to practical difficulties in the context of defamation which is communicated through the media of radio, television and newspapers. It is difficult to separate the event which gives rise to the damage from the damage itself. It may be argued that the place where the allegedly libelous article is written or some defamatory remarks are uttered by a radio or television station is also the place where the damage first occurs. On the other hand, the distribution of newspapers or the broadcast by a radio or TV of alleged defamatory statements constitutes the last event giving rise to the damage but at the same time those events complete the tort of libel and crystallise the damage.

However, for the victim of alleged defamation the fact that he or she hears broadcast remarks as well as his or her family, friends, employers etc is of the upmost importance. Similarly, neither the place of publication nor the place of distribution but the fact that the newspaper containing a defamatory statement can be bought at the local newsstand, no matter how many copies are available, is decisive for the plaintiff. Hence it may be argued that the domicile of the victim is the most important connecting factor in the choice of law context as well as from a jurisdictional point of view in the defamation by media cases.

Finally, it may be suggested that all connecting factors as to the determination of competent jurisdiction should be ignored in favour of the solution which common sense dictates, namely that the place where the plaintiff's reputation is injured should be considered as the place where the harmful event occurred for the purposes of Article 5(3) of the Convention.

Nevertheless, the fact that complex and sophisticated techniques of modern mass media make it possible that a defamatory remark broadcast from Ireland may be heard in New Zealand or that almost any newspaper in any language may be bought in any civilised place on Earth exposes the complexity of that question.

At this stage, it seems useful to examine a few decisions rendered in contracting states in the context of Article 5(3) in respect to transnational defamation.

For instance, in *Radio Monte Carlo v Syndicat National de l'Edition Phonographique* (1991) an action was brought against the owner of a radio station in Monaco for the unlawful broadcast of copyright material which was heard in France. The French court held that it had jurisdiction on the basis of Article 5(3) since the place where injury was caused was France.

In *The Unauthorised Publication of Approved Photographs* (1991) the plaintiff, a German domiciliary sued the Dutch publisher (a Dutch domiciliary) in Germany for unauthorised publication of his photograph in the defendant's pornographic magazine. The German court declared that since the Dutch pornographic magazine was not distributed regularly or even in small numbers in Germany, the mere fact that it was possible to buy copies in Germany did not justify the assumption of jurisdiction by the German court.

Even if we accept that the minimum requirement for the assumption of jurisdiction by a court is the circulation of the publication to a significant extent or a regular distribution even if only in small numbers of copies, another problem arises. In *Shevill v Presse Alliance SA* (1992) the plaintiff (an English national, domiciled in Yorkshire) brought an action for libel against a French newspaper, *France Soir*, in respect of the publication of an article alleging that the plaintiff's workplace, a *bureau de change*, had laundered drug money. The defendant newspaper had a daily circulation of 200,000 in France and 15,000 outside France including 230 copies in England and Wales. It was held that the English court was entitled to exercise jurisdiction on the ground that the libel had been published in England and that it constituted a harmful event in the light of Article 5(3). However, the plaintiff had limited her claim to the publication of the article in England and Wales. Thus any harm she had suffered was minimal. The Appeal judgment suggested that had the plaintiff not limited her claim to the publication in England, the court might have declined jurisdiction. From this case the question arose as to whether she might sue in France where by reason of the larger circulation she might expect to get larger damages. In order to clarify the meaning of 'the place where the harmful event occurred' under Article 5(3) the House of Lords referred *Shevill* to the Court of Justice for a preliminary ruling and asked seven questions.

The Court delivered its judgment on 7 March 1995. It held that the expression 'place where the harmful event occurred' under Article 5(3) in the case of defamation by a newspaper article circulated in more than one contracting state must be interpreted as meaning that the plaintiff may sue either in the place where the publisher of the defamatory publication is established or in the courts of the place where the newspaper is distributed and where the victim claims to have suffered injury to his reputation. However, the court of the place where the publisher is established has jurisdiction to hear the action for damages for all harm caused to the plaintiff. The courts of each contracting state in which the defamatory newspaper was distributed which the victim claims injury to his reputation, has jurisdiction to rule solely in respect of the harm caused in that state.

Therefore, in international libel cases through the press, the place of the event giving rise to the damage is the place where the publisher of the defamatory publication is established since the damage originates from that place. The place where the damage occurred is the place where the event giving rise to damage produces its effect upon the plaintiff. That would be the place where the defamatory publication is distributed and where the complainant has his or her good repute.

Furthermore, the Court of Justice stated that the criteria for assessing whether the event is harmful and the evidence necessary to establish the existence and the extent of the alleged harm are outside the scope of the Convention. It is up to the *lex causae* selected by the conflict of laws rules of the forum to determine that question.

In the light of recent decisions regarding the application of Article 5(3) of the Convention in general and the cases of transnational defamation in particular, a few conclusions may be drawn.

Article 5(3) of the Convention should be interpreted restrictively as being an exception to the principle. As a consequence, the domicile of the plaintiff as the sole connecting jurisdictional factor should be excluded. Therefore, in defamation cases the jurisdiction of *forum actoris* should be rejected which means that if, for instance, a defamatory letter or article was written in State A, published in State B and as a result the reputation of the plaintiff was injured in State C, States A and C have no jurisdiction over the claim even though the plaintiff is domiciled in State C.

Different approaches should be applied in determining the place where the harmful event occurred for choice of law objectives and for the jurisdictional purposes. It may be submitted that in the context of choice of law rules, the place where the plaintiff's reputation is injured constitutes the most important connecting factor. This solution is, of course, easy to state but difficult to apply in practice. Nevertheless, in the majority of disputes it would lead to the application of the *lex domicili*. On the other hand, for the purposes of Article 5(3) of the Convention a distinction must be drawn between the place where the event which originally started the sequence of events, which eventually resulted in the damage and without which the damage could not have occurred, and the place where damage occurred at an earlier point in time. In the context of transnational defamation the place where the first event in a series of events giving rise to the damage occurred, the event at the 'origin' of the damage, is the place where the defamatory statement is published and put into circulation. As to the allocation of jurisdiction to the courts of the place where the damage first occurred, an important practical difficulty arises since the damage may occur in many contracting states at the same time.

It has been clear since *Bier* and confirmed in *Shevill* that a court may exercise jurisdiction if any one element of the tort, the event which was at the origin of the damage, or the damage itself, first occurred in the territory of the court. As a result the plaintiff is allowed to bring the action in the courts of either country. However, only the court located in the place where the event which originally started the sequence of events, which eventually resulted in the damage, has the general competence to entertain all actions in respect of tortious liability and can award damages wherever they happen to take place. This general competence is justified since it is necessary to have a clear solution in the case of complex conflicts. The exceptional allocation of jurisdiction to the courts of the place where the damage first occurred must not obscure the fact that it is the place where the wrongful event took place that possesses the general competence over the claim in its entirety. Furthermore, it is also important to realise that this is the only solution which achieves a minimum of coherence in foreign tort matters under the Convention.

As to the court of the place where the damage was first suffered, it has only functional competence since that court can only assess damages which occurred within the jurisdiction.

The distinction between general and functional competence of courts in tortious matters yields strange results in cases of defamation as the damage may have occurred first in many contracting states at the same time. For instance, newspapers or magazines containing defamatory statements may be distributed in all contracting states. This situation, which is not unusual nowadays, raises many questions, most of them were answered in *Shevill*. It is submitted that the advantage of broader choice of jurisdiction offered to the plaintiff by *Bier* disappears unless the damage occurred within one jurisdiction. Otherwise, the plaintiff has to bring separate proceedings in each contracting state. To avoid the inconvenience arising out of this situation the plaintiff may commence proceedings in the court located in the place where the original event of the damage took place. However, in the majority of disputes it would be also the place where the defendant is domiciled. This solution implies the convergence of all the relevant actions in one jurisdiction. From the point of view of the objectives of the Convention it constitutes the best possible solution since, as a matter of principle, a plaintiff is always entitled to bring his action in its entirety before the court of the defendant domicile and the jurisdiction of the court of the place where the damage first occurred is exceptional and has been conferred only for convenience of litigation.

This solution, however, has in reality a wider effect. The allocation of jurisdiction to the court of the place where the damage first took place constitutes an exception to an exception (Article 5(3)) to the principle laid down in Article 2 of the Convention. Thus, for instance, if the plaintiff brings an action concerning the same wrongful act before courts in many contracting states the same claim will be divided although it arises out of a same factual situation between the same plaintiff and the same defendant. It may be argued that each judge in each contracting state will assess the damage that occurred within that jurisdiction and that each action is distinct and independent. Theoretically, it seems that in each contracting state neither the doctrine of *lis alibi pendens* nor the *res judicata* will apply. In practice the court in each contracting state will assess damages according to its domestic law including the choice of law rules which leads not only to confusion but also increases the risk of divergent decisions. Herein lies a paradox. The allocation of jurisdiction to a court located in the place where the damage first occurred, according to the interpretation of Article 5(3) of the Convention by the Court of Justice, constitutes an exception aimed at facilitating the administration of justice in contracting states. Since Article 5(3) of the Convention is *per se* an exception to a principle it seems that an exception to an exception permits not only the division of a claim arising out of the same wrongful act between the same parties, but also hinders the administration of justice in contracting states. It remains to be seen to what extent.

In the context of choice of law rules Part III of the Private International Law (Miscellaneous Provisions) Act 1995 excludes defamation from its scope of application. As a result traditional common law conflict of law rules apply. Under those rules the determination of the place where the wrongful event occurred has been examined principally from a jurisdictional point of view.

English judgments concerning the purpose of Order 11 hitherto have held that the place where the defamation is committed is the place where the defamatory statement is published. In *Bata v Bata* (1948) (1) the Court of Appeal decided that leave to serve the defendant out of the jurisdiction should be granted where the defamatory letter written in Switzerland was received in London on the grounds that publication completed the tort of libel and thence, the cause of action had arisen in England. In *Church of Scientology v Metropolitan Police Commissioner* (1976) the Court of Appeal held that where an alleged defamatory report had been written in England and sent to a German Police Authority the tort was committed in Germany.

The same approach was applied in a case of defamation by a radio broadcast from a New York studio which was heard in Ontario. The Ontario High Court stated that the tort was committed in Ontario and therefore local courts had jurisdiction over the claim (*Jenner v Sun Oil Co* (1952)).

At this stage, it is useful to remember that the assessment of damage is a matter for the *lex fori* (*Kohnke v Karger* (1951)). Thus when an action is brought before an English court as far as the recovery of damages is concerned the principle of the lowest common denominator applies, which means that the plaintiff can only recover such damages as are recoverable both under the *lex loci delicti* commissi and the *lex fori*.

Note

1 However see *Kroch v Rossell et Cie* (1937), a case involving libel in the printed media where a person having no connection with England claimed to be defamed in two French and Belgian newspapers of which only a few copies were sold in England. The Court of Appeal refused service out of jurisdiction, but Slesser J obiter held that on the facts of the case he would have been prepared to assume that the alleged tort had been committed in England. See also *Pillai v Sarkar* (1994).

* by Alina Kaczorowska

Question 36

(a) Rat Co is a Singaporean company with a place of business in England. In 1993 it established a distributor company in Bododo to sell and market a product for asthma sufferers. The product, Nicide is manufactured entirely from Bododo although the prototype of the drug is patented in England.

Sally was on holiday in Bododo when she had an asthma attack. She went to the local pharmacy and purchased some Nicide over the counter. There was no warning on the product that it was dangerous to the aged. Sally was 76 when she took the drug. She became paralysed after taking the medicine.

Sally is now back in England. She is unable to sue Rat Co in Jamaica because she is too ill to travel back to Bododo. Furthermore, she is not very well off and is not able to afford the legal fees involved. It is also unclear as to whether Bododon law provides for remedies against medical product liability as indicated here.

Sally has commenced action in tort against Rat Co in England.

Discuss how the English court will decide on the issue of jurisdiction in view of the fact that the Private International Law (Miscellaneous Provisions) Act 1995 has not come into effect.

(b) Valerio an Italian company makes underclothing in Milan. In 1991 Ulrika bought some underclothing from a retail shop in London. After wearing the underclothing she suffered from a skin ailment. The doctors have found that the ailment is caused by the fabric dye used by Valerio Co. She had to endure severe pain and itching for a long time before she recovered.

Advise Ulrika if she could sue Valerio in England. If so which law will decide whether she can claim damages for pain and suffering?

Answer plan

Both parts to the question concern the application of private international law to determine the question of jurisdiction and applicable law. In the first, the position is governed by the common law since Bododo is not a contracting state to the Brussels Convention. Under the common law, the rule of double actionability as espoused in *Phillips v Eyre* (1870) and as qualified by *Boys v Chaplin* (1971) should be discussed. Since the facts arose before the Private International Law (Miscellaneous Provisions) Act 1995 and the Act has yet to come into force, these old rules shall apply.

In the second instance the Brussels Convention comes into focus. The student should demonstrate the operation of Article 5(3) of the Convention as an exception to the general rule in Article 2. Define the 'tort or delict' and also 'where the harmful event occurred'. These concepts are fundamental to the good answer. Ignore the issue of the applicability of English law *vis-à-vis* damages for pain and suffering. It should be resolved under *Metall und Rohstoff AG* not *Boys v Chaplin.*

Answer

(a) Sally has been injured as a result of the want of proper labelling in Bododo. Here it may be concluded that whatever test of the place of a tort is used, Bododo is clearly the place where the alleged tort took place. It was in Bododo that the negligent omission took place and it was there that Sally was injured. The fact that Bododo is both the place where the damage occurred and the alleged tortious omission necessitates the application of the rule of 'double actionability' by the English court in determination of Sally's claim.

In *Phillips v Eyre* (1870), Willes J held that as a general rule in order to found a suit in England for a wrong alleged to have been committed abroad, two conditions must be met. First the wrong must be of such a character that it would have been actionable if committed in England. Secondly the act must not have been justifiable under the law of the place where it was done. The scope of this rule must be viewed against the backdrop set out in *Boys v Chaplin* (1971). In that case the condition is that in order for an action in tort of this nature to succeed in England it must be demonstrated that the act which gave rise to the claim is actionable under both the *lex fori* and the *lex loci delicti*. Transposed on to Sally's case, the alleged act or omission must be actionable both under English law (the *lex fori*) and Bododon law (the *lex loci delicti*).

While it has not been exactly easy to extract the ratio of the case or to properly define the 'rule' above, it is pellucid from Lord Wilberforce's speech that a third element should be added – the index of flexibility should be introduced to the so-called double actionability rule in the interests of individual justice. In the words of Lord Wilberforce, it is necessary to inquire as to what situations and in what contexts it was intended to apply; whether or not to apply it in the circumstances of the instant case would serve any interest which the rule was devised to address. To paraphrase, a flexible approach should be adopted when as a matter of policy a foreign rule of law ought not to apply.

Returning to the facts of Sally's case, where it is proved that the omission to provide instructions is negligent, there would be a cause of action in England had the omission taken place in this country. As for the second test it cannot be said for certain that leaving aside the financial impecuniosity and physical infirmity Sally would have been entitled to a remedy in Bododo for the alleged negligence. The position of Bododon law in this respect is not clear in terms of a cause of action.

Consequently it is important to use the flexibility element to determine if the English court may be prepared to allow the action on grounds of policy. The connection element is fundamental to the determination of the flexibility rule. Sally is not connected with Bododo as she was merely a visitor. On the other hand the defendant company manufactures the drug in Bododo and depending on the degree of control the Singaporean company has over the operations in Bododo, the connection appears to be with Bododo.

Still on the point of connection, in *Boys v Chaplin* as both parties were normally resident in England and had been only temporarily present in Malta, the English court was properly exercising jurisdiction over the dispute. It may be argued that since both parties in the present case have some residential links with England, the case may be deemed to be connected with England. This argument may however be distinguished on the ground that in *Boys v Chaplin* both parties were natural persons with their place of residence in England, in Sally's situation the person she is suing is a legal person with several places of business around the world. It may be more difficult to identify a geographic connection with England. Be that as it may, it is submitted that rules of double actionability should be construed in such a way so as to prevent multi-national companies from avoiding liability by relying on their 'mobile' place of business.

The fact that the product is registered and patented in England may be yet another connecting factor tugging the case towards England. It should not however be overemphasised in that while it shows that the product is to be protected intellectually by English law, this is all the intention there is. It was not the substance of the drug that caused the damage but the failure to label it properly. This latter omission is the operative cause of the injury.

Above all it must be cautioned that the double actionability flexible approach is a matter of the court's discretion but it may be persuaded by the fact that there is nothing contrary to public policy in denying Sally a cause of action when it is clear that she is totally unable to bring the action in Bododo.

(b) As the defendant is domiciled in the EC, the relevant provision is Article 2 of the Brussels Convention as contained in the Civil Jurisdiction and Judgments Act 1982. Under that article the general rule is that the defendant is to be sued in the courts of his place of domicile. By rights therefore Ulrika should commence action against Valerio in Italy, assuming that Italy is the country of Valerio's domicile. In the interests of justice and convenience the Convention does provide for special jurisdiction on courts in contracting states other than the place of the defendant's domicile.

Article 5(3) for example provides that in matters of tort, delict or quasi-delict there is jurisdiction conferred on the courts of the state where the harmful event occurred. A tort or delict has been very vaguely defined by the European Court of Justice in *Kalfelis v Schroder, Munchmeyer, Heugst* (1988) as including any action which sought to call in question the liability of a defendant and which was not connected with matters related to a contract under Article 5(1). From this somewhat watery endeavour, it may be submitted that as long as there has been a breach of duty owed to the plaintiff and this breach led to damage, there is a cause of action in tort or delict. Presumably, it should cover all obligations arising from a non-contractual relationship between the litigants. It is substantially limpid that product liability aside from the issue of a contractual duty is a matter of tort or delict within the ambit of Article 5(3).

Moving on to the issue of where the 'harmful event occurred', guidance may be sought from *Bier v Mines de Potasse* (1976). The European Court of Justice held that the place where the harmful event occurred is both the place where the wrongful act or omission took place and that where the plaintiff sustained damage or harm. In that case the French defendant company was alleged to have polluted the Rhine in France. The Rhine flows into the Netherlands where the pollution caused substantial damage to the plaintiff. The Court of Justice held that under Article 5(3) the plaintiff has the option of suing not only in a place other than the place where the defendant committed the act of pollution (which was also his place of domicile) but at the place where the damage ultimately materialised, namely the Netherlands. It may be contended in the present case that the dye was applied in Italy, then Italy should be the place of general jurisdiction. However the actual ailment ie the damage, was sustained in England, thus conferring jurisdiction on the English court.

As for the pain and suffering the logistics are now properly maintained by the rule in *Metall und Rohstoff AG v Donaldson Lufkin & Jenrette* (1990). In short before the rule of double actionability in *Boys v Chaplin* (1971) has to be dealt with, the current position is that the rule is to be disregarded entirely where a tort was committed in substance in England (1). Although it had been argued in Metall that all the damage has to take place in England, the Court of Appeal held that there was no justification for such a construction. All that is required is that there is some significant damage in England. From this ruling therefore the natural conclusion is that English law will be applied to determine the issue of pain and suffering.

Notes

1 See too Order 11 rule 1(1)(f) which provides that a writ may be served out of jurisdiction with the permission of the court 'if the claim is founded on a tort and the damage was sustained or resulted from an act committed within jurisdiction'. According to *Metall und Rohstoff*, once the court has decided that the tort was substantially committed within the jurisdiction, the conflict of law rules developed in *Boys v Chaplin* (1971) or any defences arising under foreign law are irrelevant.

Chapter 7

Property and Succession

Introduction

This chapter looks into the rules of private international law in relation to transfers of property, individual or universal. The first relates to transfers founded on a contractual agreement, whilst the latter is usually by will or other similar dispositions.

Students should know the distinction between movable property and immovable property. Conflict of laws is not concerned so much with the distinction between personal and real property as it is with immovable and movable property. One of the fundamental problems in this connection is the classification of movables and immovables. English private international law provides that the classification of whether the property in question is movable or immovable is left to the *lex situs*.

The general rule *vis-à-vis* immovable property is found in Article 16(1) Brussels Convention as incorporated into English law by the Civil Jurisdiction and Judgments Act 1982. The article which encapsulates the common law position, states that the courts of the *lex situs* shall have exclusive jurisdiction in proceedings which have as their object rights *in rem* in, or tenancies of, immovable property (see too *British South Africa Co v Compania de Mocambique* (1893)). The exceptions to this rule should be observed:

(a) In *Arglasse Muschamp* (1682) and *Penn v Baltimore* (1750), the position is that where the court has jurisdiction *in personam* over the defendant, it shall also have jurisdiction to entertain an action against him in respect of contract or an equity affecting foreign land (Order 11 r 1(1), Rules of the Supreme Court).

(b) In *Nelson v Bridport* (1845), the second exception is that where the court has jurisdiction to administer a trust or the estate of a deceased person, and some of the property in question includes foreign land, there is no reason why the court cannot exercise jurisdiction over the claim.

(c) A third exception is that found in the law of admiralty. In *The Tolken* (1946), in the exercise of jurisdiction *in rem* by an English Admiralty court, that court shall also have jurisdiction over foreign immovables connected with the claim.

The transfer is subject to the *lex situs* in respect of its formal validity, its essential validity and to a lesser extent the capacity of the transferor (*Bank of Africa v Cohen* (1909)).

In respect of movable property, the student should bear in mind the distinction between tangible movables and intangible movables. Some highly relevant issues in this area include:

(a) the general rule that proprietary rights in the movable are to be determined by the *lex situs* operative at the time when the property was transferred;
(b) reservation of title clauses written into the foreign contract of sale as an exception to the general rule;
(c) the problems caused by goods in transit;
(d) the application of mandatory public policy considerations;
(e) the application of Article 12 of the Rome Convention to assignment of intangible movables.

In the area of succession, the distinction between intestacy and testacy is crucial; the rule for the former is that any distribution of movable property is to be carried out in accordance with the law of the deceased's place of domicile. With testacy, the distribution of movables shall be executed according to the terms of the will, the essential validity and capacity of the parties which are to be determined by the law of the testator's domicile. The issue of formal validity is less strict, as long as the will complies with the provisions of s 1 of the Wills Act 1963.

In respect of immovables, the law is that their distribution *should* be in accordance with the *lex situs*.

Checklist

Areas which should be given particular attention include:

- the distinction between immovables and movables
- the *lex situs* and immovable property
- choice of law and validity of transfer of the property
- the issue of capacity to transfer and to receive
- the *lex situs* of tangible movables
- reservation of title, goods in transit and public policy concerns as exceptions to the general rule
- the proper law of assignment set out in Article 12 Rome Convention

- assignment of debts, validity and capacity considerations
- seizure of property by foreign governments

Question 37

Adam is a trader in artefacts and similar items. While he was in Whatzaland a year ago he bought a dinosaur skull from Poe. He has now returned to England and intends to sell the skull to the Natural History Museum.

The skull had in fact been taken out of Xantia by Poe in breach of Xantian law and was smuggled into Whatzaland. Xantian law prohibits the sale and export of fossils and pre-historic relics. The Xantian government intends to retrieve the skull in pursuance of a governmental decree. Whatzaland's law makes it an offence to trade in smuggled goods.

In another transaction, when Adam was in Xantia, he agreed to franchise his business interest to Ben. The agreement stipulates that Xantian law is to apply to any dispute arising from the arrangement. Ben is prohibited under the contract from assigning his right to any third party or to sub-contract out of the franchise. This restriction is valid under English law but not under Xantian law.

Ben has now entered into a contract with Carl purporting to grant Carl the franchise to sell antiques and artefacts in northern Xantia. This agreement is formally valid under English law but not so under Xantian law. Carl is domiciled in England.

Discuss how the rules of English private international law will apply to the events.

Answer plan

The first distinct issue here is whether the Xantian government could retrieve the skull by resorting to the English courts. The rule that an English court is slow to enforce a rule of public law as pointed out by Lord Denning in *AG of New Zealand v Ortiz* (1984) is essential to the answer. Some discussion of the conditions set out in *Lecouturier v Rey* (1910) and *Luther v Sagor* (1921) should form a good incursion into the problem.

The second issue turns on the question assignment and the assignability of intangible movables, the franchise. Here the student should identify the relevant articles in the Rome Convention, namely Articles 3, 9 and 12. The primary principles involved are: recognition of the parties' autonomy in choosing the applicable law, the use of the applicable law to determine the assignability of the franchise and the operation of Article 9 on formal validity.

Answer

It is well settled law that the *lex situs* governs the validity and effect of the transfer of tangible movables. In the present case the validity of the transfer of the skull in Whatzaland is in issue. At English law where the *situs* is constant, the position is that if the proper law of the transaction vests the proprietary interest in the transferee, then that interest in the transferee shall be recognised. Where the *situs* is not a constant as is the case here, assistance may be derived from *Cammell v Sewell* (1860).

In *Cammell v Sewell*, the English owner's goods were sold by the shipmaster in Norway after the ship was wrecked off the coast of Norway. His proprietary interest could not prevail over the right of the bona fide purchaser who subsequently brought the goods into England. It was held that although the sale in Norway was unlawful under English law, the purchaser's rights prevailed over the original owner because under Norwegian law (the *lex situs*) that transfer was valid.

It is unclear if Whatzaland's law makes the transfer of the title in skull to Adam bad even though it does prohibit the sale and purchase of smuggled goods. The question of passage of title is different from the issue of the unlawfulness of the sale; this distinction must be assessed at Whatzaland's law. If it does confer good title regardless of the prohibition, the Xantian government will be unable to recover the skull in the English courts.

On the assumption that the *lex situs* confers a good title on Adam through the sale, the fact that both Xantian and Whatzalandic laws make the act an offence is irrelevant to the extent that English law does not enforce a foreign penal law. It is envisaged that the Xantian government is likely to claim that the skull is the property of state by legislation or like manner; and should therefore be returned. This argument finds support in the general rule at English private international law that the English judge has no jurisdiction to entertain an action which affects a foreign sovereign's proprietary interest subject only to the operation of the State Immunity Act 1978. This general rule however must be seen in the context of *Luther v Sagor* (1921) and *Lecouturier v Rey* (1910).

The position is that foreign governmental laws or decrees purporting to recover or seize private property will be recognised only if the property was within the territory of the foreign state at the time of the decree or the legislation concerned. In dealing with the present case, it would be imperative to determine whether the legislation or decree was in place when the skull was in Xantia. Tangible things like the skull are situate where they are physically (*Standard Chartered Bank Ltd v IRC* (1978)). Secondly the legislation must refer specifically to the property in question and finally, the court must inquire whether the decree forms a part of the law of that place which is acceptable by English law.

According to the court in *Luther v Sagor*, before the seizure or purported seizure is to be given recognition at English law, the court must be satisfied that the decree has legal standing at the place where it was legislated. A forcible seizure by an unlawful government will not be recognised, for example. This does not arise in Adam's case.

Although the information given does not go far enough to permit the determination of the validity and currency of the decree, the rule is that if the decree was issued only after the skull had been taken out of Xantia then the extraterritoriality effect of the decree will not be enforced by the English court.

On the third condition, it was held in *Banco de Vizcaya v Don Alfonso de Borbon y Austria* (1935) that decrees which confiscate property are to be treated as penal in nature and hence, are not to be enforced. In *AG of New Zealand v Ortiz* (1982) the New Zealand authorities claimed that they were entitled to a Maori door taken unlawfully from New Zealand to England to be auctioned off. Lord Denning in the Court of Appeal held that the New Zealand statute that provided for the forfeiture of historic articles was a provision of public law and therefore could not be enforced by the English court. Moreover on further examination, the statute provided that New Zealand authorises such right only when the goods have been seised by them. The House of Lords upheld this finding but unfortunately did not venture to address the issue of whether such a statute constitutes public law unenforceable at English law.

On the franchise contract, the relevant provision of law comes from the Contracts (Applicable Law) Act 1990 which incorporates the Rome Convention 1980. Voluntary assignments are governed generally by Article 12 Rome Convention. Hence since a franchise contract is an intangible movable, Article 12(1) should apply. It provides that the mutual rights and obligations of the parties are determined by the law which under the Convention applies to the contract. This law will effectively govern the issue as to formal and essential validity.

Assuming that either party is possessed of formal and essential capacity, it is important to consider if the restriction on the assignment may be enforced in the English courts. It is ascertainable from the facts that the restriction is valid under English law but not under Xantian law. In order to resolve this issue it is important to establish whether the law that is applicable to the question of assignability is English law or Xantian law. Article 12(2) of the Convention states that the law governing the right to which the assignment relates shall also determine its assignability. What then is the law 'governing the assignment'?

In the current situation, the agreement between Adam and Ben clearly prohibits the assignment of rights derived under the franchise. The contract however expressly prescribes that Xantian law is to govern the contract. Under Article 3(1) of the same Convention, that law which is chosen by the parties will be the applicable law of the contract. Consequently, the assignment executed by Ben is not unlawful since Xantian law allows such assignment.

Upon the supposition that the franchise may be assigned or subcontracted to a third party under Xantian law, the next issue is whether the lack of formal validity at Xantian law would be fatal to the Ben. Under Article 9(2) a contract concluded between persons who are in different countries is formally valid if it satisfies the formal requirements of the law which governs it under the Convention or of the law of one of those countries. Consequently as the contract is formally valid where Carl is situated, this article ensures that the contract is enforceable in England even though it does not meet Xantian formal requirements.

In this connection it would be useful to determine what it means by 'form'. The Giuliano-Lagarde Report defines it as 'include[ing] every external manifestation required on the part of a person expressing a will to be legally bound, and in the absence of which such expression of will would not be regarded as fully effective'. Presumably if the Xantian formal requirements are set out to ensure that this 'purported intention' is evinced, then they could be properly regarded as 'formal'.

Question 38

In March 1995, Isaac bought a tractor from Harry in Erewhomes subject to the condition that 'until the legally required transfer fee of heavy vehicles has been paid, the title to the tractor remains with Harry and Harry shall have the right to claim possession of the vehicle'. Before settling the full transfer fee, Isaac drove the tractor into Erewhon and sold it to Jason. The law of Erewhon prohibits the removal of vehicles outside its territory until all transfer and registration charges have been settled.

Jason paid Isaac partly in cash and partly by assigning to Isaac a percentage of his royalties on his new album in Erewhomes. In Erewhomes the assignment of future royalties is not permitted.

Under the law of Erewhomes, the sale of the vehicle gave Jason a good title provided that he was an innocent purchaser and had no notice of the defect in title. Under the private international law of Erewhomes however this is not possible.

Jason has now brought the tractor into England. Harry wishes to recover the tractor and Isaac wishes to sue Jason in England for the outstanding royalties which he claims that Jason has failed to settle.

Discuss with reference to English private international law.

Answer plan

This question examines the scope of the transfer of tangible movables under English rules of private international law. The main part of this question revolves around the validity and enforceability of the reservation of title clause. This matter is one of considerable doubt and uncertainty. It would be prudent to examine the two well-known, non-English cases in this regard – *Goetschius v Brightman* (1927) and *Century Credit Corporation v Richard* (1962). There is the express invitation to discuss what the proper law of the transaction was when the *situs* changes. In this connection, the rule in *Cammell v Sewell* (1860) necessitates comment.

The second limb to this question, albeit the lesser of the two, requires a careful explanation of the ambit of Article 12, Rome Convention and consequently, the determination of the applicable law following Articles 3 and 4.

Answer

There are two distinct situations that warrant discussion here. One relates to the reservation of title condition placed on the sale and purchase agreement between Isaac and Harry, and its validity and subsequent enforceability at English law. The second turns on whether the assignment of future royalties could be enforced by Isaac.

Where the transfer of the vehicle is valid according to its *lex situs* at the time of the transfer, then that transfer shall be recognised in England. In *Winkworth v Christie Manson & Woods Ltd* (1980), for example, the transfer of stolen art works was recognised because under Italian law (the *lex situs*) such a transfer was valid. The fact that Isaac had unlawfully (under Erewhomes law) removed the vehicle from the jurisdiction and sold it in Erewhomes is irrelevant to the extent that the *lex situs* (Erewhomes) recognises the transfer.

On the reservation of title clause in the contract between Isaac and Harry, the rule is that the act of reserving or retaining title is not a contractual matter but a proprietary one. This proposition finds support in *Simpson v Fogo* (1863). It was held that the law of the place where the reservation took place should prevail provided that the goods were in that country when the title was reserved.

In *Century Credit Corporation v Richard* (1962) a Canadian case, a car had been sold under a conditional sale agreement in Quebec. In breach of the agreement the person in possession took the car into Ontario and sold it to a third party who resold it to the defendant. Under the law of Quebec, the reservation of title clause was valid but under Ontarian law, reservation of title was only valid if they were registered and further, a purchaser in good faith and for value was entitled to a good title under certain circumstances. There was thus a conflict between the two legal systems.

The court first identified the *lex situs* of the transaction in question – ie the sale to the defendant. That took place in Ontario. It was then decided by the court that while any attempt of Ontarian law to equip itself with extraterritorial effect over, for example the laws of Quebec is unenforceable, the situation where the transaction in question takes place wholly within Ontario should naturally be governed by Ontarian law.

If the English courts were to follow this line of approach, it would appear then that the recognition of the transaction between Isaac and Jason in Erewhomes should be enforceable because firstly it is the *lex situs* and secondly, there is no extraterritorial effect intended or caused.

Further guidance may perhaps be educed from an American case. In *Goetschius v Brightman* (1927), the law of New York provided that all reservations of title were void against subsequent purchasers in good faith unless the contract had been registered in New York. The seller sought to enforce such a clause against the buyer, a Californian resident who had taken the car in breach of the contract into New York, and sold it to a third party without the seller's consent or knowledge. Under Californian law, the original owner's title prevailed over all other derived titles. On the issue of the statutorily required registration, the New York court held that although the contract was not initially registered the original owner could satisfy this requirement by registering as soon as he becomes aware of it. This was because the statutory registration requirement could not be extended beyond domestic transactions generally.

The two cases may be reconciled on the basis that in the latter case New York law had not stated unequivocally that a valid title had passed to the third party. In the Canadian case, the position was that the registration issue was of less importance because under Ontarian law, there had been good passing of property to the third party purchaser.

The thrust of these cases on the present situation is that whether Harry loses his title when his tractor was taken into Erewhomes and sold there to Jason depends on the reason why Erewhomes law would deny him his title. Applying the opinion of Professor McClean to the present case, there are two possible reasons:

- Erewhomes, as the country where the subsequent transaction took place may say that an event which has occurred in its territory has the effect of overriding prior titles; or
- it may not recognise the transaction whereby the original owner acquired or reserved his title in the first country (in the present case, Erewhon).

If the former were the case, the law of Erewhomes governs as the *lex situs* and Harry's title is lost because the law of Erewhomes makes an innocent purchaser without notice of the defect in title capable of receiving a good title even though the transferor has no title. If it were the latter, the law of Erewhon would govern as the *lex situs* instead, and Harry should thus retain his title. The law of Erewhomes would be irrelevant to the transaction.

These propositions take the discussion back to *Cammell v Sewell* (1860) where it is the law of England to recognise a title to goods acquired in the first state until a new title overrides the original title. Two key points are to be noted; the inclination of the English courts to avoid giving effect to extraterritoriality of foreign laws and secondly, the *lex situs* always takes precedence generally. The question very frequently is determining the *situs* of the transaction. Where it is proved that Jason obtains a good title to the tractor under the *lex situs* (Erewhomes) then that title shall be similarly recognised by English law.

On the issue of the royalties, it should be pointed out that royalties are a form of intangible movables. As such the assignment of royalties is to be seen in the light of Article 12 of the Rome Convention which has been incorporated into English law by the Contracts (Applicable Law) Act 1990. Article 12 provides that the mutual obligations of assignor and assignee under a voluntary assignment shall be determined by the law which under the Convention is applicable to the contract in question.

Hence the first issue is to ascertain the applicable law to the contract made between Jason and Isaac relating to the royalties. The general rule under the Convention is that where the parties have expressly elected the applicable law for the contract, that election shall apply. Where there is an absence of an express choice of law Article 4(1) states that the law of the country most closely connected with the contract shall be the applicable law. In determining the law of the country most closely connected with the contract, Article 4(2) presumes that the country most closely connected with the contract is where the party who is to effect the performance characteristic of the contract has, at the time of the conclusion of the contract, his habitual residence.

If the delivery of the tractor to Jason is to be treated as the obligation performance which is characteristic to the contract, then Erewhon would appear to be the country with which the contract is most closely connected because that presumably is the place where Isaac (the party who is to effect that performance) has his place of habitual residence. This proposition would be in line with the Giuliano-Lagrade Report where performance characteristic of the contract was linked with that for which consideration in payment of money is due.

Article 4(2) however is not irrebuttable. Under Article 4(5), the presumption is not to be used if it appears from the circumstances that on the whole the contract is more closely connected with another country. The law of that country shall be the applicable law. It may be argued that as the contract was actually made and performed in Erewhomes, the provisions of Article 4(2) are displaced.

Accordingly, if it is the law of Erewhon that governs the substance of contract, the prohibition on future royalties under Erewhomes law would be ineffective and could not be applied by the English courts.

Question 39

'Any inability of the court to enforce the decree *in rem* is no reason for refusing the plaintiff such right and means of enforcement as equity can afford him' *per* Megarry J, *Richard West & Partners (Inverness) Ltd v Dick* (1969).

Critically examine the operation of equity on private international law in this context.

Answer plan

It is important to know the context of the quote. The 'inability of the court to enforce ... decree *in rem*' refers to the rule at common law and the Brussels Convention against the interference with another country's jurisdiction over its land or immovable property. Taking that as the starting point, it would be useful to explain the operation of that general position with reference to case law (see *British South Africa Co v Compania de Mocambique* (1893)).

Next discuss how equity intervenes to offer some form of redress for the plaintiff whose rights are rights in personam but tied with immovables in a foreign state. Examine the difficulties involved and comment on the lack of consistency evident in case law.

Answer

The general rule at common law and the Brussels Convention (Article 16(1)(a)) is that English courts have no jurisdiction when the subject matter in the dispute is the title to or right to possession of foreign immovable property. Just before the turn of the century, the House of Lords decided in *British South Africa Co v Compania de Mocambique* (1893) that the Judicature Act 1873 and the subsequently drafted Rules of Court prevented any English court from exercising jurisdiction over an action to determine the title to or right to possession of any immovable property situated outside England and Wales. The quote taken from Megarry J is however a reflection of the more flexible approach and practice of the Court of Equity to grant relief even though the action may involve such a title claim or right to possession.

This essay will examine the rationale of equitable relief principles *vis-à-vis* the so-called Mocambique rule (and/or Article 16 of the Brussels Convention) and consider the extent to which these principles have been applied.

The rationale behind the English law rule of restraint is that to exercise jurisdiction over immovable property situated in another country is an unwarranted interference with that state's territorial sovereignty. On the other hand, where the matter concerns personal rights there is no conflict with the principle of territorial sovereignty for an English court to exercise jurisdiction over that person who has submitted to jurisdiction or is within jurisdiction. In the latter case, the rights involved are rights *in personam* generally and jurisdiction over these rights is not interventionist in nature as far as international comity between states is concerned. The problem arises however when these personal rights connote or implicate rights over immovable property in a foreign country.

The basic rule as espoused in *Re Smith* (1916) is that the enforcement of such personal rights may be lawful provided that the *lex situs* over the immovable property is not affected.

In that case the court ordered specific performance of the undertaking to create an effective mortgage over immovable property in the West Indies. This was permissible in that case because the specific performance ordered was based on the personal relationship between the parties and was not founded on rights *in rem*.

There is however inconsistency in judicial approach and practice in this regard. In *Bank of Africa v Cohen* (1909), the *lex situs* (the Transvaal) prohibited the transfer of land as security without the surety first renouncing certain protectionary legislation. The surety, an English domiciled married woman had not done so and the court found that the surety agreement could therefore not be enforced in England. Although the legislation dealt with her personal rights, the court appeared to have taken a rather strict approach.

This inconsistency which is unfortunately too often a side product of the application of equity, has motivated some of the later decisions to prescribe certain conditions before applying or refusing to apply equity in this manner.

The first rule is that jurisdiction *in personam* must be established. This may be achieved by showing that the defendant is in England when the writ is served or because he expressly or by implication submits to the jurisdiction or secondly, where leave to serve notice of the writ out of jurisdiction under Order 11 r 1(1) RSC has been obtained.

Respect for the *lex situs* is of fundamental importance. Hence the second condition. According to *Re Courtney, ex parte Pollard* (1840) Lord Cottenham stated that before jurisdiction may be exercised, 'the law of the country where the land is situate should not permit, or not enable the defendant to do what the court might otherwise think it right to decree'. It would be useless and unjust to direct him so to act. In that case the mortgagor deposited the title deeds to land in Scotland with the mortgagee and undertook to take steps to ensure that the security is good. Under English law, the deposit of title deeds was tantamount to an equitable mortgage but not at Scots law. The mortgagee subsequently attempted to enforce the mortgage and succeeded on the basis that there was nothing to prevent a valid mortgage being created over Scottish land, the mortgage being a right *in personam* and there was also a personal duty on the mortgagor to do so.

The emphasis on rights *in personam* is taken further in *Re Hawthorne* (1883) where the court held that there 'must be some personal element, something more than a mere a naked question of title to foreign land'. In that case the title to a property in Germany was in dispute. One of the parties sold the property and received part of the purchase price. On whether the other person could compel him to account for the money, the court declined jurisdiction. Jurisdiction cannot be exercised unless there is some 'personal equity running from the plaintiff to the defendant', according to Professor McClean. These rights *in personam* must be recognisable at equity, where in *Norris v Chambres* (1861), for example, the court had to decline jurisdiction because the person against whom equitable relief is sought was not privy to the equity. There the seller had agreed to sell land in a foreign country but had later transferred it to a third party instead. Although the third party had notice of the agreement between the seller and the original buyer, the court could not wield any jurisdictional control over him. This is not an easy issue for the courts, thus limiting further the scope of equity in this realm. The position in *Norris v Chambres* was not followed in *Mercantile Investment Co v River Plate Ltd* (1892) where the third party's notice of a charge on the land in question was subject to equity and jurisdiction was exercised accordingly.

Yet another difficulty in relying on equity is the fact or rule of practice that English courts will not issue any equitable relief unless it can effectively supervise the execution and enforcement of the decree. In *Grey v Manitoba Railway Co* (1897) the court was invited by the mortgagee to order relief against the mortgagor who had land in a foreign country. The court refused to order a sale of the land in question because there was little likelihood of effective supervision of the execution of such an order.

Where fraud or other unconscionable conduct is alleged, the court is quite prepared to order equitable relief where to do so would not be repugnant to the control of the *lex situs* over the property. In *Webb v Webb* (1991), for example, the court had little hesitation in ordering a trustee in a constructive trust situation to perform his obligations even though the property involved is immovable property situated in a foreign country.

In conclusion it may be opined that while equity does in fact equip the common law courts to grant relief to a person whose rights are dependent or connected with the immovable property in a foreign state, there are four major difficulties; the cardinal priority of avoiding encroaching on the foreign country's territorial sovereignty, the problem with defining that connection with the immovable property, identifying the existence of an equitable element and thirdly the practical matter of supervision of the granted equitable remedy. Further the remedy sought being that which is founded on equity, all the conventional equitable norms or maxims shall apply.

Question 40

Siti, who was domiciled in Highland married Abdul, a domiciliary of Lowland. She then moved to Lowland to be with Abdul. By an ante-nuptial agreement Siti who was then under the age of majority by the law of Highland covenanted to settle her property on her husband. According to the law of Lowland, the settlement is valid but under the law of Highland a woman cannot settle her property on marriage.

The law of Highland provides that the married woman's property is to be divided equally between her husband and children.

Assuming that Siti and Abdul were subsequently domiciled in England until Siti died in 1992, how would you advise Abdul regarding the settlement?

Answer plan

The emphasis of this question is the operation of a marriage settlement contract and questions of validity, formal and essential.

The student should be versed in the general rule that matrimonial property rights as created by an ante-nuptial agreement are governed by the terms of that agreement (*Duke of Marlborough v Attorney General* (1945)). The exclusion of the Rome Convention should be pointed out in this regard.

There is also the added issue of the distinction between rights accruing to immovable property as against movables.

The proposition that capacity is to be determined by the law of the matrimonial domicile rather than the proper law of the settlement should be examined critically. The three cases usually cited in support, *Re Cooke's Trusts* (1887), *Cooper v Cooper* (1888) and *Viditz v O'Hagan* (1900) should be discussed in the light of opinions of writers.

Answer

Generally the effect of marriage on the property of the wife or the husband will depend on whether there exists between them a marriage settlement or ante-nuptial agreement. According to Dicey and Morris where there is no marriage settlement and where there is no subsequent change of domicile by the parties to the marriage, the governing law so far as movables are concerned is the law of the matrimonial domicile, which is normally the husband's domicile at the time of the marriage. Were there has been a change of domicile, the rights of the spouses *vis-à-vis* movables will be governed by the law of the new domicile, except in so far as vested rights have been acquired under the law of the former domicile. On immovable property, in *Welch v Tennant* (1891), the implication is that the *lex situs* shall apply.

In our situation there is a marriage settlement made between Siti and Abdul. The terms of the contract will govern the substantive rights of the parties to all property within its terms, whether the property was then owned or subsequently acquired. This is notwithstanding any change in domicile. The determination of whether the property in question is within the governance of the contract is a question of construction based on its proper law.

The proper law of the ante-nuptial contract between Siti and Abdul is the law of the matrimonial domicile when the agreement was made. Consistent with the rule in *Duke of Marlborough v*

Attorney General (1945), the law of the matrimonial domicile is that of the husband's domicile. This is to say that the proper law is that of Lowland and accordingly, the ante-nuptial contract is valid.

At this juncture it might be added that the Rome Convention as incorporated in the Contracts (Applicable Law) Act 1990 has no application even though an ante-nuptial contract is a contract properly enforceable at law. By virtue of Article 1(2)(b) of the said Convention, contracts relating to the 'rights arising out of a matrimonial relationship' are expressly excluded from its operation.

Before the claimant is entitled to enforce the ante-nuptial agreement in England, he or she must not only show the agreement is valid under the rules of private international law but also that the parties had the necessary capacity to enter into the agreement. The question is determining the relevant law that is to govern the issue of capacity. It has been suggested on the authority of *Re Cooke's Trusts* (1887) and *Cooper v Cooper* (1888) that the question of capacity should be settled by reference to the *lex domicilii*, ie the law of the domicile of the party alleged to be incapable. In the present case, the law of Highland should apply. This would make the ante-nuptial contract null and void as it is the law of Highland that when Siti entered into the agreement she was not of the age of majority.

The contrary view is to be found in Professor Morris' argument (1). The argument as modified is that there is no reason why capacity should not be governed by the law of the settlement, an analogy to be drawn from the Rome Convention rules and commercial contracts.

An assessment of the three cases is necessary. In *Re Cooke's Trusts*, the question of capacity to enter into a notarial contract in French form was not to be determined by the proper law of the contract but by the *lex domicilii* of the maker. Professor Morris argued that this case as an authority is not particularly cogent because it was based on an erroneous assumption that under English law marriage settlements made by infants are not void but merely voidable.

Although in *Cooper v Cooper* while Lord Halsbury and Lord Macnaghten allowed the widow to repudiate the contract on the basis that she was a minor when she made the ante-nuptial contract, both judges were inconsistent in their finding of validity of the infant's marriage settlement at Irish law. Whilst Lord Macnaghten found that such contracts are void *ab initio*, Lord Halsbury thought they were simply voidable (2). The position as observed by Lord Lindley in *Viditz v O'Hagan* (1900) was that in *Cooper v Cooper*, the claimant succeeded in repudiating the settlement after the lapse of much more than a reasonable time, if the fact of her change of domicile between the execution of the settlement and the repudiation is shut out. In *Viditz v O'Hagan*, the Court of Appeal had to consider the ante-nuptial agreement entered into by an Irish domiciled girl under the age of 21. She married an Austrian domiciled man. The settlement was expressed in English form. The parties then moved to Austria and became domiciled there. About 30 years later, they applied to revoke the settlement by a notarial act in Austria. The court held that the revocation in Austrian form was valid because the wife never possessed the capacity to make an irrevocable settlement either before or after her marriage. She could never under Austrian law confirm or ratify the settlement, she could only repudiate it, which she did.

The clear inference according to Professor McClean is that the indication is that the House of Lords in *Cooper* did not shut out consideration of the proper law of the settlement. Hence it is no authority for saying that the capacity to make a marriage settlement is governed by the law of domicile of the party alleged to be incapable. He therefore submitted that such capacity is to be governed by the proper law of the contract, which is the system of law most closely connected with the contract, and not the law intended by the parties.

If the court finds that the ante-nuptial contract is null and void, the rule relating to movable matrimonial property ought to apply in the absence of a marriage settlement. This means that once the domicile is changed, the law of the new domicile will be used to determine Abdul's rights. Under the circumstances, his rights will be governed by English law, the law of the new domicile.

In terms of immovable property, the rights of the parties would appear to be governed by the law of the matrimonial domicile. There is no direct authority on this issue. Some assistance may perhaps be gained by referring to *Chiwell v Carlyon* (1897). The court held that the land bought by the husband in Cornwall was subject to South African (the original domicile) community of property where there is no marriage settlement on the disposition, even though the parties were then domiciled in England. If this case is followed, the denouement, it would seem, is that the law of Lowland shall govern any property rights accruing to Abdul *vis-à-vis* immovable property.

One last issue is perhaps that of formal validity. The law as set out in *Guépratte v Young* (1851) and *Van Grutten v Digby* (1862) is that where the settlement conforms with the law of the place where it is executed or the proper law, it meets the requirement of formal validity.

Notes

1 See (1938) 54 Law Quarterly Review 78.

2 It should be pointed out that in *Edwards v Carter* (1893), the House of Lords held that at English law a minor's marriage settlement agreement was neither void nor voidable whenever the minor wishes to repudiate it, but voidable only within a reasonable time after the minor had attained the age of majority.

Question 41

In October 1994, Matt committed suicide in Popia. He had been suffering from acute depression for more than 10 months. A week before he killed himself he visited his mistress, May. Matt was domiciled in Manna while May is domiciled in England.

He made a videotape containing the following instructions in her presence:

Please make sure that my freehold cottage, The Rose Cottage, in Luton, England is left to my dear daughter, Mo. I should also want my younger girl, Marie to have my collection of rare books on Mannan history now kept on loan by the Mannan National Archive. And you, May, shall have the residue of my movable property.

May then signed on the videotape label stating that she witnessed the making of the 'will'. Under Popian law such a recording constitutes a formally valid will.

In 1995, the Mannan ruler decreed that all rare books shall vest in the state upon the death of the owner. The decree was to have effect as of 1 January 1990, Manna's Independence Day.

There is also a Mannan statute to the effect that no Mannan testator may leave his property to a mistress. Furthermore, it is illegal for Mannan nationals to own freehold property overseas.

Mo is domiciled in Manna and her sister, Marie is domiciled in Ireland.

Discuss the legal implications of the above events under English rules of private international law.

Answer plan

In matters of testacy, the distribution of the property of the deceased will generally be executed according to the terms of the will. The question is when there is an international element to the will, how should the validity of the terms (essential validity) and the formal validity of the will itself be determined?

The rule as to the capacity to make a will is that the capacity to make a will relating to movables must be determined by the law of the testator's domicile whilst the capacity to make a will of immovables is arguably governed by the *lex situs*.

On essential or material validity, the position is very much the same. The problem however emerges when the court has to characterise the issue as one relating to capacity or form.

Answer

The first issue is whether Matt's will satisfies the formal validity of a will made overseas. Section 1 of the Wills Act 1963 provides that a will shall be treated as properly executed if its execution conformed to the internal law of force in the territory where it was executed. In this context, under s 6 'internal law' refers to the law that would apply in a case where no question of conflict of laws arose. Since it is pellucid that the will was made on video in Popia whose law provides that such a will is valid, the will satisfies the element of formal validity.

Before moving on to the issue of essential validity, the question of which law is to determine the personal capacity of the testator should be resolved. It is conceivable that this may indeed be in issue since Matt was under severe depression when the will was made. The rule at common law, is that the law of the testator's domicile determines whether he has personal capacity to make a will of movables (*In bonis Maraver* (1828); *In bonis Gutteriez* (1869) and *In the Estate of Fuld (No 3)* (1968)). Following this rule, the law of Manna is to be applied to determine if Matt had the legal capacity to make dispositions by will. On the law that governs the capacity in making a will of immovables, it may be suggested that in line with the *dicta* in *Bank of Africa v Cohen* (1909), the *lex situs* should govern. This would mean the law of the place where the freehold cottage is situated should govern the issue of Matt's legal capacity to dispose of the cottage to Mo. The *lex situs* is therefore English law. Under English law, unless it can be proved that he was labouring under bodily or mental illness so as to deprive him of the soundness of mind to make a will, mere depression should not be enough.

On the issue of material or essential validity, a similar distinction between a will for movables and immovables should be made. In *Whicker v Hume* (1858) the issue is to be determined by the law of the testator's domicile at the time of his death *vis-à-vis* the gifts of movables. Thus, the material validity of the disposition of the rare books and the residue of the movable property is to be adjudged under Mannan law, the law of Matt's domicile when he died. The fact that he died in Popia is immaterial.

The gift of immovables is to be governed by the *lex situs* (*Nelson v Bridport* (1846)). Thus, the gift of the freehold to his daughter being a disposition of immovables is to be determined by English law. Under English law, the gift would have been valid materially. The seeming difficulty is whether Mo, being a Mannan domiciliary, who by Mannan law is prohibited from owning land abroad, could still acquire title to Rose Cottage. It may be argued that this is a question of capacity and therefore falls to be governed by the relevant *lex domicilii*. It is however submitted that the issue cannot be severed from the original disposition of immovables and therefore must be governed by the *lex situs*. If this is accepted by the court, then Mo will have the essential capacity to take the gift. It has been held in *Re Miller* (1914) that the incidents of the estates owned by the testator should be determined by the *lex situs*. Similarly an analogy could be extracted from *Duncan v Lawson* (1889) where the question of whether the testator may make a gift to charities was held to be governed by the *lex situs*. The essence is how severable the disposition is from the issue of capacity.

On the gifts of the movables, Mannan law will apply. The gift to May may be caught by the Mannan statute prohibiting the leaving of property by will to mistresses. It could however be argued in favour of May that the Mannan law simply turns on the issue of the mistress's capacity to inherit property under a will and is therefore not a question relating to the essential validity of the will. This being the case, the law of the beneficiary's domicile should govern the issue of her capacity (*Re Hellman* (1866)).

The gift of the collection of rare books falls to be considered by Mannan law. Under Mannan law which is the *lex causae*, the gift would have been permissible but for the retrospective decree. In *Lynch v Provisional Government of Paraguay* (1871), a change in the *lex causae* having retrospective effect according to Lord Penzance is not relevant as English law adopts the law of the domicile 'as it stands at the time of the death'. This rather wide characterisation of the position of English private international law may be criticised on the basis that it does not give effect to the transitional law of the *lex causae*. Also to exclude such law regardless of its content is untenable (1).

Subsequent to *Lynch*, the court in *Re Aganoor's Trust* (1895) adopted very much the same judicial attitude. In that case, the testatrix's legacy was valid under Austrian law which was the law in force in Padua at the time of her death. However when the Italian Civil Code with retrospective effect came to replace the Austrian code, the trust substitutions she had purported to do by will became unlawful. The court disregarded the new legal position on the basis that the change in the *lex causae* after the death of the testatrix is irrelevant.

An interesting contrast may be made with a case on succession to immovables. In *Nelson v Bridport* (1846), Lord Langdale MR held unequivocally that he had to apply the law of Sicily as it existed from time to time and not as it was at the time of the original grant of the entail in issue and/or at the time of the death of the party concerned (2). Taken in this context, Marie has a right to the collection of rare books held by the Mannan Archive. There is, however, the practical issue of whether the Mannan government will relinquish its possession of the collection in recognition and enforcement of the probate granted in England.

Notes

1 For a criticism of the rule, see FA Mann (1954) 31 British Yearbook of International Law 217 and Grodecki (1959) 35 British Yearbook of International Law 58.

2 According to Professor McClean (*Morris, Conflict of Laws*, 4th edn), if it is true that in succession to movables no account is to be taken of subsequent changes in the *lex causae* made after the death of the testator, that proposition is subject to an important qualification so far as the formal validity of wills is concerned. This is because s 6(3) Wills Act 1963 states that regard shall be had to retrospective alterations in the *lex causae* which enable the will to be treated as properly executed. The same regard shall be had to retrospective amendments in the *lex causae* which invalidate the will.

Question 42 *

'In modern law it is a quite unnecessary complication to have different conflict rules for interstate succession to movables and immovables' (Dicey and Morris, *Conflict of Laws*, p 1025).

Comment.

Answer plan

It is necessary to explain the principle of scission and the complications it creates:

- it requires the classification of the item of property as a movable and an immovable: *Re Berchtold*
- it requires application of different laws to the same estate
- it may lead to unfair results: *Re Collens*, contrast with *Re Thom*
- finally the solutions of the Hague Convention on the Law Applicable to Succession to the Estates of Deceased Persons of 1989 should be examined

Answer

English conflict of laws rules relating to intestate succession recognises the principle of scission according to which the intestate succession to the immovables is determined by the law of the country where the immovables are situated (*lex situs*) and the intestate succession to the movables is governed by the law of domicile of a deceased person at the time of his death. In contrast, under the principle of unitary succession a single system of law is applied for both movables and immovables, testate and intestate succession. Only common law countries, France, Belgium and Austria adhere to the principle of scission. The Hague Conference on private international law favours the principle of unitary succession which is adopted by the Convention on the Law Applicable to Succession to the Estates of Deceased Persons of 1988 (1).

The principle of scission creates many unnecessary complications. First, it involves the classification of the item of property as a movable or an immovable. The distinction is not always easy. In *Re Berchtold* (1923), the propositus died intestate domiciled in Hungary. He left a freehold interest in English land which was subject to a trust for sale. As he died before the conversion took place it was necessary to determine whether the freehold interest was to be considered as an interest in an immovable and thus governed by the *lex situs* or on the basis of the doctrine of conversion (according to which the land directed to be sold and turned into money is to be regarded as that species of property into which it is directed: *Fletcher v Ashburner* (1779)) as a movable (money). It was therefore governed by the law of domicile of the deceased person at the time of his death. Although it was argued that the unsold land was already considered as money in the eyes of equity, the court held that there was no connection between the doctrine of conversion and the classification of the subject matter of ownership and that the unsold land was an immovable property irrespective of the binding direction for its conversion into money. Although the classification is governed by the law of the situs, by deciding that the freehold interest in land was an interest in immovable property, the English court avoided consulting Hungarian law which may have led to a different solution. Furthermore, sometimes a legislation decides *a priori* whether a subject matter of ownership is to be considered as immovables or movables (*Re Cutcliffe's Will Trusts* (1940)).

Secondly, the principle of scission divides a single unit, that is, a whole estate comprising movables and immovables, into as many separate legal entities as the number of different laws applicable. Each legal entity is autonomous and does not take into consideration what happens to other items of the estate. For example, if the estate of a deceased person is composed of an immovable property scattered around the world: in London, Paris, Greece and Argentina and in order to decide the question of intestate succession to movables the court will apply the doctrine of renvoi, many legal systems will be involved. In addition, the same individual may accept succession to movables in one country and refuse the succession to immovables in another country.

Finally, in the intestate succession to immovables the order of descent or distribution provided by the law of the situs is applied regardless of the domicile of a deceased person. This may lead to unfair and surprising results. In *Re Collens* (1986) the propositus died interstate domiciled in Trinidad and Tobago leaving assets in Trinidad, Tobago, England and Barbados.

According to the law of Trinidad and Tobago his widow was entitled to a third of the estate and the children from his first marriage to two-thirds of the estate. The widow accepted $1 million as her share of the assets in Trinidad and Tobago under a deed of compromise. In connection to immovables in England the question arose whether she was entitled to claim the statutory legacy due to her under s 46 of the Administration of Estates Act 1925 (as amended) (at that time £5,000) in addition to her share of assets agreed under the law of domicile of the deceased. Although Sir Nicholas Browne-Wilkinson VC regretted that he could not exclude her from the statutory legacy, the meaning of the English statute was clear and left no room for doubt: she was entitled to £5,000 in addition to the sums already received under the deed of compromise. However in a Canadian case of *Re Thom* (1987) it was decided that a widow could claim only one of the two statutory legacies.

It is submitted that the principle of scission should be abandoned in favour of the principle of unitary succession governed by the law of the habitual residence of the deceased person at the time of his death. The solution adopted by the Hague Convention on the Law Applicable to Succession to the Estates of Deceased Persons is modern, fair and appropriate to solve today's problems posed by the intestate succession. As such it should be part of English law. The traditional common law rules in this area were suitable before 1926 when English domestic law of succession distinguished the succession to land from the succession to personality, notwithstanding the fact that even before 1926 this solution had produced unfair results (*Re Rea* (1902)).

Note

1 The Convention on the Law Applicable to Succession to the Estates of Deceased Person is not in force. It has been opened for signatures on 1 August 1989. Form, capacity and matrimonial property are excluded from its scope of application. The Convention recognises the principle of unitary succession for movables and immovables. The law of habitual residence of the deceased person, at least five years before his death or in default his nationality, is applicable to succession. The *propositus* may select the law of his habitual residence or his nationality as applicable to the succession of his estate at the time of drafting his final will and testament.

* by Alina Kaczorowska

Question 43 *

James, who was domiciled in England died intestate while recuperating from a serious illness in France. He left a collection of impressionist paintings in a safe deposit in Brussels, a house in Italy, a mortgage on a house in Paris and in London as security for a loan granted to Hans. James owned shares in a German company. However, a few days before his trip to France he executed their transfer by way of gift to his daughter Maria. The shares certificates were sent to Germany to be registered but under German law, a company incorporated in Germany could not register the transfer without the consent of the Treasury. James had signed and sent off the necessary forms to obtain the consent but he died before the consent was granted.

Determine the system of law or systems of law which will be applicable to the distribution of above mentioned items of his estate.

Answer plan

James left the movables and immovables. Thus the principle of scission applies. The following points should be examined:

- his collection of paintings – the application of the law of his domicile at the time of death
- house in Italy – the application of the *lex situs*
- mortgage on a house in Paris and London – in this respect it is necessary to determine whether a mortgage is considered as a movable or an interest in an immovable: *Re Hoyes* in order to apply the appropriate rule
- shares – the most important question is whether the transfer is valid: *Re Fry; Colonial Bank v Candy*, if not, the shares are part of his estate and should be distributed according to the law of his domicile at the time of death. If the transfer is valid, Maria is a new shareholder.

Answer

James owned both movables and immovables. The principle of scission will apply to his succession. His movable property will be distributed according to the law of his domicile at the time of his death (*Pipon v Pipon* (1744); *Sommerville v Sommerville* (1980)). Although he died in France, at the time of his death he was domiciled in England. Thus, English law will govern the succession to the movables of an intestate. The fact that his collection of paintings is in Brussels not in England may only be of some relevance if he died without any next-of-kin. This is not the case as he has a daughter Maria. However, if a person dies without a next-of-kin the general rule whereby the intestate's movables are distributed according to the law of the country in which the *propositus* was domiciled at the time of his death, is abandoned in favour of the right of the Crown or of a foreign country to take ownerless property as *bona vacantia* or as a *jus regale* or as *ultimus heres* (*Re Maldonado's Estate* (1954)).

Secondly, James owned a house in Italy. The classification poses no problem. A house is *par excellence* an immovable. The succession to immovables of an intestate is governed by the law of the country where the immovables are situated. Thus, the succession to his house will be determined by Italian law (*lex situs*). When English rules of private international law refer to Italian law under the doctrine of 'Total *Renvoi*' which is adopted in England, Italian law means the law which an Italian judge would apply if he were seised of the matter. Thus, it is necessary to determine how an Italian court would deal with the intestate succession to immovables situated in Italy but owned by an English domiciliary. According to Italian law the succession is governed by the national law of the deceased person. Thus, an Italian court would refer the matter to English law. English law then remits the question to Italian law (*lex situs*). Since Italian law rejects the single *renvoi* doctrine, the Italian court will not accept the remission. Consequently, the Italian court would apply English internal law (*Re Ross* (1930)) and therefore the succession to his house in Italy will be governed by English domestic law.

As for the mortgage on a house in London it is necessary to determine whether the mortgage is regarded as a movable or an interest in an immovable. Under English domestic law mortgages are considered as personalty. In this respect *Re Hoyes* (1911) is the leading authority. In that case the propositus died in 1888 domiciled in England. He left one-third of his real and personal property after the death of his wife to charity. He owned, *inter alia*, $16,340 invested in legal mortgages of freehold land in Toronto, in the province of Ontario, in Canada. The question before the Court of Appeal was whether the charitable gift was valid under the Mortmain Act 1736 in force at the time of testator's death. Under both laws, the law of Ontario and the law of England, the Mortmain Act 1736 was in force and under both laws a mortgage was regarded as personalty. First it was necessary to determine whether the mortgage on land was a movable or an immovable. Judge Farwell LJ decided that in order to classify the mortgage it was necessary to take into consideration the objectives of the Mortmain Act 1736. According to ss 1 and 2 of the Act '... gifts or alienation of land, tenements or hereditaments, in mortmain, are prohibited or restrained by Magna Carta ... as prejudicial to and against the common utility'. Therefore, the gift was considered as a public mischief, contrary to and prejudicial to the public utility and as such it was void. For that reason the mortgage was classified as an immovable. Since the succession to the immovables is governed by the law of the country where the immovables are situated, the mortgage on a house in London will be governed by English law (*lex situs*). However, the classification of mortgages in France may be different. The *lex situs* will decide. According to French law, mortgages are immovables. Consequently, an English court will refer the matter to French law (*lex situs*) and by applying the 'total *renvoi*' doctrine decide exactly as the French court would if it was seised with the matter. French private international law adopts the principle of scission. The intestate succession to immovables is governed by the law of the country where the immovables are situated. As it is situated in France, French law will accept the renvoi.

In relation to shares the main problem is whether the transfer of shares was valid (1). It is, however, not an incidental question since the three conditions required for its existence are not satisfied:

- the main issue must be governed by a foreign law which has been selected by English conflict of laws rules;
- the subsidiary question must involve some foreign element which has arisen separately and which has its own independent choice of law rules;
- the solution to the subsidiary question reached under the law selected by English conflict of law rules must be different from one determined by corresponding rules adopted by the country whose law governs the main question.

The main issue which is the intestate succession to movables, is not governed by a foreign law. Indeed, James was domiciled in England at the time of his death and thus English law applies.

Shares in a company are regarded as intangible movables. Although, in general, a share is represented by a certificate and thus it may be argued that it is a document of value which has a separate physical entity, under English law only the entry of a share on the register of the issuing company constitutes legal ownership. The transfer of shares gives rise to two problems: the first concerns the effect of the transfer as against the company and the second regards the effect of the transfer as against the parties to the transfer and persons claiming under them. The first question is solved by reference to the *situs* of the shares. In this respect the fundamental principle is that shares are situated in the country where they can be effectively dealt with as between the owner and the company. As a result, a share is situated in the country where the register of shareholders is kept (*Attorney General v Higgins* (1857); *Erie Beach Company Ltd v Attorney General for Ontario* (1930)). Usually, it is the principal place of business of the company but under s 362 of the Company Act 1985 an English company may keep its register in branches. All transactions affecting shares in that country are recorded in the branch register (*Standard Chartered Bank Ltd v IRC* (1978)). It is also necessary to mention that the place of incorporation of a company determines the way the shares in a company may be transferred. Thus if the country where the register is kept and the country where the company has been incorporated are different, the application of the *lex situs* of the register is possible only because the law of the country of incorporation tolerates this situation, but this may be changed at any time (*Braun v The Custodian* (1944); *Spitz v Secretary of State for Canada* (1939)). In our case the company has been incorporated in Germany and the register is kept in Germany. Thus the *lex situs* of shares is Germany.

As to the second question, the transfer of rights and the validity of the transfer is governed by the proper law of the transaction which is the law of the country where the rights were created that is the place where the certificate has been delivered. In our case it is Germany. However, according to German law a consent of Treasury is necessary in order to register the transfer. Unfortunately, James died before the consent was granted (*Re Fry* (1946); *Colonial Bank v Candy* (1890)). Therefore, the transfer is invalid and the shares are still part of James' estate. Shares as intangible movables will be distributed according to English law, the law of James' domicile at the time of his death.

Note

1 At present, the assignment of intangible movables is governed by Article 12 of the Rome Convention on the Law Applicable to Contractual Obligations (in force in the UK since 1 April 1991). However, it seems that this question is outside the scope of the application of Article 12 of the Rome Convention because of Article 1(2)(e).

* by Alina Kaczorowska

Chapter 8

Family Law *

Introduction

Conflict of law rules relating to family matters are constantly challenged. The reason is obvious. It is the area of private international law which concerns the essential and fundamental structure of any society – the family. It reflects the political, sociological and religious peculiarity of each state. National legislation in family law is increasingly affected by the internationalisation of every day life resulting in the growth of international conflicts in this area. Furthermore, conflict of laws in family matters is of potential interest to everybody. Nowadays, we travel abroad, marry abroad, we live in multi-national, multi-faith and multi-racial societies. Even the notion of marriage is subject to different definitions. In 1866 (*Hyde v Hyde*) private international law refused to recognise the existence of polygamous marriages. Today, it struggles with new issues such as homosexual marriages or the capacity of transsexuals to marry. Even the self-evident notions of father or mother pose difficult problems. The old problem of proving paternity, which in the eyes of conflict of laws rules is a matter of procedure and as such governed by the *lex fori*, has been resolved beyond reasonable doubt through DNA profiling but in cases of the new artificial reproductive technology such as donor insemination, egg and embryo transfer and surrogacy, it is not always evident who the mother or the father of a child is.

On the other hand, transnational divorces are more common. In England one in three marriages ends in divorce. This rate is similar in many countries. The recognition of overseas divorces, judicial and extra-judicial, constitutes an important consideration of English private international law.

Children from broken multi-national families are at risk of being abducted by one of their parents. Once again, private international law by way of international conventions helps to restore the *status quo* and brings children back home as promptly as possible.

* by Alina Kaczorowska

Finally, inter-state adoptions are almost the only option for British couples as the number of children available for adoption in England declines steadily. Once again, the rules of private international law are vitally important in the recognition of overseas adoption. The clash between old and new is constantly present in conflict of laws in family matters.

Checklist

- marriage: its meaning, formal and essential validity of marriage
- matrimonial causes: polygamous marriages, recognition of overseas divorces, annulment of marriage
- legitimacy and legitimation and the rights to succession
- international abduction of children
- new challenges in family law: transsexual marriages, transsexual's capacity to marry, new insemination technology and the rights to the succession of children born as a result of artificial insemination

Question 44

Janusz a Polish officer married Isabelle, a French national in Rome in 1946. At that time Janusz was a member of the Polish Army serving in Italy with the British Army. They were married by a Polish Roman Catholic Priest according to Catholic rites. Recently Isabelle has commenced proceedings in England to declare her marriage invalid. She claims that:

- the marriage is invalid under Italian law since it has not been registered in Italy;
- it is invalid under Polish law since Janusz did not obtain the authorisation of the Commander of Polish Forces in Italy to marry Isabelle;
- it is invalid under French law since Isabelle at the time of marriage was only 14 years old.

Janusz argues that Isabelle lied about her age at the time of their marriage. She told him that she was 20 years old, although to him she looked at least 25.

Advise Isabelle.

Answer plan

The question concerns both formal and essential validity of marriage. First it is necessary to determine the formal validity of the marriage. The formal validity concerns issues like the form of ceremony which may be civil or religious, registration of a marriage, witnesses, the time and place of celebration, the presence of a priest, prior medical examination, parental consent etc.

The fundamental principle in this area is that the *lex loci celebrationis* applies. Thus if a marriage is valid under the law of the country where it was celebrated it would be valid in England, provided statutory and common law exceptions do not apply. As to the essential validity of marriage it relates to such matters as consanguinity, affinity, bigamy, lack of age, lack of consent etc. In English private international law the controversy lingers on whether the capacity to marry is to be determined according to the ante-nuptial law of domicile of each party (the dual domicile theory) or the law of the intended matrimonial home (the matrimonial home doctrine). Case law is inconclusive but it seems that the doctrine of the dual domicile prevails. The following points should be examined:

- the *lex loci celebrationis* and exceptions to its application
- marriage of military forces in belligerent occupation: *Taczanowska v Taczanowski*
- the parental consent in relation to the authorisation to marry given by the Commander of Polish Forces in Italy: *Simonin v Malloc; Ogden v Ogden*
- minority as an incapacity: s 2 of the Marriage Act 1949, *Pugh v Pugh; Mohamed v Knott*

Answer

The formal validity of marriage is governed by the *lex loci celebrationis*. This is a fundamental rule of English private international law (*Brook v Brook* (1861)); and in modern time *Berthiaume v Dastous* (1930). Thus if a marriage is valid under the law of the place where it was celebrated it would be valid in England. In *Herbert (Lady) v Herbert (Lord)* (1819) it was held that 'Every marriage must be tried according to the law of the country in which it took place'. Recently the rule has been applied in

McCabe v McCabe (1994). In that case an Irishman domiciled in England who was living in London with an Akan woman domiciled in Ghana, at the suggestion of her uncle visiting them, consented to a marriage ceremony in Ghana according to the tribal custom of Akan (a tribe which lives in Ghana). The uncle asked the Irishman to give him a bottle of gin and some money (as 'aseda') and took it to Ghana where the ceremony was performed. The parties were neither present at the ceremony nor represented by proxy. The Court of Appeal based on expert witnesses testimony on the ceremony of marriage of Akans decided that they were validly married. The only requirement for contracting a valid marriage under the Akans custom was the consent of the parties (however consent is not a formal requirement!) and their families. According to expert witnesses neither the ceremony nor the 'aseda' were essential.

In respect of Isabelle's first claim, it seems that since their marriage was not valid under Italian law it would not be valid in England. However, it was decided in *Starkowski v AG* (1954) that a marriage void at the time of celebration may be validated by subsequent changes in the law of the place of celebration, that is, if a legislation subsequent to the ceremony validates the marriage retrospectively. In *Starkowski v AG* two Polish nationals domiciled in Poland went through a religious ceremony of marriage in Austria in 1945. Their marriage was void according to Austrian law since only civil marriages were regarded as valid. However, subsequent Austrian legislation validated such religious marriages if they were registered in a public register. In *Starkowski v AG* one of the parties had registered the marriage. Thus its validity was upheld. If the parties have neglected to satisfy the requirement of registration then the marriage would be void in England (*Pilinski v Pilinski* (1955)). At first glance it seems that Isabelle has a good point in relation to the formal validity of marriage. The marriage was neither valid nor subsequently validated by Italian law.

However, the rule *lex loci celebrationis* suffers few exceptions. Some are statutory, some are derived from the common law. The common law exceptions are relevant to our case. In this respect it is recognised that in some exceptional circumstances a marriage celebrated in breach of the formal requirements of the law of the place where it is solemnised, would be valid if it satisfied the form accepted by the common law. The first exception applies when there is extreme difficulty in conforming to local custom. The parties must show that there was not only difficulty but that it was virtually impossible to celebrate their marriage in conformity with the local law. In our case this exception is not applicable since the parties could comply with the requirements of Italian law.

The second exception, on the other hand, is relevant to our question since it concerns marriages of military forces in belligerent occupation. In this respect the leading case is *Taczanowska v Taczanowski* (1957) where two Polish nationals domiciled in Poland went through a marriage ceremony in Italy in 1946. The husband was serving in the Polish 2nd Corps in belligerent occupation of Italy. The religious ceremony was celebrated by a Polish Army Chaplain, a priest of the Roman Catholic Church. The marriage was formally invalid according to Italian law. The Court of Appeal decided that since the parties were not in Italy of their free will but as members of the military forces in occupation of Italy they were not presumed to submit to the local law. Accordingly, English common law was applied and their marriage was upheld to be valid. The theory of submission produces uncertainty as to the validity of marriage and for that reason its has to be construed very narrowly. In *Merker v Merker* (1963) Sir Jocelyn Simon P stated that the principle in *Taczanowska v Taczanowski* should be applied to cases of:

> 'Marriage within the lines of the foreign army of occupation (which constitute, so to speak, an enclave, within which it is reasonable to hold that the local law has no application), or of persons in a strictly analogous situation to the members of such an army, such as members of an organised body of escaped prisoners of war.'

As a result, in *Lazarewicz v Lazarewicz* (1962) the marriage was declared void because the wife was a national of a conquered country. In that case a Polish corporal serving with the Polish forces in Italy married an Italian woman. They were married in a Polish refugee camp by a Catholic priest. The case was distinguished from other cases on the basis that the parties submitted to Italian law.

In our case Isabelle is a French national, not an Italian. It is submitted that the principle in *Taczanowska v Taczanowski* will apply and consequently their marriage, although invalid under Italian law, will be held as a valid marriage under English common law.

The next question to examine is whether the lack of authorisation of the Commander of Polish Forces in Italy in relation to Janusz's marriage invalidates the marriage. In this respect, it is necessary to determine whether the authorisation relates to the formal or essential validity. It is submitted that an authorisation from a superior officer can be compared to parental consent. Under English law parental consent is considered to be a formal requirement and is thus governed by the *lex loci celebrationis*. Historically, the English courts made no distinction between form and capacity to marry, and thus parental consent became only a matter of form. In the XVII century many English couples went to Scotland to get married since under Scottish law no parental consent was necessary. Once the distinction was made, English courts had to find a justification for validating those marriages and as a result parental consent has been classified as a formal requirement. Furthermore, English private international law rejects the doctrine of evasion of law, that is, if the marriage is contracted abroad in order to escape mandatory provision of national law it will be considered as valid in England. In *Simonin v Malloc* (1860) the marriage was solemnised in England without the parental consent required by Article 154 of the French Civil Code. It was held valid in England although it was void in France (see also *Ogden v Ogden* (1908). It is submitted that the lack of authorisation constitutes a formal requirement and as such is determined by the *lex loci celebrationis*. Italian law does not contain this requirement and thus it has no effect on the validity of marriage. In any case the marriage would be invalid under Italian law.

Finally, Isabelle claims that she was only 14 at the time of marriage. Age is considered to be an essential requirement. In England, s 2 of the Marriage Act 1949 (re-enacting the Age of Marriage Act 1929) stipulates that a marriage between persons, either of whom is under the age of 16, is void. However, different countries have a different perception of the minimum age for contracting a valid marriage. As to the lack of age two principles are established. First, that a marriage solemnised in England will be void if one (or both) of the parties are under the age of 16 regardless of their domicile. Secondly, if one party is under the age of 16, neither of them is domiciled at the relevant time in England, their marriage was celebrated abroad and is regarded as valid under local law, then it will be valid in England. In this respect in

Mohamed v Knott (1969) the marriage celebrated in Nigeria between parties domiciled there was held to be valid even though the wife was only 13 at that time. As to the English domiciliaries it seems that case law on the subject is rather limited. The one case in this area is *Pugh v Pugh* (1951). In this case a British officer, domiciled in England but stationed in Austria and a Hungarian girl of 15 domiciled in Hungary got married in Austria. Their marriage was valid under the Hungarian and Austrian law. However, it was held void in England since the husband was domiciled in England and thus the Age of Marriage Act 1929 applied.

It is submitted that no matter what law will be applied to determine Isabelle's capacity to marry, that is her ante-nuptial law (French law) or the law of a common domicile (which may be English or Polish) the result will be the same: her marriage will be held invalid for lack of age. Whatever Janusz believed or thought about her age at the time of marriage is irrelevant.

The marriage between Janusz and Isabelle is void on the ground that Isabelle, at the relevant time, lacked the capacity to marry as she was only 14. As regards the formal requirements, the *lex loci celebrationis* is displaced in favour of the common law of England.

Question 45

Anna, domiciled in England, is an anthropologist. She went to Zimu-Zimu an island in the Pacific to conduct research on the customs and traditions of the Kumu-Kumu, inhabitants of the island. They are a rare tribe who practises polyandry. During her stay she met Atu, a member of the tribe and in 1990 she married him in a ceremony performed according to rites of the Kumu-Kumu. Two years later she was attracted to Batu and decided to marry him. Once again she went through the traditional marriage ceremony of the Kumu-Kumu. They all lived happily until Anna had to go back to England for a few months. She is worried as to whether her marriages will be recognised in England and wants to know more about the way English private international law deals with polygamy in general and polyandry in particular.

Advise Anna.

Answer plan

In the first part polygamy should be discussed; especially how the English private international law has changed since *Hyde v Hyde* was decided in 1866. Also the recognition of polygamous marriages and its limitations are relevant in answering the question. The second part should focus on Anna's problem. In this respect the most important question is whether she has capacity as an English domiciliary to contract a polygamous marriage. Two cases are important in this area: *Radwan v Radwan* and *Hussein v Hussein,* since they give indications as to the meaning of s 11(d) of the Matrimonial Causes Act 1973. Furthermore, s 5(1) of the Private International Law (Miscellaneous Provisions) Act 1995 which embodies the recommendation of the Law Commission and abolishes the notion of potentially polygamous marriages (*de facto* monogamous) should be discussed. It should be noted that although most parts of the Act have not yet come into force, s 5(1) has been in effect since 8 January 1996.

Answer

The polygamous marriage may take two forms: polygyny – a man may have more that one wife during the length of his first marriage and polyandry – a woman is entitled to have more than one husband during the subsistence of her first marriage.

It used to be of great importance to determine the nature of a marriage as the parties to polygamous marriages could not commence proceedings for matrimonial relief. The hostility to polygamy was expressed by Lord Penzane in *Hyde v Hyde* (1866) when he said that: 'the matrimonial law of this country is adopted to the Christian marriage and is wholly inapplicable to polygamy' and as a result it was not proper for an English court to be 'creating conjugal duties, not enforcing them, and furnishing remedies when there was no offence'. He meant that under English law the religious nature of the marriage is unimportant. The relationship between man and woman is essential. Thus a marriage must have two main characteristics: it must be a voluntary union of indefinite duration between man and woman to the exclusion of all others. Also in *Hyde v Hyde* a very important distinction has been made: a marriage is considered under English law to be polygamous if either party is entitled to have another spouse although in fact it may be a monogamous marriage. Thus *de facto* monogamous marriage which is by its nature polygamous, is still polygamous for the purposes of law even though a husband has never exercised the right to take a second wife or ever intended to do so (*Hyde v Hyde*, *Sowa v Sowa* (1961)). In cases of concubinage it was decided in *Lee v Lau* (1967) that a marriage (under customary Chinese law) which allows a husband to take *'tsipsis'* (concubines or secondary wives) during the length of the marriage but not to remarry was considered as polygamous.

Since *Hyde v Hyde*, English law has changed greatly in respect of polygamy and many, but not all, obstacles have been removed in order to give parties to polygamous marriages similar rights to those enjoyed by monogamous marriages. A valid polygamous marriage is recognised in England (*Mohamed v Knott* (1969)) for many purposes. Children from *de facto* (*Baindail v Baindail* (1946)) and actually polygamous marriages (*Hashmi v Hashmi* (1971) are regarded as legitimate. Furthermore, s 1 of the Matrimonial Proceedings (Polygamous Marriages) Act 1972 provides that parties to a polygamous marriages are entitled to matrimonial relief such as decree for divorce, judicial separation, and declaration under Part III of the Family Law Act 1986 which may involve the determination of the validity of a marriage. Section 47(1) of the Act states that the matrimonial law of England applies to polygamous marriages and thus the approach in *Hyde v Hyde* is abolished. The Social Security Contributions and Benefit Act 1992 provides in s 121(1)(b) that a polygamous marriage shall be treated as a monogamous marriage for any day, but only for any day throughout which it is *de facto* monogamous. A husband to a polygamous marriage who maintains his wife or wives is entitled to a deduction of tax under s 257(1) of the Income and Corporation Taxes Act 1988. The Matrimonial Homes Act 1983 applies to a polygamously married wife (*Nabi v Heaton* (1981)) as well as s 17 of the Married Women's Property Act 1882. The Law Commission and many academics agree that the Fatal Accidents Act 1976 should be applied to a wife or wives of a polygamous marriage.

In Anna's case, it is necessary, first, to determine whether, as an English domiciliary she has capacity to enter a polygamous marriage. In this respect s 11(d) of the Matrimonial Causes Act 1973 states that marriages celebrated after 31 July 1971 shall be void if at the time of marriage either party was domiciled in England and Wales. However, the construction of this statutory provision which seems clear and straightforward has produced unexpected results in *Radwan v Radwan* (1973). In that case a polygamous marriage was celebrated in the Egyptian Consulate in Paris between a woman domiciled in England and a man domiciled in Egypt. The parties decided to set up a home in Egypt and they did. Cumming-Bruce J considered that s 11(d) of the Matrimonial Causes Act 1973 applies only if either party is domiciled in England and the parties intend to have their matrimonial home in England. He justified his conclusion on the basis of s 14 which applies the substantive law of another country if English conflict of laws rules determine its application. Thus according to *Radwan v Radwan* the capacity to contract a polygamous marriage is governed by the law of the intended matrimonial home. On the basis of *Radwan v Radwan*, Anna would have capacity to contract a polygamous marriage. The question however remains whether she has acquired a domicile of choice in Zimu-Zimu and this is quite uncertain. The decision of the Court of Appeal in *Hussein v Hussein* (1983) and its implications are also relevant to Anna's case. In that case it was decided, *inter alia*, that the capacity to enter into an actually polygamous marriage is governed by the ante-nuptial domicile of each party which means that Anna could not contract a polygamous marriage.

The conflicting decisions in *Radwan v Radwan* and *Hussein v Hussein* have prompted the Law Commission to amend s 11(d) of the Matrimonial Causes Act 1973. The Private International Law (Miscellaneous Provisions) Act 1995 has been enacted to incorporate the recommendations. The new 1995 Act provides in s 5(1) that an English domiciliary should have capacity to enter a marriage outside the United Kingdom which though polygamous in form is *de facto* monogamous. Section 5(1) came into force as of 8 January 1996.

The rule applies to all marriages wherever celebrated provided the marriage has not been declared void by a nullity decree or a party to a polygamous marriage has not entered a later marriage which would be rendered invalid by the retrospective validation of the earlier one. What the Act abolishes is the old division between a polygamous and potentially polygamous marriage. As a result s 11(d) will apply to polygamous marriages as in Anna's case. However, even under new legislation she will lack capacity to contract a truly polygamous marriage, that is, she will not be entitled to have two husbands and, if she does, she may be guilty of the crime of bigamy as defined in s 57 of the Offences against the Persons Act 1861.

Question 46

Critically examine the difference between void and voidable marriages and assess the conflict of laws rules on the nullity of marriage.

Answer plan

The main points that should be examined are:

- the differences between a void and a voidable marriage
- the grounds for annulment of void and voidable marriages – ss 11 and 12 of the Matrimonial Causes Act 1973
- the jurisdiction of English courts in nullity proceedings – s 5(3) of the Domicile and Matrimonial Proceedings Act 1973
- the controversial issues regarding grounds for annulment in conflict of laws: consent (*Apt v Apt; Szechter v Szechter)* and physical incapacity (*Ponticelli v Ponticelli*)

Answer

There are three main differences between a void and a voidable marriage. The first and the most important is that a void marriage is null *ab initio*. In other words a void marriage has never existed in the eyes of law, and 'spouses' are cohabitees. A voidable marriage, on the other hand, is described as 'one that will be regarded by every court as a valid subsisting marriage until a decree annulling it has been pronounced by a court of competent jurisdiction' (*De Reneville v De Reneville* (1948)). The second difference is that a void marriage can be challenged by anyone and no proceedings are necessary in order to nullify a void marriage. In contrast, a voidable marriage can only be challenged by the parties themselves by nullity proceedings or otherwise. Finally, a void marriage has retrospective effect while a voidable marriage is retrospective only at common law. A decree granted after 31 July 1971 nullifies the marriage prospectively from the date of the decree absolute.

The grounds for annulment of a void marriage celebrated after 31 July 1971 are enumerated by s 11 of the Matrimonial Causes Act 1973. The list is exhaustive and includes the following cases:

- the parties are within the prohibited degrees of relationship (consanguinity and affinity);
- either party is under the age of 16;
- the parties have intermarried in breach of certain requirements as to the formation of marriage;
- either party has been already lawfully married at the time of the marriage (bigamy);
- the parties are not respectively male and female;
- if either party was at the time of the marriage domiciled in England or Wales and contracted a polygamous marriage outside England and Wales.

Section 12 of the Matrimonial Causes Act 1973 stipulates that a marriage celebrated after 31 July 1971 will be voidable on the following grounds only: the marriage has not been consummated due to the incapacity of either party to consummate it or to a wilful refusal of the respondent to consummate it; either party did not validly consent to it, whether in consequence of duress, mistake, unsoundness of mind or otherwise; either party although capable of giving a valid consent was suffering (whether continuously or intermittently) from mental disorder within the meaning of the Mental Health Act 1959 of such a kind or to such an extent as to be unfit for marriage; the respondent was suffering from venereal disease in a communicable form or was pregnant by some other person than the petitioner at the time of the marriage.

However, the last two grounds can only be invoked if the petitioner was not aware of the respondent's venereal disease or pregnancy at the time of marriage.

The jurisdiction of English courts in the annulment proceedings is governed by s 5(3) of the Domicile and Matrimonial Proceedings Act 1973. Thus in relation to nullity petitions the courts in England have jurisdiction if either party was domiciled in England on the date of commencement of proceedings or was habitually resident throughout the period of one year ending with the date when the proceedings have been commenced or if either part died before that date but was at death domiciled in England or habitually resided in England throughout the period of one year ending with the date of death. Under s 5(5) an English court has additional grounds of jurisdiction notwithstanding that the requirements of s 5(3) are not satisfied if proceedings are pending for the same divorce, judicial separation or nullity of marriage. This subsection concerns the supplemental or cross-petition. Thus if neither party is domiciled or has habitual residence in England but an English court has entertained the original proceedings and the petition is still pending, the court has jurisdiction over the supplemental or cross-petition.

Once an English court has jurisdiction to entertain proceedings it has to classify the defect affecting the marriage and decide whether it is an issue of formal or essential validity. The classification as a matter of procedure is governed by the *lex fori*. This stage is sometimes crucial for the outcome of the case since different laws classify the same defect differently. For example in *Solomon v Walters* (1956) a marriage celebrated in Nevada did not satisfy the requirement of parental consent of the *lex loci celebrationis*. Although under the law of the parties' domicile, parental consent was not required, the *lex fori* held that as parental consent was a question of form, it was to be determined by the *lex loci celebrationis*. As a result, the marriage was nullified and the law of Nevada was applied. The conflict of laws rules in nullity, apart from a few exceptions, are simple. If the defect concerns the formal validity of marriage the *lex loci celebrationis* applies; if the essential validity is challenged the ante-nuptial law of domicile of the concerned party governs the matter. The most controversial question in this area is whether the lack of consent should be considered as a formal or as an essential requirement. In this respect it seems that the English courts have primarily applied the *lex fori* ignoring the distinction between jurisdictional and conflict of laws rules. Case law on nullity where a foreign law was applied is scarce and controversial.

In *Apt v Apt* (1948) the question of validity of proxy marriage was at issue and the Court of Appeal made a distinction between the consent itself and the way of giving consent. The latter was considered as a formal requirement. The marriage was held valid and the *lex loci celebrationis* was applied. In *Way v Way* (1950) an English domiciliary married a Russian national in a ceremony which took place in Russia falsely believing that under Russian law spouses had a duty to live together. He thought that he would be allowed to stay in Russia or that his wife would be allowed to join him to live in England. It was held that: 'questions of consent are to be dealt with by reference to the personal law of the parties rather than by reference to the law of the place where the contract was made'. However, in that case the marriage was held valid by Russian law, the ante-nuptial law of domicile of the wife which was also the *lex loci celebrationis* and English law, the ante-nuptial law of domicile of the husband. Similarly in *Szechter v Szechter* (1971), a Polish professor, domiciled in Poland, divorced his wife and married his secretary (also a Polish domiciliary) in order to rescue her from prison and help her to emigrate. She was serving a prison sentence for 'anti-state activities' and was suffering from ill health. In England the secretary petitioned for nullity wishing that the marriage of her rescuer would be resumed. The marriage was invalid for duress under Polish law, the ante-nuptial law of both parties and the *lex loci celebrationis*, and under English law. Although Polish law was applied the same result would be reached by applying English law.

Another interesting case is *Vervaeke v Smith* (1983) in which the test of the most real and substantial connection was applied to determine the 'quintessential validity' of marriage. According to Lord Simon the law of the territory with which the marriage had the most real and substantial connection was the law of the intended matrimonial home. He believed that his solution would clarify the law applicable to consent.

It is submitted that marriage although a special contract, is still a contract. For that reason the *lex loci celebrationis* is inappropriate since the place of contracting has nothing to do with the consent of parties. The consent should be determined by the law of the ante-nuptial domicile of the party who alleges to have lacked consent. It is unnecessary to refer to the ante-nuptial law of domicile of both parties (however the question of consent was not discussed in *Sotomayer v De Barros (No 2)* (1879)) in which the dual domicile rule was applied to determine the capacity to marry).

Another controversial or rather undecided question is the law applicable to physical defect or incapacity: wilful refusal to consummate the marriage and impotence. The difficulty is exacerbated by two factors: in some countries those defects are not considered as grounds for annulment. For example wilful refusal is not considered as a serious enough reason to justify the annulment of a marriage in Italy. In *Ponticelli v Ponticelli* (1958) the husband was domiciled in England, the wife in Italy and they married by proxy in Italy. The husband wanted to nullify the marriage on the ground of wilful refusal to consummate it by the wife. The court applied the law of the domicile of the husband and annulled the marriage. Secondly, those defects were actually post-nuptial defects.

It is submitted that it is easier to decide what law should not be applied in cases of wilful refusal and impotence than to determine the appropriate one. It seems that the recommendation of the Law Commission will provide a satisfactory solution, that is, the application of the ante-nuptial law of domicile of the person who alleges to be incapable. Furthermore, it is the law which determines all issues relating to essential validity of marriage.

Question 47

> 'Those who can afford to travel abroad may have their foreign divorces recognised ... whereas those who cannot afford to make the journey are left with limping marriages.'

Discuss the above observation in the context of divorce proceedings conducted under religious laws commenced in England and concluded abroad.

Answer plan

The concept of a 'limping marriage' should be explained, especially in relation to the 1970 Hague Convention on the Recognition of Divorces and Legal Separations. The different form of religious divorce, and mainly the Muslim *talaq* and the Jewish *get* should be examined. The distinction between overseas divorces obtained by means of judicial proceedings and other proceedings and the situation where no proceedings are involved should be discussed. The application of the Family Law Act 1986 to overseas divorces, including religious divorces is important. Finally the following decisions are particularly relevant:

- *R v Secretary of State for the Home Department, ex p Fatima* (1985)
- *Berkovits v Grinberg* (1995)

Answer

Lord Diplock in *Quazi v Quazi* (1980) stated that a 'limping marriage' is one which is recognised as dissolved in one jurisdiction and considered as subsisting in another. Indeed, a limping marriage is a result of discrepancy and divergence in rules of conflict of laws both jurisdictional and choice of laws, which refuse to recognise a divorce or an annulment of marriage obtained in another country. This situation creates many legal problems which have impact not only on the parties themselves, since they do not know whether they are still married or divorced or bigamist or depending on the country their marital status changes, but on their partners from new relationships. More importantly the legal status of their children from previous and subsequent unions is unclear. In order to alleviate the 'acute misery and frustrations' that 'limping marriages' create, the Hague Conference on Private International Law adopted in 1970 the Convention on the Recognition of Divorces and Legal Separations which was implemented in the United Kingdom by the Recognition of Divorces and Legal Separations Act 1971.

In relation to the religious divorces, different religions offer different approaches to the question of termination of marital relationships during the lifetime of the spouses. This question is of a considerable importance since England has became a multi-faith society, a fact which was recognised by the Archbishop of Canterbury, Dr George Carey in relation to the revision of the coronation oath. It is impossible to examine all different forms of religious divorce but the most important should be discussed. The Roman Catholic Church has not changed its view on divorce for centuries. Marriage is a sacrament and as such its sanctity cannot be challenged under any circumstance. Thus no earthly authority can terminate a valid marriage as man does not have the right to separate what God united. The Church of England, however, makes concessions for human weakness although since the promulgation of the Matrimonial Causes Act in 1857 secular jurisdiction replaced the Ecclesiastical courts. Other Reform Churches on the continent also permit divorce. The Eastern Catholic Church is very generous in this respect. Marriages in the Eastern Church may almost be dissolved at will. A marriage may be terminated if the original commitments in the sacrament are no longer in existence, where it is morally dead, psychologically hateful and there is no love between the spouses.

In Islamic law, divorce is permissible. Although Islamic law (the *Sharia*) is basically the same in all Muslim countries, there are marked differences between Sunnis and Shia's. The fundamental form of divorce for both sects is the unilateral repudiation of a wife by the husband known as the '*talaq*' (which means 'I divorce you'). Under the classic Muslim Sunni no formalities are required. Thus, the talaq may be explicit by words (it involves the pronouncement of the word *talaq* three times), in writing (the *telegnama*) or by a gesture when the husband is incapable of expressing his wish by words or in writing. The most common form of repudiation for Sunnis is the revocable *talaq*. Thus certain times must elapse, usually as Sura Bagara II, v 228 specifies: 'Repudiated women shall wait ... for three monthly periods' before *talaq* is effective. For Shia's talaq is irrevocable and immediately effective. Consequently, it requires a specific form. The husband must expressly tell his wife that she is repudiated *(talaq)* and point in her direction. Two male witnesses are necessary and the *talaq* can be pronounced only in the time when the wife is in a period of menstrual purity during which no sexual intercourse occurs. Although Islamic law recognises other forms of divorce, for example, the termination of a marriage by mutual consent of the spouses at the request of the wife called *khula* or its judicial form (*tafriq*) the husband in many countries retains his right of unilateral repudiation. On the other end of the scale are Muslim countries which have abandoned the *Sharia* and have secularised their family law on the European pattern (Turkey, Tunisia etc).

Finally, Jewish law allows for divorce which is called the '*get*'. The fundamental requirement of the Jewish law is the mutual agreement of both spouses. The Jewish procedure for divorce is very complicated, time-consuming and involves considerable hardship for both spouses. A special document also called the *get'* must be drafted, mutual consent be proved and then the husband must appear in person before the Rabbinical Court (*Beth Din*) which is composed of three judges specialising in family law. At this stage the *get* document is scrutinised once again and where there is a mistake, the entire procedure must be repeated. The *get* document terminates the matrimonial bond once it is officially delivered by the husband or his proxy to the wife in the presence of witnesses usually judges of the Rabbinical court in order to make sure that the wife accepts the document of her own free will. Since Jewish law is personal law for Jews, regardless of their place of residence, they must apply to the Rabbinical Court and follow the get procedure.

The question whether such religious divorces are recognised in England is governed by the Family Law Act 1986. According to s 44(1) no divorce obtained in the British Isles shall be effective unless it takes the form of a judicial decree. As a result an extra-judicial divorce pronounced in a foreign embassy in London is considered as obtained in the United Kingdom and consequently non-recognised. In *Radwan v Radwan* (1973), an Egyptian national married to an English woman repudiated her by *talaq* in the Egyptian Embassy in London. Their divorce was not recognised under s 44(1) of the Family Law Act 1986.

As regards overseas divorces, a distinction is made between overseas divorces obtained by means of judicial proceedings or other proceedings and where there are no proceedings. When a divorce is obtained by judicial or other proceedings the jurisdictional basis for recognition is much wider than if there are no proceedings. For overseas' divorces belonging to the first category the following requirements must be satisfied for their recognition: they must be effective under the law of the country where they were obtained and at the date of the commencement of the proceedings, either spouse was habitually resident or domiciled in, or was a national of that country. The crucial question is what constitutes proceedings under the 1986 Act. In this respect there is no definition in the 1986 Act itself but it seems that some formalities are necessary such as registration, conciliation proceedings etc, external to the parties. In *Chaudhary v Chaudhary* (1985) Oliver LJ said that proceedings 'must impart a degree of formality and at least the involvement of some agency, whether lay or religious, or recognised by the state as having a function that is more than simply probative' which is not the case when both spouses by a private act or one of them even if the act is solemnised by the party and witnesses, are present at the declaration of divorce. Consequently a 'bare' *talaq*, that is when the husband unilaterally repudiates the wife by pronouncing three times the word *talaq* and which is immediately effective does not amount to the proceedings (*Chaudray v Chaudray* (1976)). Where there have been no proceedings, that is, when a divorce takes all similar forms to the 'bare' *talaq*, on the issue of recognition s 46(2) of the Family Law Act 1986 may be referred to. Thus it will be recognised if it is effective under the law of the country in which it was obtained and at the date the divorce was obtained both parties were domiciled in that country, or if only one party to the marriage was domiciled in that country, the divorce must be recognised as valid under the law of domicile of the other party. Furthermore, it will be recognised if neither party was habitually resident in the United Kingdom throughout the period of one year immediately preceding that date.

However our question concerns the situation where one of the parties is present in the United Kingdom while the other spouse is abroad and the religious divorce has been obtained by way of proceedings which are commenced in the United Kingdom and concluded abroad. In *R v Secretary of State for the Home Department, ex parte Fatima* (1985) the appellant was a Pakistani national, resident in the United Kingdom who pronounced *talaq* in England against his wife (who was in Pakistan) and made a statutory declaration in this respect before a solicitor in Bolton, England. A copy of the document was sent to Pakistan to the wife and the Chairman of a local union council. In Pakistan under the 1961 Muslim Family Laws Ordinance a husband who pronounced the *talaq* must notify in writing, as soon as possible, his decision to the Chairman of the relevant local union council. The wife has to be informed about her husband's decision. The Chairman of the Local union must then within 30 days of receiving the notice, set up an Arbitration Council in order to commence reconciliation proceedings. If they fail, 90 days after the notice of the *talaq* was delivered to the Chairman, the *talaq* is effective. In *Fatima*, the appellant obtained a divorce in Pakistan. Once his marriage was dissolved he wanted to marry Ghulam Fatima. However, she was refused leave to enter the United Kingdom and the immigration officers declared that the appellant was still validly married. The appellant argued that his marriage with Fatima could take place within a reasonable time since the *talaq* was effective as 'obtained' in Pakistan although pronounced in England. The House of Lords held that the pronouncement of the *talaq* amounted to the institution of the proceedings. However, the proceedings, in order to be effective, 'must be a single set of proceedings which have to be instituted in the same country as that in which the relevant divorce was ultimately obtained'). As a result, the divorce was not obtained overseas and the so called 'divorce by post' by Pakistani nationals residing in the United Kingdom is not recognised.

The entry into force of Part II of the Family Law Act 1986 has not changed the position of English law in this respect. However, it was uncertain whether the divorce obtained by a Jewish *get* in similar circumstances would also be refused recognition in the United Kingdom. In *Berkovits v Grinberg* (1995) it was held that the marriage is considered to be dissolved when the *get* is handed to the wife, the writing of the *get* is a step in proceedings and that all proceedings must be conducted in a country outside the United Kingdom in order to be recognised under s 46(1) of the Family Law Act 1986 as an overseas divorce. Consequently, when the proceedings are commenced in England but the *get* is delivered in another country the principle of Fatima applies.

It is submitted that when the divorce proceedings conducted under religious laws were commenced in England and concluded in another country, the divorce although valid under religious laws would not be recognised in England. Section 46(1) of the Family Law Act 1986 applies only to divorces obtained by a means of a single set of proceedings conducted outside the British Islands. Consequently, the statement that 'those who can afford to travel abroad may have their divorces recognised ... whereas those who cannot afford to make the journey are left with limping marriages' is true in the context of divorce proceedings conducted under religious laws which were commenced in England and concluded abroad. For that reason In *Berkovits v Grinberg,* Wall J said that there were strong arguments of policy against the conclusion which the construction of the Family Act 1986 required.

Question 48

Jane, domiciled and resident in Belgium, a devout Catholic, has always dreamt of getting married in Lourdes. When she met John, an English domiciliary and also a Catholic, they decided to marry in a Catholic ceremony in Lourdes. Their marriage took place in 1975 and was performed by a Catholic priest according to Catholic rites.

Jane and John decided to set up a home in Belgium. In 1976 their daughter Faith was born. Soon after their marriage started to deteriorate. In 1977 John decided to get a divorce and consulted a solicitor on the matter. He was told that his marriage was void since under French law only civil marriages are valid. John left Jane and their daughter Faith, and moved back to England. In 1988 he married April in a Registry Office in London. They had a son Malcolm in 1989. In 1995 John died intestate.

Discuss the succession to movable property of John's children Faith and Malcolm.

Answer plan

In order to answer the question it is necessary to deal separately with legitimacy and succession to movable property. Legitimacy concerns the determination of John's children's status. Succession is a question of construction of words like 'children' or 'issues' under the relevant Act of Parliament (John died intestate) in order to determine whether Faith and Malcolm can inherit their father's movable property. The position of illegitimate children under English law has been gradually improved although the Family Law Reform Act 1987 has not abolished the distinction between legitimacy and illegitimacy. For the purposes of succession it is not conclusive if a child is considered to be legitimate under a foreign law. For example, only a child born in lawful wedlock can succeed as heir to English real estate. Conversely, statutory rules may disregard the distinction between legitimate and illegitimate children and allow children to succeed regardless of their status. The following points should be examined:

- distinction between legitimacy and legitimation
- s 1(1) and (2) of the Legitimacy Act 1976
- ss 1, 18(1)(4) of the Family Law Reform Act 1987

Answer

At the time of birth a child acquires the status of a legitimate child if he or she is born in lawful wedlock. Legitimation is where a child born as illegitimate becomes legitimate as a result of subsequent events such as the marriage of his parents after the birth (the only event under English domestic law which renders a child legitimate), parental recognition etc.

The first question concerns the status of John's children. The traditional manner of determining the question of legitimacy is to examine whether the marriage of a child's parents is valid. Until the passing of the Legitimacy Act 1959 the English rule of domestic law was that when a child was born of parents whose marriage was valid at the time of his birth he was considered as a legitimate child. In this context Faith is not a legitimate child since the marriage of her parents was void for the lack of form. Jane and John celebrated their marriage in France in breach of French law according to which only civil marriages are valid. Since the matter is governed by the *lex loci celebrationis* (French law), their marriage is void. However, the traditional test has been displaced by statutory provision and developments in common law. As to the statutory provision the concept of putative marriage has been introduced by the Legitimacy Act 1976 s 1(1) which states:

> 'The child of a void marriage, whenever born (1), shall ... be treated as the legitimate child of his parents if at the time of the insemination resulting in the birth or, where there was no such insemination, the child's conception (or at the time of the celebration of the marriage if later) both or either of the parties reasonably believed that the marriage was valid.'

Section 28 of the Family Law Reform Act 1987 further develops this section by setting up a rebuttable presumption in favour of children of void marriages: if one of the party to a void marriage reasonable believes that at the relevant time the marriage was valid, the child is regarded as legitimate. This presumption is not retrospective as it applies only to children born after 4 April 1988, the date of coming into force of that section and thus it is irrelevant to our case. However under s 1(1) of the Legitimacy Act 1976 Faith may be considered as a legitimate child since both her parents believed that their marriage was valid at the time of her birth. The bad news is that s 1(1) of the Legitimacy Act 1976 is subject to s 1(2) which provides that the Act applies only to the child whose father was domiciled in England at the time of the birth, or if he died before the birth, his last domicile was in England. At the time of Faith's birth both her parents were domiciled in Belgium. As a result she cannot rely on s 1(1) of the Legitimacy Act 1976. This solution yields strange results. The legislation legitimates children whose fathers were domiciled in England at the relevant time but denies the benefit of a status of a legitimate child to a person who would have been born in England but whose father was at the time of birth domiciled abroad.

According to Dicey and Morris it would not be appropriate to draw any inference from s 1(2) of the Legitimacy Act 1976 as to the choice of law issue as the rule only establishes the territorial scope of English domestic law (pp 860–61) and constitutes solely an assumption of law in an Act of Parliament which is not necessarily correct or binding on the courts. In this context, it is submitted that if the law of the parent's domicile at the relevant time recognises the concept of a putative marriage and thus confers the status of a legitimate child to a child born of a void marriage it is difficult to accept that an English court would not follow the solution of that law. Secondly, we may accept the theory of Professor North which is that the domicile of a child, in order to determine his status, should be governed by the law of his domicile of origin and the validity of marriage of his parents should be irrelevant. In this respect where parents have the same domicile at the time of his birth, no problem arises. However if they have a different domicile one enters a vicious circle since if a child is legitimate he acquires the domicile of origin of his father and if he is illegitimate, the domicile of his mother. In those circumstances it is impossible to ascertain the domicile of a child without answering the question of his legitimacy. According to North in order to break the vicious circle, the domicile of the natural father should prevail in favour of this solution it can be said that it is admitted in cases of legitimation (*Goodman's Trust* (1881)). In *Re Bischoffsheim* (1948) a testator gave a share of residue to the children of his granddaughter Nesta. Nesta, domiciled in England had married her deceased husband's brother, also an English domiciliary in New York in 1917. Their marriage was void under English law but valid under the law of New York. It was held that at the time of marriage they still have English domicile but acquired a domicile of choice in New York by 1920 when their son Richard was born. The question was whether Richard was the legitimate child of his mother in order to be entitled to succeed under the will of a testator who died domiciled in England. The court held that the validity of Nesta's marriage to her second husband was irrelevant to the question of succession and that the legitimacy of Richard should be established by reference to his domicile of origin (the domicile of his parents at the time of his birth). Thus there is no reason to treat legitimacy and legitimation differently which indeed was confirmed in *Motala v AG* (1990) which was reversed by the House of Lords on a different aspect). In addition, the introduction of the concept of the putative marriage further enhances this approach (see also the decision in *Re Jones, Royal Trust Co v Jones* (1961)).

As to our case, to ascertain the domicile of origin of Faith is not difficult as her parents were domiciled in Belgium at the time of her birth. Thus, the Belgian law will decide whether she is legitimate or illegitimate. If Belgian law makes no distinction between legitimate and illegitimate children as is the case in New Zealand (Status of Children) Act 1969, she should be considered as legitimate in England. In this context it is interesting to mention the decision of the Supreme Court of Canada in *Re MacDonald* (1962) in which it was held that a child considered as illegitimate in Mexico (a child of an unmarried couple) should have the status of a legitimate child in Canada.

In relation to Faith's rights to the intestate succession to movables (only) her position is not affected by her status. If she is recognised as a legitimate child she should succeed to property under English deeds, wills or intestacy as if she were legitimate by English domestic law (*Re Bozzelli's Settlement* (1902)). However if she is still considered as an illegitimate child ss 1 and 18(1)(4) of the Family Law Reform Act 1987 provide that on the intestacy occurring on or after the entry into force of this Act (4 April 1988) references in the intestacy rules, in Part IV of the Administration of Estate Act 1925, to any relationship between two persons are to be interpreted without regard to whether the persons of either of them, or of any person through whom the relationship is deducted, were at any time married to each other.

As to Malcolm, the marriage of his parents is valid and he is the legitimate son of his father.

The intestate succession to movables will be distributed according to the law of the deceased domicile at the time of his death and since John's last domicile was in England, English law applies.

It is submitted that Faith and Malcolm for the purposes of the intestate succession to the movable property of John enjoy exactly the same rights.

Note

1 However the child must be born after the marriage was entered into (*Re Spence* (1990)).

Question 49

Anna, a British national, married Isaak, an Israeli national, in 1984. They set up a home in England. Their children Paula and Jane were born in 1985 and 1986. Both children have a dual nationality: British and Israeli.

In 1988 as their marriage broke down Isaak returned to Israel to live with his parents. Their divorce became final (*nisi*) in 1987. Both Paula and Jane have remained in the custody of their mother. In September 1995 Isaak came to England to visit his children. At that time Paula was sick and stayed with Anna but Jane went with Isaak for a weekend. She never returned. She was taken away by Isaak and is still with him in Israel.

Isaak refuses to bring her back to England. He claims that Jane is perfectly happy in Israel living with him and his parents and that her return, taking into account the fact that Anna is mentally unstable, will represent a risk to Jane's health and welfare.

Anna wants to know what she can do in order to get Jane back. Advise her, taking into account that Israel is a contracting state to the Hague Convention on the Civil Aspect of International Child Abduction 1980.

Answer plan

The Hague Convention on the Civil Aspect of International Child Abduction 1980 which is in force in the United Kingdom applies in our case. The main features of the Hague Convention should be examined. Article 13(b) is especially relevant as it concerns the refusal of the abductor to return the child if he alleges that there is a grave risk that the return would expose the child to physical or psychological harm or otherwise place him in a intolerable situation. The interpretation of Article 13(b) by courts in contracting states is very important:

- *B v K (Child Abduction)* (1992)
- *Macmillan v Macmillan* (1989)

Answer

Many factors contribute to aggravate the problem of international child abduction: marriages between parties of different nationalities, the growing number of broken marriages (in the United Kingdom, more than one in three marriages ends in divorce), the facility to travel and set up a home abroad etc. In the United Kingdom around 350 children are abducted each year.

The question of abduction of children in the United Kingdom is regulated by various legislation which may be relevant to our case. The United Kingdom has ratified two conventions in this area:

- the Hague Convention on the Civil Aspect of International Child Abduction signed at the Hague on 15 October 1980; and
- the European Convention on Recognition and Enforcement of Decisions concerning Custody of Children and on Restoration of Custody of Children signed at Luxembourg on 20 May 1980.

Both Conventions are implemented in the United Kingdom in the Child Abduction Act 1984. The Child Abduction Act 1984 considers abduction as a criminal offence in England and Wales. Further, the Children Act 1982, in force since 14 October 1991, provides that the fundamental principle in proceedings concerning children in England and Wales is the welfare of the child and thus the courts should always take into account the child's best interests.

First, the question of Jane's return will be examined. Jane has already been taken abroad by her father. Fortunately for Anna, Israel is a contracting state to the Hague Convention. The main objective of this Convention is to facilitate the speedy return of an abducted child and the recognition of custody rights in contracting states. According to Article 1 of the Convention the contracting states should take all appropriate measures to secure implementation of the Convention and shall use the most expeditious procedures available. The Hague Convention has been very successful in returning children. In 1994 the Lord Chancellor's Department intervened in 160 cases of abduction to the United Kingdom and 163 cases of abduction from the United Kingdom to the Hague Convention countries. All together in 1994 in 18 cases the return was refused (in all other cases the return was ordered or effected voluntarily and 105 cases were pending). The Hague Convention applies if the following requirements are satisfied: a child must be under 16 and habitually resident in a contracting state prior to the abduction. The applicant, in our case Anna, must exercise right to custody in relation to the child and finally the Convention must be in force in both contracting states. All requirements are fulfilled in the case of Jane.

The Hague Convention comes into operation when the removal or retention of a child is wrongful. In this respect Article 3 of the Convention states that it happens when (a) it is in breach of rights of custody attributed to a person, an institution or any other body, either jointly or alone, under the law of the state in which the child was habitually resident immediately before the removal or retention and (b) at the time of the removal or retention those rights were actually exercised, either jointly or alone, or would have been so exercised but for the removal or retention. The House of Lords held in *Re H; Re S (Abduction; Custody Rights)* (1991) that the removal is wrongful when a child is removed without the other parent's consent and was wrongful at the point of removal.

It is very important for Anna that she exercises the custody rights over Jane. Indeed, the Hague Convention draws the distinction between rights of custody and rights of access. Only the rights of custody include the right to determine the child's place of residence. Furthermore, the expression 'right of custody' has been widely interpreted by the courts when there was no order or any other official custodial status (*Re B (A Minor) (Abduction)* (1994)). Finally, fortunately for Anna the prompt return of a child who has been wrongfully taken away is a primary consideration of the Hague Convention, not the welfare of the child. Thus Article 12 of the Convention requires the mandatory return of a child within 12 months of abduction. Once the mandatory period expires, the return may be refused if it is demonstrated that the child has settled into his new environment. Jane was abducted in August 1995 and thus the mandatory period has not yet expired. As a result, apart from exceptions contained in Article 13 of the Convention, the court of a contracting state in which the child has his habitual residence has exclusive jurisdiction to make decisions on the merits of the case and the requested state must solely order the return of the child. The rule on jurisdiction is absolute and the Israeli court cannot exercise any discretion but order the return of Jane. Sometimes this rule produces an interesting result. In *H v H (Child Abduction: Stay of Domestic Proceedings)* (1994) it was held that although England was the appropriate forum for the determination of the child's future, under the Hague Convention the child had to be returned to France, the place of his habitual residence and French courts had jurisdiction to investigate the merits of the case. Under the Hague Convention the doctrine of *forum non conveniens* does not apply.

However, Article 13 may change the Anna's situation. It provides that a judicial or administrative authority of a requested state may refuse the return of the child if the person opposing the return establishes: (a) that the other party was not actually exercising the rights of custody or consented to or subsequently acquiesced in the removal or retention or (b) that there is a grave risk that the return of a child would expose him to physical or psychological harm or otherwise place the child in an intolerable situation. In our case Issak bases his claims on Article 13(b). Furthermore, in the context of Article 13(b) the child's views may be taken into account by a requested state (Israel) if the child is of age and maturity at which it is appropriate to do so. The court must decide those issues since no age is mentioned by the Convention. However, the objectives and the spirit of the Convention require the prompt return of wrongfully removed children and the investigation on the merits should be conducted by the court of the child's habitual residence. As Jane is only 10 years old the chances of her opinion being taken into account by the court are slim. However, in *Re R (Minor) (Abduction)* (1991) when a 14 year old girl threatened to commit suicide if sent back, the court did allow her to stay.

In the light of Article 13(b) the question arises as to Isaak's chances of retaining Jane in Israel. It seems that it will be extremely difficult for Isaak to prove that the return of Jane to England constitutes a grave risk to her mental health for many reasons. In England there has been only one case where the party was able to prove that the return would place the child in an intolerable situation (in *B v K (Child Abduction)* (1992)). In this case the court decided that the child should return without his older sister who succeeded in convincing the court that to let her stay would constitute a grave risk within the meaning of Article 13(b) (see also the unreported case of *Re C* (1990)). No adjournment would be allowed in order to gather information, thus encouraging the delaying tactics of the abductor (*Re E (A Minor) (Abduction)* (1989)). Case law indicates that the defence under Article 13(b) has been strictly interpreted by the courts in contracting states (1). Only where the applicant has a history of mental illness or of alcohol abuse is it possible for the abductor to succeed (*Macmillan v Macmillan* (1989)). Nothing in our case indicates that Anna has any mental problems. Secondly, as already discussed, the objective of the Convention is the return of the child and not his welfare (*Re S (Minor) (Abduction)* (1991)). Furthermore, Isaak can bring proceedings in England once Jane is back home and seek to obtain the custody rights. Article 19 of the Convention provides that any decision regarding the child under the Convention should not be taken into account in any subsequent custody hearings. Finally, even if Isaak succeeds in proving that Anna is mentally unstable, the Israeli court exercises a discretion in deciding the return of a child under the Convention.

On the practical side, under the Convention contracting states shall establish a Central Authority to discharge the duties imposed by the Convention. In England and Wales the Child Abduction Unit of the Lord Chancellor's Department is the Central Authority for processing the application. Thus Anna should contact the Unit which will help her to prepare a formal application for return of Jane and will send it to the Central authority of Israel. It is important to emphasise that under the Convention no payment for legal proceedings is required although expenses relating to the return of the child are not covered. Anna should indicate in her application that an order for travel costs should be made against Isaak.

It is submitted that Anna should expect a prompt return of Jane. The Hague Convention although criticised for not taking into account the best interest of a child constitutes a very efficient mechanism for returning unlawfully removed or retained children (2). So far it has been ratified by 43 countries. Its effectiveness will certainly encourage more countries to become contracting states. In this context, Article 11(2) of the UN Convention on the Rights of the Child 1989 recommends the ratification of the Hague Convention, while its Article 11(1) urges all states to take appropriate measures to prevent child abduction.

Notes

1 See the Second Special Commission Report on the application and effectiveness of the Hague Convention as summarised in (1994) 33 ILM 225, at 241.

2 See the Reports of the two Special Commissions on the application and effectiveness of the Hague Convention as summarised in (1990) 29 ILM, 219, 224 and (1994) 33 ILM 225.

Question 50

James who was domiciled in England, had married Anna, a French national, in 1991. They set up a family home in England. They wanted to have a child but both had medical problems. Anna could get pregnant but could not give birth to a child. James and Anna decided to use artificial insemination techniques. Anna asked her friend Maria, domiciled in California, to be a surrogate mother. An embryo created with the gametes of Hans, a friend of James, and Anna was implanted in Maria's womb. Maria gave birth to Mark in 1993 and handed him over to James and Anna.

In 1994 James noticed that Anna often wore his clothes and his aftershave. He was worried but Anna assured him that she was doing it just for fun. However, in 1995 Anna declared that she was really a man and would shortly have sex realignment surgery in Switzerland. She left James and Mark and returned to France. After a successful operation Anna has become Steve.

In the meantime, Maria died intestate in California without the next of kin, leaving movable property in France and her house in Los Angeles.

James is very confused. He wants to know:

- whether he is still married to Anna and, if so, how to legally terminate the marriage
- whether he is legally Mark's father
- whether Mark can succeed to the immovable and movable property of Maria

Advise James.

Answer plan

Each issue should be addressed separately. The answer will be rather speculative as there is no authority on many of the issues. However, the following points should be examined:

- on the matter of transsexuals: *Corbett v Corbett* (1970); *Rees v UK* (1986); *Cossey v UK* (1990)
- regarding the validity of marriage: s 11(c) of the Matrimonial Causes Act 1973
- the determination of the legal status of Mark: The Human Fertilisation and Embryology Act 1990
- the question of succession: *Johnson v Calvert* (1993)

Answer

The traditional perception of marriage, parentage and family crucial to conflict of law rules in family law matters, risk being challenged. On one hand, the new artificial reproductive technology such as donor insemination, egg and embryo transfer and surrogacy, results in uncertainty as to who are the legal parents of a child. In international adoption or in succession matters those questions are of real importance. The notion of 'mother' which used to be self-evident is no longer easy to determine. On the other hand, the acceptance of relationships between two individuals of the same sex will have to be legally recognised sooner or later. In some countries homosexual 'marriages' are accepted (in Denmark and Norway, for example, a form of registration which produces legal consequences similar to marriage is available to homosexual couples). This is not so in England. There is also the issue of transsexuals. Do they have the capacity to marry a person of the opposite sex but originally of the same sex? What happens if a person already married changes his or her gender during the marriage? This essay emphasises the fact that private international law is a fascinating area and how it must respond to the changes in our society like any other branch of law.

The first issue concerns the effect of a sex operation on the validity or even existence of the marriage. Anna had the change of sex operation which resulted in giving her the outward appearance of the other sex. She has legally changed her name to Steve. Could she still be treated as being married to James? There is no authority on this matter. The definition of marriage provided by Lord Penzance in *Hyde v Hyde* (1866) according to which marriage is 'the voluntary union for life of one man and one woman to the exclusion of all others', however, may prove instructive. The question is whether Anna is still a woman. This question, as any question concerning personal status, will be answered by reference to the law of the respondent's domicile. Anna (or Steve) is now domiciled in France. If under French law she is considered a man then James is married to a man.

The Matrimonial Causes Act 1973 provides that marriage in England is void if the parties are not respectively male and female (s 11(c)). In *Corbett v Corbett* (1970) it was decided that for the purposes of marriage, a sex change operation cannot be given legal effect. In England the original gender survives the sex change operation. In other words a transsexual has no capacity to marry. In *Rees v UK* (1986) The European Commission of Human Rights has unanimously stated that: '... the right to marry guaranteed by Article 12 refers to the traditional marriage between persons of opposing biological sex' and thus a contracting state is not in breach of Article 12 if it disqualifies a transsexual from marrying. The Commission was divided on the question of whether the issue was formal or substantial. If it was formal then after the sex operation a contracting state should allow that person to legally change the status. Otherwise a contracting state would be in breach of Article 8 of the Convention. Thus under a new status there was no reason why that person should be prevented from marrying a person of the opposite sex.

Where, on the other hand, it was a substantive question then the essence of marriage was at stake; this essence including 'the physical capacity to procreate'. As a result, on this ground the right to marry should be denied to transsexuals. However, in *Cossey v UK* (1990) the Commission decided that there was a violation of Article 12 (10 votes to 6) and rejected the distinction between the capacity to marry and the capacity to found a family. The European Court of Human Rights disagreed and reaffirmed the decision in *Reeds v UK* and decided that the denial of the right to marry to transsexuals did not violate Article 12. It appears that slowly the perception of marriage has changed in Strasbourg.

It would appear that James is married to another man. It seems difficult to imagine that a court in England, as it happened in *Hyde v Hyde* would decide that there is no marriage and deny matrimonial relief. His marriage will most likely be annulled under s 11(c) of the Matrimonial Causes Act 1973.

In Mark's case, his biological father is Hans. However, James was married to the 'mother' (if Anna is considered as a mother) at the time of his birth. The Human Fertilisation and Embryology Act 1990 provides a definition of a mother and a father. Both definitions apply for all legal purposes. A mother is 'the woman who is carrying or has carried a child as a result of the placing in her of an embryo or of sperm and eggs, and no other woman, is to be treated as the mother of the child'. Thus, in England, the surrogate mother has parental rights over the child. Maria is the legal mother of Mark. As to the father the 1990 Act specifies that in cases of artificial donor insemination and egg or embryo transfer the husband or the partner, providing he consents, of the woman who becomes pregnant is considered to be father. Thus neither James nor Hans is legally a father of Mark. James has to adopt Mark.

Finally, the question of succession has to be examined. The principle is that the intestate succession to the immovables is determined by the law of the country where the immovables are situated (*lex situs*) and the intestate succession to the movables is governed by the law of domicile of the deceased person at the time of his death. Maria was domiciled in California and the immovables property is situated in California. The law of the state of California will determine whether Mark is entitled to succeed. In this respect in *Johnson v Calvert* (1993) where a surrogate mother refused to give up her child after the birth, the Supreme Court of California held that the surrogate mother had no parental rights and the biological parents were considered as parents for all legal purposes. Therefore, Mark is not considered as Maria's son under the law of the state of California.

It is submitted that in the future many interesting cases will have to be decided concerning the two issues. Traditional rules of conflict of laws are not appropriate to solve such complicated issues. Although national legislation has been introduced in many areas, the inconsistencies between them may produce unjust results. In our example Mark legally has no father. Under English law his mother is Maria, under the law of California Anna is his mother. As a result, depending on jurisdictions, he may end up with three fathers: James, John and Steve and two mothers Maria and Anna, or he may be an orphan. It is necessary to harmonise national legislation and the best solution is to unify law at the international level by way of international conventions.

Index